Intuition, in its highest form, is nothing less than the voice of God within you. It is one of God's greatest gifts. To recognize, honor, and develop constant communication with this inner voice is the foundation of mystical life. Your own intuitive gifts can catapult you to new heights of human awareness and interaction, and lead you to spiritual understanding. Sacred and secular then become one. Your conscious awareness expands and encompasses many layers of reality. Your intellectual pursuits and intuitive understandings unite to blaze a trail of profound wisdom and insight.

This is intuitive living. This is the path of the 21st-century mystic — a path awaiting you, a pioneer in the creation of new paradigms of spiritual living for the next century.

# ON BECOMING A
# 21st-CENTURY
# MYSTIC

# ON BECOMING A
# 21st-CENTURY MYSTIC

## Pathways to Intuitive Living

### ALAN SEALE

Skytop Publishing
New York, NY
1997

ON BECOMING A 21st-CENTURY MYSTIC

Skytop Publishing/1997

Copyright © 1997 by Alan Seale.

Cover design by David Dann.

Grateful acknowledgment is made for permission to reprint excerpts from the following works: *Hands of Light: A Guide to Healing Through the Human Energy Field* by Barbara Brennan. Published by Bantam Books, 1988. Reprint permission from Bantam, Doubleday, Dell Publishing Group, Inc. *Wheels of Life — A User's Guide to the Chakra System* by Anodea Judith. Published by Llewellyn Publications, 1990. Reprint permission from Llewellyn Publications. *The Drummer's Path* by Sule Greg Wilson. Published by Destiny Books, a division of Inner Traditions International, Rochester, VT, Copyright © 1992 by Sule Greg Wilson. Reprint permission from Inner Traditions International. *Creating the Work You Love* by Rick Jarow. Published by Destiny Books, a division of Inner Traditions International, Rochester, VT, Copyright © 1995 by Rick Jarow. Reprint permission from Inner Traditions International. *Martha: The Life and Work of Martha Graham*. Published by Random House, 1956. Reprint permission from Random House, Inc.

Library of Congress Cataloging-in-Publication Data

Seale, Alan.
    On becoming a 21st-century mystic : pathways to intuitive living / Alan Seale. —
  1st ed.
      p.  cm.
      Includes bibliographical references and index.
      ISBN: 0-9657736-1-2     Library of Congress Catalog Card Number: 97-91818

      1. Spiritual life — New Age movement.
      2. New Age movement. 3. Mysticism
      I. Title. II. Title: On becoming a twenty-first century mystic

BP605.N48.S43 1997          229'.93
                        QBI97-40554

Published and Printed in the United States of America

Skytop Publishing
P. O. Box 134
Cathedral Station
New York, NY 10025

0 9 8 7 6 5 4 3 2 1

*To my Papa,*
*Rev. Dr. James M. Seale,*
*who, by his life, has shown me*
*that there is a place to go,*
*but has let me discover my own trails.*


*To "Cousin Lucy" Clay Woodford Winn,*
*who, in my childhood, taught me to live in truth,*
*and, even now from spirit,*
*continues to teach me of Love.*


*To Sonia Smith,*
*who, by sharing her own journey*
*and transition back to spirit,*
*helped me find my path.*

# Contents

## Part I
## The Path of the 21st-Century Mystic

# Part II
# Spiritual Self-Discovery and Transformation

# Part III
# Working with Spirit —
# Embracing Intuitive Living

# Acknowledgments

The whole of my life to this point has led to this book. As I meet each step of the journey, I find new understanding and grace. For this I am eternally grateful. The first thanks must go to Spirit. In that all-encompassing realm of being, I have come to know who I am and the wonders of all possibility.

There are many people to thank for their profound impact on my growth, my work, and my life as I have taken this journey with Spirit. First are my parents, Jim and Mary Dudley Seale, who provided a home in which love of God was primary. There have been many important teachers — Dr. Ginger Grancagnolo, Joey Crinita, Rick Jarow, Rev. Daniel Neusom, Rev. John William King, and Rev. Charles Burnham. But perhaps the most important teachers of all have been the students in my classes and workshops, and those with whom I have been privileged to work in counseling and readings. I thank each of them for the gifts of wisdom and love they have shared with me.

Although I have had very little or no personal contact with these people, for their books and performances which have given me great inspiration, healing, and love, I must thank Ram Dass, Emmanuel and Pat Rodegast, Bartholomew, White Eagle, Stephen Levine, Neale Donald Walsch, Paul Winter and Paul Halley and the Paul Winter Consort, and Susan Osborn.

From what seems now like the distant past, I must thank Muzetta Swann, Carolyn Harris, and Charlotte Miller, three very important women who helped me see my own possibilities and encouraged and supported me to begin teaching in the spiritual and creative realms. And to Jim Pulley, who, in 1991, let me know in no uncertain terms that I was giving up on the teaching journey, and pulled me back to the pathway after a period of inner conflict. (He also introduced me to the world of computers, which has made the writing of this book much less daunting!)

Thanks to Bill Lewis for helping me fulfill my dream of a

mountaintop home; and to him and Arlene Shrut for the fantastic musical collaborations we have shared, all of which fed my relationship to Spirit, just as Spirit filled our music. There must also be a special thanks to Simon Chaussé whose love and encouragement brought the beginnings of this book into being five years ago.

A huge thank you to Lynn McCann, my editor. You always knew just the right thing to say to bring out the best in me. Thanks also to David Dann for his cover design and guidance in the layout and design of the book. And thank you to those who read various parts of the manuscript and/or contributed in various ways: Len Belzer, Sandra Bilotto, Jeff Binford, Dr. Kathleen Calabrese, Wendy Coad, Rev. Charmaine Colon, Cat Conrad, David Edelfelt, Jean Frédéric, Stephanie Gunning, Martin Hennessy, Ken Hornbeck, Rev. Terry Drew Karanen, John Klapper, Rev. Kathy Medici, Laura Meyers, Dorothy Neff, Rev. Joel Rosow, Anthony Saridakis, Rev. James and Mary Dudley Seale, Rebecca Shore, Arlene Shrut, Donna Slawsky, Emily Squires, and Ann Weeks.

Finally, to my fellow traveler, Myra Winner — thank you for all you are to me. You have given me many gifts for my journey.

Alan Seale<br>
New York City<br>
March 30, 1997

# Prologue

# The Language of Love

Many years ago, Spirit spoke to me of a new language —
> the language of Love —
>> and explained that it was actually the original language of
>> all creation,
>>> but seemed to be a new language for our time.

And so I asked,
> How do I learn the language of Love?

Spirit replied,
> *There is nothing to learn. There is only 'to be.'*

And I said,
> But 'be' what?

Spirit replied,
> *Be You. Be You in the largest sense of You.*
> *Be You in your truth, in your power, in your strength.*
> *Be You as you know yourself in God and God in you.*

I asked,
> What are the words of this language of Love?

Spirit responded,
> *There are no words. And there are all words.*
> *When you come to know your heart*
>> *and can live there in your essence,*
>>> *in God,*
>>>> *you will know and speak the language of Love.*
> *The vocabulary of the language of Love is not verbal.*
> *This is a language of intention, of thought, of movement, of color,*
>> *of sound, of action, of faith, of wisdom, of integrity.*

15

*Speaking this language means letting Love be the essence*
*of every word you speak,*
*every breath you draw,*
*every action you take,*
*every aspect of your deepest faith.*
*It is the sharing of your innermost being.*
*It is a silent language that speaks louder*
*than any words will ever speak.*
*It is the language of Spirit. When you speak the language of Love,*
*you can commune with the highest realms of Spirit.*
*You will know Spirit's guidance*
*in every moment of your existence.*
*This language of Love can be yours, if you choose.*
*It is yours to explore and find your way into.*
*It is your language to live.*
*It is your language to experience.*
*It is Love.*

I spoke once more to Spirit, asking,
How do I get to this place of 'being?'
And Spirit said very simply,
*Go home. Go home to your heart.*
*Sit deep in your heart and listen.*
*Your heart is your home.*
*Your heart is where you must live.*
*Only in your heart can you know Love.*
*Only in your heart can you find peace.*

And, in that moment, I began to know the path of the 21st-century mystic.

# Introduction

This is a book about life — your life, my life, all of our lives together. It's a book about awareness — becoming aware of yourself at the depths of your being, of others around you, and of all that surrounds you. It's a book about spirituality — an exploration of your spirit that is at the same time human and divine, and the development of your own personal sense of spirituality. It's a book about Spirit, which I define simply as "the all of the everything that is." You might also call it God or Source, Love, the Universal Creative Force, the Great Mystery, Universal Wisdom, or Higher Power. I will use the term Spirit throughout this book to represent this great mystery that cannot be defined.

This is a book about communication — communication with yourself, with others, and with Spirit. It's a book about intuition, which, in its highest form, is nothing less that the voice of Spirit within you. Intuition, fully developed, is the most profound level of communication — a direct knowing or understanding, whether through words, images, or feelings, of the presence of Spirit and Its profound guidance. It is one of God's greatest gifts. This book will help you uncover the presence of Spirit in the moment-to-moment living of your life, and develop that highest level of communication called intuition.

This is a book about understanding Love as a potent energy force that has created the universe, and continues to create and sustain us all, creatures of all kinds, and all matter in space. The journey that we are about to undertake together will help you know deep in every cell of your being that *you* are Love made manifest on Earth. As you honor yourself as Love, you will awaken your innate intuitive wisdom. Your journey will open doors to a mystical process within you of moving back to soul, nurturing yourself toward a place of balance between ego and soul. It is a journey into your essence — a journey to a more profound understanding of your oneness with the divine. It's a

17

journey that involves opening, developing, and using your intuitive gifts, just as you use all your other talents or abilities, to enrich every day of your life.

You will find many tools in this book to help you move along through the journey. There are many exercises, some of which are activities, while others are meditations for you simply to experience. You will find explanations of universal concepts, often made clearer or expanded upon by direct teachings from Spirit. You will learn and grow, be challenged and be fed. At times you will have a direct experience of a shift of perception or understanding within, and other times the process will be much more subtle. Try not to judge your experience or have preconceived notions of what your experience should or should not be. Step into this path with an open heart and mind, and allow the mystic within you to begin making itself known. What you experience could be the magnificent unfolding of *you*.

# A Time of Great Change

As we move into the 21st century, life seems to keep "speeding up." We see it most clearly in the domain of science and technology. The new computer on which I write this book is outdated within weeks of its purchase. Global communication networks, cybertechnology, and methods of doing business are constantly being updated, so that "state-of-the-art" is almost a meaningless term.

We also see religious and cultural belief systems that have reigned for centuries being questioned, shaken, endangered, rejected, revised, transformed, and re-discovered in a relative wink of an eye. Political systems and empires rise, and topple. It seems that what once took 500 years to develop in human consciousness became possible in 250, then 100, then 25 years. Only a few generations ago, the set of beliefs into which you were born — about life, about what's right and wrong, what works and what doesn't — would last you a lifetime. Now, however, we are faced with constantly changing values. Life seems to be an ongoing process of re-evaluation.

This accelerated rate of growth and change unsettles us. It provokes us constantly to take stock of our lives, to question our beliefs and our models, to examine our ways of thinking, feeling, and acting. It demands that we embrace change rather than resist it, that we become actively engaged in the process of our lives. We are challenged to develop a more "enlightened" way of living — one that requires awareness of all that is around and within us. This means awareness not only of what is readily apparent to the physical senses, but also what is available to us through our inner, specifically our *intuitive* senses.

This book is about learning to listen to intuition, the voice of Spirit within you. The purpose is to find your own sense of order and structure in your personal, professional, emotional, and spiritual life. You are invited to enter into a spirituality that has no rules — a spirituality that is large enough to allow each person to find their freedom and their truth in their own divine process of human development.

For me, this has entailed an in-depth and ongoing exploration into the essence of my being, digging around in the hidden aspects of myself, searching out my own sense of the divine and its role in my life, establishing a clear and powerful relationship with Spirit, and walking hand in hand with Spirit through every day. I have come to know this as the journey of the 21st-century mystic.

We will be using a number of terms which may benefit from a working definition to establish our common ground. For example, we have defined Spirit as "the all of the everything that is." With this as a starting point, your own definition of Spirit, and other terms we use, will grow and gain dimension, as we go on.

# Mysticism and Mystical Experience

These two terms, mysticism and mystical experience, seem inseparable to me. You cannot have one without the other. However, let's first look at them individually for a better understanding. Traditionally, mysticism has been defined as belief in a higher power or God, and the pursuit of becoming one with that higher power. There are, of course, many different types of mysticism and different understandings of mystical union. However, the underlying search for the One seems to be the fundamental essence of most mystical traditions.

To me, mysticism is an acute awareness of Spirit, and of its influence on and movement through daily life. A mystic recognizes both the power and the playfulness of Spirit, and constantly seeks to work with this potent force in the creation of their life. The mystic understands that the oneness of all of creation is found in this fundamental creative energy. The mystic recognizes that Spirit moves through life on many levels of conscious awareness, and seeks to perceive and comprehend these many levels all at once. Simply put, the mystic wants the close-up view and the larger perspective *at the same time*. Because of this multi-level awareness, the mystic trusts their experience of Spirit without the need for scientific or rational explanation. This is not to suggest rejection of rational thought, but rather an embrace of life lived within a realm of possibilities that goes far beyond deductive reasoning.

Mystical experience has been defined as an experience in which one transcends ordinary consciousness, moving to a much larger awareness beyond time, space, and their present physical reality. Mystical experiences, by their nature are beyond verbal description, but the transcendent aspect seems to be common among all cultures and religions. They are deeply spiritual, but not necessarily religious. Although the idea of a mystic or mystical experience often conjures up images of monks or ascetics living in secluded monasteries or mountain caves, many people have some kind of mystical experience at least once in their life.

I define mystical experience as "that which is very real to the experiencer, but cannot be explained by the rational mind." We all have these experiences from time to time, but do not necessarily identify them as mystical. They may be as obvious as a vision or a spirit visitation, or as subtle as a dream, or what we often dismiss as coincidences. Coincidences are rare. When we look inside a coincidence, we often can see the synchronicity at work within that experience. In some unexplained way, everything has fallen into place to create that moment. Your rational mind may not be able to comprehend what has happened, yet some deeper part of you knows that something very significant has just occurred. From the simple and subtle to the profound, mystical experiences are happening all the time. They are great opportunities for us to listen, look, feel — to learn or understand something about ourselves and this mystery called life at a deeper level.

Mysticism and mystical experiences transcend religious form. When you dig down through the dogma and philosophies of the religions of the world to get to their mystical roots, you find that they are all virtually the same. All religions or belief systems are, fundamentally, pathways in search of the One. They may each give a different name to this One — God, the Creator, the Great Mystery, Tunkashila, Allah, the Universal Force or Universal Mind, the Great Spirit, to name some of the more familiar ones — but nevertheless the fundamental concept is the same. All are in search of the sacred and of living in the sacred essence.

# Intuition — The Inner Voice of Spirit

Intuition has been defined as an unexplained inner knowing, a hunch, or a gut feeling or response. In the Western mainstream culture, it has often been given little, if any, credence. It certainly has not been considered information on which to rely for any matters of consequence.

For me, however, intuition is much more than this. It is a process of tapping into your deep sense of inner wisdom. This is the place inside of you where you know your oneness with All. At its highest level, the intuitive voice is the part of you that is one with the Great Mystery, that is Love. It is the voice of God within. Intuitive awareness develops hand-in-hand with your willingness to step beyond the intellectual mind, so that you may *know* and *experience* the infinite possibilities that exist beyond the bounds of ordinary consciousness. The way to this inner wisdom is through your own personal spiritual and mystical journey — embracing this inner voice as Spirit, and allowing it to lead you as teacher, counselor, guide, and friend.

This inner voice of Spirit is the foundation of mystical life, and the fundamental essence of this book. In our culture we are not encouraged to develop an awareness of this inner voice. We are, in

21

fact, often afraid to make a decision or take an action because of a "gut feeling" or hearing an inner voice saying, "Do this." And if we do, we are usually very hesitant to admit it to anyone else. We are not taught to trust that inner voice. Yet Spirit is alive and well and dwelling deep in each of our hearts. Through the inner journey and a willingness to accept that there is more to life than what we perceive with our outer senses and the reasoning mind, we can step fully into the mystical journey and enter a world of endless possibilities.

# The 21st-Century Mystic

Historically, it was often thought in many belief systems that only a chosen few could aspire to be mystics. Only a few were thought to be blessed with intuitive gifts, the ability to be aware of and access other realms of consciousness, that deep inner voice. However, as we approach the end of the 20th century, more and more people are awakening to a call from within to walk the mystical path, to open to the boundless possibilities of the greater world that seems hidden to normal conscious awareness. "Seems" is the important word here. The boundless possibilities lie within everyday, moment-to-moment living. It does not matter whether you choose a life in the public eye or one of quiet and privacy. Simply in the living of your life you will introduce others to new paradigms of spiritual living. This is path of the 21st-century mystic — this is the journey of this book.

As I searched for a way to define my process and the work that was evolving with my students, my inner voice suggested the term "21st-century mystic." As I studied historical concepts of what made a mystic, I began to more clearly understand this modern-day path.

The 21st-century mystic is one who comes to experience and know oneness with God through a journey involving five steps:

1) spiritual awakening — an opening in conscious awareness to the existence of a universal force that is the creator and sustainer of all.

2) self-exploration — embarking upon a journey to uncover and know the divine essence of your being.

3) removing blocks — recognizing, acknowledging, and working through emotional blocks and inner resistance or fears that hinder a full awareness of your own divinity, and the constant flow of Love through you.

4) intuitive development — developing the intuitive mind as an aspect of Spirit, of Love, of God, of the Great Mystery.

5) surrender — complete surrender to the guidance of Spirit. This surrender is not at all a passive process. It is, in fact, extremely active, in that it is a process of being in a profoundly heightened state of awareness, receiving the guidance of Spirit, and responding in the appropriate way through attitude and action.

These steps are not necessarily undertaken in any particular order. Every person has their own unique experiences, perhaps starting with number two followed by number one, then four and three, and then back to number two, and on and on it goes.

The 21st-century mystic is one who chooses to embark upon an expedition into self, accepting the challenge to explore on many levels of awareness at once. This explorer goes to the far outer limits of conscious awareness and then pushes out from there to discover every aspect of being. When we choose this path, we dive deep into our hearts to plumb the depths of our souls, through which we come to know God — not necessarily a God we have been taught to believe in by family, society, or institutions, but rather a God or Spirit or Universal Mind with whom we find our own very personal relationship. As 21st-century mystics, we embrace the intuitive mind as an aspect of the divine within us, and integrate the intuitive mind with the conscious or rational thought process for a more complete awareness and experience throughout every day. We learn to listen and respond to this divine inner voice of Spirit, allowing it to be the guiding light for our lives.

The 21st-century mystic's path does not necessarily replace any particular religious or spiritual belief system, but rather transcends it. This has been true for mystics from all traditions throughout history. Our sense of spirituality comes out of experience and faith, not out of what someone else tells us to think or feel. The mystical path is one of exploration and discovery, letting go of presuppositions. Rather than forcing an experience to fit into the framework of a particular belief, we let the experience show us its inherent spiritual message. We come to this spiritual truth through daily living. The mystic comes to know Spirit through experience rather than dogma, and, at times, may even reject all beliefs or thoughts in order to allow Spirit or mystical/ spiritual experience to enter in.

Too often, we encounter people who say, "I know what I believe," and that is the end of the discussion. They have not given much thought or consideration to their beliefs, but at the same time wish to go no further, and certainly do not want you to question or challenge their beliefs. They have found a very safe place within those beliefs. However, for the mystic, the actual statement of belief becomes the "jumping off point" for examining and understanding the belief as it relates to life, rather than the statement of belief being the "end point" of the journey. The 21st-century mystic embraces all of life as the spiritual teacher — an unfolding spiritual process, moment by moment, constantly offering gifts and insights, deeper and more profound understanding. The 21st-century mystic does not look at life through a fixed lens of beliefs, but rather lets life experience itself lead to personal truth.

# Using this Book

This book is designed as a workbook or guidebook for your personal mystical journey of self-discovery, co-creation, and intuitive development. It is structured in such a way to guide effectively both the novice in this realm as well as the individual who has been actively walking the spiritual path for many years. You will find that there are many layers to this work, many stages in the journey. Therefore, this is not meant to be a book that you will read only once. When you have come to the end of the book, perhaps you will take some time off to let things settle. Then you start again at your new level of development. You will find that the exercises and meditations speak to you in profoundly different ways at different stages of your own growth and development. Many of my students, having completed the third level of classes, ask to return to the first level to begin their journey again. As you begin the book for the first time, you may want to read it all the way through, and then come back and work your way through the exercises. Or, you may just want to start at the beginning and slowly proceed, doing all the exercises and meditations as you come to them.

Treat this book as a workbook, highlighting sections of text that are significant to you, and making notes in the margins. This will allow you to find discussions of particular concepts again quickly so that you can work with those ideas over and over. This book is meant to be used, not to sit on a shelf in pristine condition.

# Finding a Partner
# or Organizing a Study Group

Although you can do a tremendous amount of this work alone, you will find some exercises for which you need a partner, and some, especially in Part III, where a group is recommended. With this in mind, you may want to invite an adventurous and like-minded friend to join you for this journey. Or, you may want to organize a study group and work through the book with your friends and fellow spiritual explorers.

A partner or a group can become a powerful support for you in your journey. As you move through the self-discovery process, you will go deeper and deeper within yourself, uncovering joy and love, as well as pain and conflict. However, because of this deep exploration, building trust and safety within the group is essential. You will need to nurture this support system, allowing it to develop in its own time, so that everyone feels safe there.

Another advantage of working in a group is that together you are able to raise a very high level of energy, often facilitating much deeper work within individuals. In order to build this high level of energy, commitment to the group is essential from every member of the circle. It does not work for members to come and go. Each must make a commitment to on-time, regular attendance, and being fully present during your time together. I also suggest that you establish a specific seating arrangement in the class and keep this arrangement for the duration of your work together. If someone is absent from a session, leave an empty chair in their place in the circle. The reason for assigned seating is that you are building energy. You will begin to get used to the energy of the circle, and find that it builds faster and faster with each succeeding meeting.

All of this is to say, choose carefully who you invite to join you on this mystical journey so that you build a loving, supportive, and committed circle of people. And then enjoy your time together, for you will be sharing a magnificent unfolding.

With or without a group, however, you can certainly approach this book as your own personal curriculum for transformation. Take your time and go step-by-step, working through the exercises and meditations. You can read through many of the exercises to get a sense of them and then proceed. However, some are intended to be guided meditations. I suggest that you either pre-record these meditations on tape so that you can minimize distraction and set your own pace, or that you and your partner guide each other through the exercise. If you choose the latter, do not discuss the exercise until you have each had your turn, so that neither of you influences the other's experience. You can also use the meditation tapes that are available as a companion to this book.

If you choose to create your own meditation tapes, speak in a voice quality and pace that will facilitate a meditative state. You may want to record the first couple of meditations once and then listen back to see how the tape sounds. Ask yourself what could be improved in order to create the best possible meditative experience for you. You may want to go through the printed text, highlighting words or phrases you want to stress. Then tape it again. After doing this for a few meditations, you will know exactly how you want to create your tape the first time through.

# Journal Writing

I ask my students to keep a daily journal, writing at least three pages a day. I recommend that you do the same as you begin this journey. Three pages often seems like a lot, but you will find as time goes on that you begin working out the issues of your life through these journal pages, and that you gain powerful insights and clearer perspectives through the process of writing. At times, you may also begin to realize that you are not the one doing the writing. This is one of the most effective ways to begin your direct communication with Spirit. An easy and open dialogue can evolve out of your own reflective process without you trying so hard to get Spirit to speak. Spirit is there ready to help and guide you, offering love, nurture, and support if you can step back and let it happen. Following meditation, you may also want to record the experiences of your inner work in your journal, particularly if you received insights or clarity around certain issues, so that you may come back to work further with this understanding.

# Meditation

I also ask that my students establish a meditation discipline. If you do not already have an established meditation practice, I encourage you to begin a regular practice now. The particular method you use is not as important as the fact that you do it. There are a number of meditations in this book. They are very simple at the beginning and become more involved as we progress. They will help you establish your practice and open to the profound guidance and teaching available to you through your own meditation.

If at all possible, it is helpful to meditate at the same time and in the same place every day. This helps build an energy around that time and place, which will help you go deeper and deeper in your consciousness, and access higher and higher states of awareness. If you are working with specific spirit guides and teachers, you are in effect making a standing appointment with them for working together every day. And they will keep that appointment! We will talk more about direct work with spirit guides and teachers in Chapter 18.

Meditation is a process of heightening attention and awareness. It is about tuning in, not tuning out. It is about being awake — really awake — more awake than you have ever been. The goal of meditation is to heighten awareness, not to escape from the world. It is about finding your deep, inner point of stillness. Mystical experience occurs from within this point of stillness, a place where all conscious mental activity ceases. In our Western tradition, we tend to get caught in rational thought, which keeps us from the highest levels of consciousness. Mystics see the rational thought process as just another mental activity to be transcended in order to get to that ultimate point of stillness.

Meditation is a discipline of mind and body in order to access that point of stillness. It is a process of purification. As you are able to focus and reach the states of inner quiet, you begin to also be in touch with your inner states of disquiet. As you work through the unresolved issues that cause the disquiet, transforming them to quiet, purification occurs. You have then raised yourself to a higher level of consciousness.

# Open Mind, Open Heart

However you choose to approach meditation and the information and work of this book, try to come to it with your mind and heart open and fresh. Let go of preconceived ideas of how it "should" be — how you should behave, think, or feel in response to these concepts or experiences. Try to come into the work as an empty vessel waiting to be filled with the Love of the universe.

Allow yourself to work through this book and the individual concepts and exercises at your own pace. Respect your feelings at every step of the way. If an exercise or concept feels overwhelming in some way, or just uncomfortable for you in that moment, respect that feeling and move on. Take from this book what feels comfortable to you and leave what does not. However, remember that uneasiness will not always mean to retreat. At times you may come to an exercise that challenges you, yet you also know it is a step you now must take. The exercises you skip over may come calling out to you at a later point, and you will know then that you are ready to take that step. As my fellow musician, Jorge Alfano, says, "There's nothing wrong with fear — it's just a sign you are crossing over into the unknown." So, know your feelings and let your own inner wisdom be your guide.

We have said that this work has many layers. Some of you will be starting on the surface layers as you pick up this book, while others of you will have already progressed to much deeper layers. Give yourself permission to be wherever you are in your journey. Don't try to force yourself to be somewhere you are not. Don't try to push yourself faster than you are ready to go. At the same time, be sure to acknowledge the tremendous work you may have already done, and celebrate the accomplishments you *have* made in your spiritual path.

# And So We Begin

At the beginning of most travels, it is suggested that you fasten your seat belt and get ready for the ride. For this journey, however, I'd like to suggest that you might want to *take off* your seat belt in order to be free to fly. Be comfortable and free to move around, so that Spirit can move around within you. Just as I allowed myself to be guided by Spirit in writing this book, I hope you will allow Spirit to guide you in reading and working.

The sections of the text that are in italics have come directly from Spirit. Just one note of explanation here — you will notice that Spirit often refers to itself as "we." "They" have explained themselves as a collective consciousness of the Universe, again, as "the all of the everything that is." So, lest you get confused that "we" is a committee sitting in the spirit world, "they" are simply the great wisdom of the universe that lives within each of us.

Enjoy the gifts that I have received from Spirit, as well as your own gifts. When you open and commit to the mystical journey, to working with Spirit in the development of your intuitive awareness, the gifts are many, and the possibilities endless. All good wishes for your journey.

# Definitions

**intuition** — a process of tapping into one's deep sense of inner wisdom, the place inside of you where you know your oneness with All. At its highest level, the intuitive voice is the part of you that is one with the Great Mystery, that is Love, that is the voice of God within.

**intuitive living** — living moment-to-moment in an awareness of Spirit and the intuitive mind as a fully integrated aspect of your total being.

**mystic** — one who seeks a constant awareness of Spirit throughout every moment of daily life.

**mystical experience** — that which is very real to the experiencer, but cannot be explained by the rational mind.

**mysticism** — an acute awareness of Spirit, its influence on and movement through daily life.

**Spirit** — the all of the everything that is. It may also be called God, Source, Love, the Universal Creative Force, the Great Mystery, Universal Wisdom, or Higher Power.

**spirituality** — a sense of one's personal relationship with the divine, with God, with Spirit, or the ultimate Creative Force of the Universe.

# Part I

# The Path
# of the
# 21st-Century Mystic

Love is the face and body of the Universe.
It is the connective tissue of the universe,
the stuff of which we are made. Love is the
experience of being whole and connected
to Universal Divinity.

— Barbara Ann Brennan
*Hands of Light*

# 1

# Finding the Path

*Welcome to this wondrous journey into you. Me, you might ask? Yes, you. For if you want to find Spirit, if you want to find God, if you want to know Love and how this marvelous universe works, you must take the journey into you. As you do, you will begin to uncover extraordinary parts of you that you never knew were there. And you will come to much more profound understandings about parts you thought you already knew very well. The deeper you go in spiritual self-discovery, the higher you can fly in conscious awareness of all that surrounds you, seen and unseen, heard and unheard, known and unknown, thought and unthought. Sounds simple? It is. Sounds difficult? It is.*

*For now, welcome to the path — your path. It belongs to no one but you. Sometimes it will feel like you are creating it as you go, and other times it will appear to have been created for you. This is the mystical path, plain and simple — a path of co-creation, serendipity, miracles, and day-to-day, moment-to-moment human experience.*

We all have experiences of Spirit and intuition in our own ways. There is no single way. What is important is that each person who so desires finds their way, finds their own sense of spirituality and its unfolding journey, comes to know their own intuitive process, their own sense of Love and its movement through their life. This book is a result of my own spiritual and mystical journey to date. It has been a journey of awakening to the essence of who I am and the truth that is me, leading to the constant and powerful presence of intuitive understanding — profound communication with myself and with Spirit.

The words on these pages and the ideas they present all have come from some aspect of "doing the work" — daily meditation, Spirit Circles, teaching classes and workshops, clairvoyant counseling sessions and readings with individual clients, long and solitary drives from my country house to my city office and studio, walking the Earth, living with and in Spirit. What I want to share with you is the richness of life that can come from developing your intuitive gifts through a more acute awareness of Spirit, a process that involves self-discovery and leads to self-empowerment. This journey moves far beyond the fascination level of "psychic phenomena" and enters the domain of the soul. Developing intuitive gifts is an in-depth process of journeying to the core of your being and removing any and all obstacles that might separate you from the fullness of Love. The more we work through and let go of our own excess baggage, the clearer and brighter the soul shines out, and the easier it is for us simply to become one with Spirit, the Universal Mind or God-force, granting access to all of the knowledge and wisdom that is there for us.

# My Own Journey

I certainly can't say that my journey with Spirit has been without doubt, skepticism, frustration, or conflict; but I must also say that I can't imagine not taking the journey. From my earliest years, I was a creature of curiosity and vision, always seeking the next step, the next place to go in order to perfect a skill or to find out who I really was. Growing up in Kentucky and Indiana, I followed my father through many of his daily activities as a Protestant minister. As active as I was in all of the church affairs, I found myself still searching for more. I knew that there had to be a bigger picture. It wasn't until many years later that I would begin to see into the other realms of possibilities.

I look back now and realize the ways I was working with Spirit or acting on intuitive wisdom even as a child, the ways I could "see" and "know." One particular event stands out in my memory. I was 9

34

or 10 years old and my parents were away. Mrs. Heaton was staying with my sister and me. I was awakened in the middle of the night by the blaring of the volunteer fire department siren in our small town and knew instantly that Mrs. Heaton's house was on fire. Moments later the telephone rang, a call from her neighbor to tell us the news.

With this and other experiences, I assumed that everyone could see and know things. As I realized that they didn't, I avoided talking about mystical experience and had no encouragement to explore these spiritual gifts. Mystical experience, working with Spirit, and direct communication with God or the universe were not part of everyday conversation in small towns in central Kentucky.

My conscious awakening began in the early 1980s. I had completed graduate degrees in church music and voice performance, joined the voice faculty of a well-known college conservatory, and began serving as organist and choirmaster in a church. As I taught singers and dealt with some of my own personal issues, I began to realize that I was embarking on a journey that perhaps not everyone was actively pursuing. I realized that I was searching deeper inside myself and striving harder for an understanding about life and its mysteries than most people I knew. I began seeing many parallels between the freedom of singing and the freedom of life; yet I was still trapped within the confines of a former belief system.

Over the next several years, I began reading books, practicing meditation, and taking classes and workshops. I began to embrace the possibilities of other realms of awareness, and of the validity of experiences which had no rational explanation. As my daily meditation practice developed, I began to feel as though somehow I was being "taught." I would perceive thoughts or understand concepts that I had never considered or understood before. I received a lot of guidance for helping a friend, Mac, who had recently been diagnosed with AIDS. Spirit helped me understand the powerful spiritual healing that was occurring in the midst of Mac's debilitating illness. For many years, he had been a very angry man. Through his illness he was able to let go of his anger, so that when death came two years later, he was a very peaceful man. Walking that difficult daily path with Mac was much easier with the guidance and insight from Spirit. As we sat and talked and struggled with his anger, fear, depression, and sadness, I would often think, "How can I possibly help him — I have no words

35

or answers." And then Spirit would give me the words or lead me to a deeper place of compassion from which to listen.

As time went on, I began to understand the unfolding of my own life from a much larger perspective. It was as if Spirit was communicating with me through thought-forms. I would just "know" which choice to make, what my next professional steps should be, where I needed to go and who I needed to see. On many occasions, I found myself going someplace simply because an inner voice said I had to go. Once there I would meet someone important to my journey, or have a conversation that would lead to a shift in perception about something in my life. Only then would I know why I had felt so compelled to go there.

After a year or so of this form of communication, I began to hear specific words, as if a voice was speaking to me. The voice, as I perceived it, was not inside my head, but rather just above my head, speaking directly down into my thoughts. I was not hearing Spirit speak through my outer sense of hearing or my ears, but rather through an inner sense of sound perception.

At this point, I placed a tape recorder beside my meditation chair. When I began to perceive that voice speaking, I turned on the tape recorder and simply spoke what I was hearing. After a while, I discovered I no longer needed first to listen to the voice and then repeat the information, but could simply let the voice speak *through me*. There was tremendous energy and love within this experience. As I listened back to the tape, transcribing the wisdom and guidance from Spirit, I was hearing my own voice, yet obviously another energy moving through it. I continued this process for many months, receiving the teaching from Spirit, transcribing the tapes, and yet not being sure what I was to do with this.

Not yet working with a teacher on a regular basis, I traveled to see Joey Crinita, a fantastic spiritualist medium from Toronto. I had taken workshops with Joey and knew that he could help me better understand what was happening in my meditation. As I shared my transcriptions with him, Joey helped me see that within them was an entire weekend workshop, and that Spirit was asking me to teach this material. I experienced tremendous resistance to this assignment, thinking that I could not possibly be ready to do such a thing. But, in spite of my resistance, I organized and taught several workshops.

36

People spoke of the powerful healing energy there was in my singing and in my teaching, and how much love they felt just being in my presence. Over the next couple of years, I taught more workshops, and the work was both satisfying and appreciated. However, I also accepted a lot of ego stroking, and basked in that for awhile, until something in me screamed out, "Stop! What are you doing?" Suddenly I was confronted with fear and confusion because I didn't know why I had this gift of communicating with Spirit, why I should have these unexplainable mystical experiences, why I had been given what seemed to me to be a tremendous responsibility, and I didn't want any part of it. I just wanted to lead a "normal" life. What was "awakening" inside of me made me very uncomfortable — so uncomfortable that I just wanted to go back to sleep. I stopped teaching classes and all intentional or conscious communication with Spirit.

Some months after ceasing these activities, I was singing a recital for a university audience, and, for the first time in my life, experienced stage fright. Well-prepared and very excited about singing a program of songs that I loved, I went bounding out onto the stage as was my habit, started the first song, and suddenly was terrified. I had never experienced such anxiety in my life. In that moment I thought that I would never be able to get through the concert. I wanted to run as fast as I possibly could from the stage, from the hall, from singing, from anyone I knew, from God, from everything. I didn't know why I was afraid, or what I was afraid of; I just knew that I would have done anything in that moment to get out of there. Over the course of the next several months, this problem only got worse. Each concert was paralyzing to me. I would somehow make it through, and tapes and reviews would tell me that they were actually quite wonderful concerts, but I was miserable. Finally, after a New York City concert of love songs on Valentine's Day, I said to myself that if this was how it was going to be, I had to stop singing. I couldn't take it anymore.

Through all of my doubts and resistance, I had at least maintained my meditation practice, but had refused any direct communication with Spirit. I came home from the concert hall that night and ranted and raved at Spirit, demanding some understanding about what was happening to me. I was all ready for a fight, when Spirit very gently and lovingly responded, *Welcome back*. That was certainly a surprise to me. The answer was so still and peaceful and embracing. *Welcome back.* Spirit went on to explain that what was happening to me was a result of abandoning my gifts. What was manifesting as fear was actually my resistance to allowing Love to flow through me in my singing. I would get on the stage and all that Love energy would come surging up through my body, and I would subconsciously try to push it back down. I interpreted the resulting inner conflict as fear. If I would only let go of the resistance and resume my communion with Spirit, my fears would dissolve.

I knew then that I had no choice but to actively resume my spiritual quest, my mystical journey. I began to work with a series of teachers in the Spiritualist tradition who helped facilitate my journey so that I would no longer step in the way of its unfolding. Spirit also worked through several friends who encouraged and finally convinced me to begin teaching classes again, and one of them offered his home for a workshop.

As I began to teach and resume my personal work with Spirit, it was like coming home again — home to me, the essence of me. For so long, I had been running away from home. I had been trying desperately to create a "normal" life for myself — one that I thought would be simple and without risk or challenge, one that would be "comfortable." But that was not to be my path. The lesson for me was surrender — surrender to Spirit, and surrender to the mystic within to guide me through a journey that was mine, not someone else's. Incidentally, the performance fears vanished immediately, as well.

My journey remains full of challenges, conflicts, "growth opportunities," but it also remains full of joy and love and, at times, even bliss. My life has become a constant dialogue with Spirit. I begin every day in meditation, thanking Spirit for being with me and guiding me through every activity — teaching voice lessons, counseling clients, singing, writing, composing, making decisions, teaching classes. With each passing day, I feel more peaceful, and less attached to outcomes — peaceful with being led by Spirit through each experience, and peaceful with exploring my intuitive gifts and seeing where I seem to be led next. I am very often surprised at where I find myself, for Spirit's guidance often leads me to unexpected turns. However, those turns have opened into wondrous new avenues of possibilities. My singing has expanded beyond the classical realm to also include cabaret and musical theater as I have opened the door to the songwriter within me. A CD recording of my songs has been released. I continue to teach singers and work with performers helping them recognize and release physical and emotional energy blocks in their work. I have completed seminary training and been ordained as an Interfaith Minister. I look at my father and realize that we are doing the same work, but following different pathways. Spirit is working with me in many ways, and works with us all in many different ways, speaking many languages so that all may, in time, hear the words. And each hears the words in his or her own time.

# A Life-Long Path

The mystic's journey is life-long. Though some of the concepts presented here may seem simplistic — "just do this and everything will be perfect" — I fully realize that their application in daily living is often very difficult, and, at times, seemingly impossible. However, it is in day-to-day living that we face our inner struggles, conflicts and growth, and take the small steps that all go together to make up the journey. It is also in our day-to-day living that we learn to trust our intuitive guidance. As Mark, one of the students in my classes, says so clearly, "Doing the work means living in an awareness that every experience of every day is a part of the learning and growth process."

# It's Not Always Easy

Spirit is pure Love. The mystic's journey in its fullest sense means surrendering to Spirit — an ultimate giving over of your life to Spirit, and how It wishes to work through you. Spirit is the supreme teacher and healer. But It does not always create an easy pathway for us. Sometimes Spirit flows through us with the gentle healing balm of a peacefully flowing river. At other times It rages through us like a torrential rapids, seeming to create havoc in our lives. Both kinds of experience are often part of the healing and learning process. Spirit creates pathways through which we can learn — pathways that can lead to clearer understanding of ourselves and our circumstances, and to a higher level of awareness. When we surrender fully to Spirit, we become at the same time student and teacher, parent and child, lover and beloved. The mystic's path is not one of avoiding fears or conflicts, or of keeping them carefully managed and "under control." The mystic's path is one of walking through fears, inner conflicts, personal issues, so that we can see them clearly, heighten our awareness, and open to the vast intuitive knowledge, wisdom, and guidance that the universe makes available to us through working with Spirit.

# Sacred and Secular Become One

This journey is about allowing mystical experiences to enter our lives — experiences of joy and bliss and satisfaction that are inexpressible in words, but that to us are holy and sacred; experiences in which we know our oneness with the divine at the very depths of our being. It is about letting Spirit enter in and work through us. As a Western civilization, we have separated the sacred and the secular in our lives. However, in indigenous cultures, where there is more of an Earth-based spirituality, there is no distinction between sacred and secular. Some modern-day religions consider these Earth-based spiritual beliefs primitive or pagan, but it seems to me that they are pretty enlightened. They honor the sacred nature of all of creation — the wisdom of the Great Mystery that flows through every plant, animal, element, person. The sacred is an integrated part of everyday life of all people, not just a selected few. In these indigenous cultures, supernatural experiences begin in childhood and are encouraged by the elders as a part of daily life. It is considered quite normal to work with Spirit, to see beyond the realm of physical sight, to experience precognitive dreams.

In our "sophisticated" Western world, filled with technology and intellectual pursuits, and our intellectualization of spirituality, we have lost touch with this "reality" of living. Through embarking on the mystical journey, we can reawaken the mystic within us, and build trust and faith in our intuitive selves. The journey is about coming

40

back to the simplicity and love and depth of Spirit and knowing our union with the divine. Angela, another student in my classes, says, "I've learned that meditation and living must ultimately be the same. The great revelations, enlightenment, and spiritual awakenings that I've experienced in class and in my meditation are of little value unless I bring them down to earth and into my everyday living."

# What's in it for me?

You might ask, why should I embark upon the path of the 21st-century mystic? Why should I take this journey? Why should I want to develop my intuitive awareness? Students come into classes, workshops, and private sessions with these same questions, yet something in them is demanding that they enter the journey. Each student has a different experience as they move through the process, but all who commit themselves to the work experience tremendous transformation. Sarah, a physician, found that opening the door to Spirit "created a wonderful framework through which to discover the different dimensions of self." Joe, an administrator, said, "This work has been more than a learning experience. It's been a shift in the living of my life. Through opening to my own gifts, I've discovered lots of exciting possibilities about a person I'd suspected was in waiting. So many new paths are now in view. I'm very excited about them as I am beginning the journey." Jackie, an actor, said, "Opening my intuitive self has opened up so many possibilities for me. I think the most wonderful thing is that it has shown me the options that I didn't know were there. I still have to do the work, but now I know I can." Robert, an educational counselor, said, "My life feels so directed now. It all seems so much easier, because I have so many tools to rely on, and have learned to trust my intuitive self. For so long I just dismissed any intuitive abilities at all, losing out on so much valuable guidance." Dina spoke of working with Spirit and the mystical journey as "the greatest nurturing experience you'll ever have." Most of the students come to the end of the first series of classes saying there is no turning back now — what's the next step? And then we move on.

Because of my own experiences and observing the exciting

transformation and growth in the lives of others, I can only say that embarking on the mystical path will change your life. You will experience personal growth and transformation that you never dreamed of before. You will come to know your own wisdom, and know that when you feel your oneness with all of creation, you receive the highest teachings through your own inner guidance. Spirit speaks to us in many ways — through dreams, meditation, thoughts, interactions with others, even through the newspaper or television. Our responsibility is to be open and aware of the messages as they come.

Doing this work does not mean that your life will be magically transformed into constant bliss and happiness. In fact, sometimes life will get even more challenging because you are more aware of all of its many facets. However, your response to your life will become vastly different. You will find a clearer understanding and perception of the difficulties and challenges in your life, as well as the marvelous aspects of your journey. You will find that you have many more tools to help you in facing the challenges and creating change so that you can move through these challenges more quickly and with less angst.

The first changes you experience will be in your perception more than in your life circumstances. However, change in perception is the essential first step to changing any life circumstance. While mid-way through a second-level class, Charlotte described her experience as a "clearing and cleansing process." She reflected, "I have felt as if my soul was tearing apart when I allowed the energy to unblock and move. It brought back so many memories that I had buried. I had fooled myself into thinking they were gone. At these painful times I was not sure if the process would ever be complete for me. I could only trust that I was right where I needed to be in order to grow and move on to the next level. As time went on a much greater awareness of myself came into place which allowed me to drop the chains of the past and step into the fullness of myself and my oneness with God. I can't yet find words to describe the tremendous healing that is now taking place."

# The Point of Stillness

As human beings, we yearn to experience our wholeness within, and our oneness or sense of connectedness and belonging to something larger than ourselves. I have found that I most fully experience wholeness and oneness when I can simply allow myself to just "be" wherever I am emotionally, embracing my feelings and circumstances. I call it coming to my point of stillness. When you reach that point of stillness deep inside, you know your wholeness. You also come to know your "aliveness." We often tend to look for our aliveness outside of ourselves through our activities. But the real aliveness comes from deep within our stillness. That is where we feel the pulsing of Spirit through our beings. Through our point of stillness we learn to work with Spirit.

When we begin to live from within this point of stillness, we begin to realize that working with Spirit is something that we already know how to do. We begin to realize that the inner voices of intuition are voices we have heard before. We all have "hunches" about how something will turn out, a "gut feeling" about what is the right decision. But we tend not to trust those feelings because we haven't worked with them enough to *learn* to trust them, to learn how they can serve us. So, you may need to reawaken that knowledge of working with Spirit and your intuitive self — to take the time to settle in and remember that somewhere inside you are answers to every question you have, guidance for every aspect of your life.

It sounds so simple, yet it is often so difficult. As you move through this book, when the concepts seem simple and at the same time overwhelming, try to keep your awareness focused on the simplicity. Awareness is everything. Fixing problems is not the answer, for then we are only treating symptoms. As we can open our awareness to possibilities and perceive patterns in our lives, we can begin to allow those patterns to shift simply through our awareness of them, and then we begin building a strong foundation for living.

Take a few moments now to do the following exercise to find your own inner point of stillness.

# Exercise #1
# Point of Stillness Meditation

Sit quietly with your eyes closed, back straight, feet flat on the floor or legs folded in a lotus position, and hands resting comfortably on your lap. Take a few deep breaths, allowing your body to relax, and then let your breath find its own natural, relaxed, easy rhythm. Begin paying attention to your breath as it passes your nostrils. Bring all of your attention to that point of focus — breath passing through your nostrils. There is nothing else in your conscious awareness except the breath.

You may notice a great deal of "chatter" going on in your mind as you attempt to focus solely on your breath. It's okay. Just notice it. Then step by step, layer by layer, go beneath the chatter. Let your breath help you to drop deeper in your consciousness. On the inhalation, feel as if the floor of your current layer of awareness opens, and on the exhalation you simply float down to the next deeper, quieter layer. Continue this process until you realize you have come to a place of absolute quiet and stillness. You may have to pass through many layers of outer chatter before you finally reach this place. It's all right. Don't worry about how long it takes. Just keep breathing and floating down to deeper and deeper layers.

As you are floating deeper, you may notice that you begin to feel calmer, more centered, and more grounded. You may feel your heart open. You are simply opening to you — your essence. You may become cognizant of several layers of awareness and consciousness at once. You may begin to understand on a whole new level the meaning of "still waters run deep" — that on the surface there is lots of chatter, but the deeper you go the quieter it gets. Take your time to float for awhile, and then when you feel as though the meditation is complete for now, open your eyes.

This exercise helps you reach your point of stillness. It also helps you see how far below the surface you are still chattering — how far you have to go to get to stillness. It is also a great check-up exercise to do from time to time just to see how you are doing. There is no judgment on what you find — just a recognition that you've come closer to living in your point of stillness, or perhaps drifted a little farther away. If you have drifted, just let the exercise serve as a call back to that still, silent place inside that is your essence.

# 2

# The Enlightened Journey

Every moment of our lives, every activity of our day, every interaction with another, every feeling or emotion, reaction or response to the world around us, is a part of our spiritual journey. Everyone is on this journey. Some are more aware of it than others, but everyone is proceeding through their own set of opportunities for self-discovery and co-creation, all leading to that ultimate goal of enlightenment.

In my meditation, Spirit has defined enlightenment as *a state of being in which we can allow Love to flow through us in every moment of our existence.* Enlightenment is a constant opening to and becoming one with Love or Spirit, letting this powerful force guide us through our lives. Through that constant flow of Love, we are open to the infinite source of knowledge, wisdom, and guidance from Spirit. Intuitive living begins with consciously setting foot on the pathway of Love, exploring every aspect of our lives, and releasing any block that might be impeding the Love flow. The greater the flow of Love through our beings, the greater our potential for intuitive awareness.

## Self-Awareness

The mystical journey begins with awakening awareness of ourselves. This may appear at first glance to be a simple concept. However, many of us are painfully unaware of ourselves — of our feelings, our bodies, our overall state of well-being. For instance, we may not realize until hours or even days after a particular encounter that we were angry or hurt by what was said or done. Or, we may experience a reaction such as anger immediately, yet not know why we are angry. In a physical activity such as moving a heavy object or in athletics, we may push ourselves beyond the sensible limit because we are not hearing the body's clear message that it is being overtaxed. This lack of awareness affects our health, our relationships, our work, our spiritual lives — every part of us. An ancient Chinese proverb says: "God's wind is always blowing, but you must put up the sail." So we begin this journey by examining ourselves, by putting up the sail, and inviting Spirit to enter in, to fill out the sail, and be the guiding force on our pathways.

When a child is born, their consciousness is still very connected to the spiritual world. During the first few months and years of life, they begin to develop their own personality and sense of self in the physical world, yet still often maintain an ability to see through the "masks" of adults and situations. We have all heard the expression, "Out of the mouths of babes . . ." referring to the amazing wisdom or perception of children. There is a beautiful story of parents looking into the nursery and finding their four-year old leaning over the edge of his new-born sister's crib, asking "Please tell me about God — I'm beginning to forget."

Children are often aware of energy fields and spirits, and understand the truth of situations very simply and clearly. However, in our Western culture and beliefs, we do not encourage children to continue developing these perceptual abilities. Their "imaginary playmates" or other "fantasies" may be strongly discouraged by parents and other adults. Their honest perceptions of situations sometimes make us adults uncomfortable in the spotlight of such naked truth, so we discount the children's perceptions in order to protect our carefully crafted "realities." This sends a clear, albeit often unconscious, message to the child that their perceptions must be wrong and that they should stop using these abilities. At the least, our culture's lack of acknowledgment of mystical experience encourages our children to close the door on their "visions," their "knowings and understandings," and their "perceptions." As adults, we have gotten stuck in our "seeing is believing" frame of mind, and lost our sense of that mystical world beyond the outer senses.

Times are beginning to change, however. More and more people are awakening to a conscious awareness of their spiritual journeys, and to the great wealth of wisdom and guidance available through opening to "another world of possibilities" — a world that the five outer senses may not perceive, but in which the inner senses flourish. Concepts of mysticism and mystical experience are being introduced into our western world once again. The principal goal of this book is to help you, the reader, remember that you have an open passageway to the mystic within — a passageway that can take you into a realm of endless possibilities, wisdom, guidance, nurturing, and Love.

# Soul and Ego — A Powerful Partnership

We find this open passageway through the soul. The soul is the aspect of you that is connected to Spirit, the aspect of you that is Love. It is your divinity. Soul and ego join together to make up the total you. Ego provides the way of action in the world. Ego is the physical body and personality, the vehicle through which your soul lives in the physical world. Ego is mind, analytical thought process, while soul is heart. Both are essential. In a healthy ego-soul balance, Love flows through the soul, guiding the way through lessons and growth, and the ego responds with the appropriate action in the world. However, when things get turned around and ego takes control, dictating its needs and desires and insisting that they be met, frustration arises because soul and ego are at odds with one another. This can manifest in many ways, as in my experience of fear while performing. My soul was desperately trying to be the channel for Love, while my ego was saying, "No, this is too much for me. I'm losing control of this situation. I must be in charge and keep things comfortable and safe."

Cultures and societies and their rules are formed out of ego's need to create a framework for existence in a physical world. There are many rules, and tremendous energy is spent enforcing those regulations. Traditions are established, and the ego finds great comfort and stability in those traditions. However, soul knows nothing of rules and traditions. It only knows its journey of unfolding Love. Soul is always seeking growth and development — new experiences that will continue to challenge us and offer opportunities for advancement in understanding and knowledge, and open us to Love. Life challenges are Spirit's way of providing this growth and development for the soul. The ego may resist the challenge or the impending change, but the soul, through its persistent yearning or nudging, insists on going forward. This creates the tension and fuel for growth, and for increasing spiritual "aliveness."

Unfortunately, in our Western culture and society, we tend to encourage and nurture ego more than soul. We are very attached to our concepts of success and the importance of appearance and how we are seen in others' eyes. This often leads to an abandonment of soul's needs and desires in favor of ego's apparent need for a more socially acceptable appearance. As we get farther away from honoring soul, ego begins to control, and soul loses its place within active consciousness. This creates a separation between soul and ego, and a split begins to develop within the individual's consciousness. Ego takes off in its determination to "succeed," whatever that may mean in the situation,

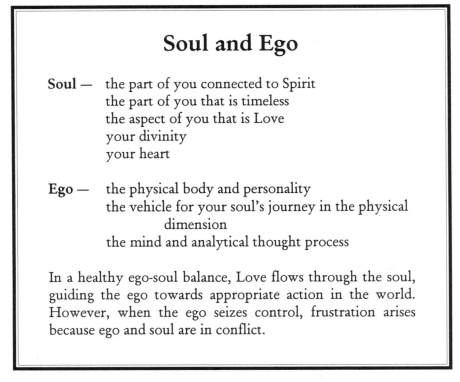

# Soul and Ego

**Soul —** the part of you connected to Spirit
the part of you that is timeless
the aspect of you that is Love
your divinity
your heart

**Ego —** the physical body and personality
the vehicle for your soul's journey in the physical
dimension
the mind and analytical thought process

In a healthy ego-soul balance, Love flows through the soul, guiding the ego towards appropriate action in the world. However, when the ego seizes control, frustration arises because ego and soul are in conflict.

and the yearnings of the soul are pushed down and covered over with activities and responsibilities of the ego's creation.

As we open to our spiritual journeys, however, we become more aware of this separation, and realize that we can make choices about how we live our lives. We begin to have greater understanding of our desires, needs, fears, angers, and quests for power as symptoms of this separation of ego and soul. As the journey continues, we explore deeper levels of these two parts of self, and can begin the process of ending the separation and bringing them back into balance.

Linda went through an angry and seemingly final separation from her husband of only one year. She experienced an emotional "bottom" and suffered terrors as if a wild animal had seized her, shaken her, and left her for dead. In fear and despair she sought the guidance of Spirit through meditation, and became acquainted with the still point of her soul. In that quiet place she knew that no matter what the eventual outcome, her deepest desire was for reconciliation and a continued journey with her partner. She was able, with the help of Spirit, to "let go" of the result she wanted, and, miraculously, her wish was granted. The journey continues not without difficulties, but with continued healing, balance, and enlightenment.

Our fundamental task in the spiritual journey is healing the separation between ego and soul so that our lives come into balance, and we can get on with the journey toward enlightenment. Spirit interjects here to say,

> *There is no separation of ego and soul in the enlightened being. But please don't think that to be enlightened is such a lofty position! In fact, to be enlightened is a very humble position. Enlightenment simply means light from within — light from within that comes from God or Source or whatever you wish to call the higher power of the universe. In the enlightened being there is full recognition and embrace of soul as supreme connection to God, and full surrender to the guidance, love and light that comes from that divine Source, from the truth of every being. Ego surrenders to soul. Surrender does not mean "is not active," for ego remains very active. Without ego, soul cannot function in the physical realm. The body is a part of ego. Language, clothes, house, job, every physical aspect or component*

*of your life is part of ego. All these aspects must surrender to the supreme leadership of soul, which is in direct partnership with God, and respond by living out the soul's desires.*

Where do all of the many and varied activities of our lives fit into this balance process? They are all ego components. The soul is simply and purely Love. Everything else in our lives is a creation of ego. In a healthily balanced state, ego creates in response to soul's desires. However, when we allow any aspect of our lives to become a creation of ego alone, with no regard for the needs or the voice of soul, we alter the divine hierarchy and place ego above soul. In this imbalance, inner conflict arises.

This first step of self-awareness entails getting back in touch with our souls, that aspect of us that is timeless, that is one with Spirit. The more we are in touch with our souls, the more the highest powers of creation are available to us, and the greater our communion and co-creation with Spirit. Much of our process through this book is about moving back to soul, working with soul energy, relating to the world more and more from soul rather than from ego, and becoming fully aware of our essence. Our culture encourages the ego journey, all of which happens outside of ourselves — the journey of career, responsibilities, successes, appearances. However, the journey of the soul is inside — allowing our lives to be created out of soul essence, tapping into the divine creative spark, the place inside of us where God lives. When our attention is focused on this soul journey and being guided by Spirit, the ego journey unfolds naturally with much less stress and anxiety. We come to know the difference between activity "aliveness," a constant flurry of outer activities and busy-ness, and spiritual "aliveness," feeling alive and invigorated at our deepest core essence.

# Enlightened Living

Henry David Thoreau said, "Only that day dawns to which we are awake." Moving back to soul requires a commitment to being awake and heightening our awareness in every realm. Being awake and aware means experiencing *through* our senses rather than simply *with* our senses. It means going beyond our five outer senses of seeing, hearing, touching, tasting, and smelling, and exploring the inner aspects of these senses. Through the soul, we can transcend all barriers of the physical dimension, and move beyond the realm of physical time and space into a realm of all possibilities. When we step into soul, we immediately open the door to that timeless and boundary-free dimension where we can access the all-encompassing wisdom and guidance of the universe.

This is the mystical path. This is enlightened living. Being awake and aware allows us to see where our emotional limits are, where we have set boundaries, or even created emotional barriers and armoring. With this clearer perception, we can begin to push past our limits, take down our emotional barriers and armoring that we have created as our ego protections, and uncover our essence and our true gifts from Spirit. Gifts from Spirit include our talents and special abilities, but also our intuitive awareness. As we embark upon and commit to this mystical journey, our clarity of understanding and perception unfold. Intuition is nothing more than tapping into the part of you that is one with God. Our whole purpose in this book is that you find your oneness with God — that you learn to live your life from a point of stillness, the point of oneness with Spirit, with Love — ultimately, that you recognize that you are Love, and therefore not only can access, but, in fact, *are* all the wisdom of the universe.

The journey is not always an easy one. There is an unfortunate idea that once one "becomes spiritual" everything in their lives becomes easy. No, in fact, in some ways our lives become more difficult, because we choose to open our eyes to the truth of our being, which often brings realizations of how we may have been *running from* our truth. We begin to understand that allowing Love to flow freely does not always create easy circumstances in our lives. Love is the healer. Love will create the experiences necessary for our learning and growth, all leading to our full and complete understanding of our oneness with God. Sometimes conflicts and challenges are necessary to facilitate growth and understanding.

Committing to the journey means moving deeper and deeper into previously unknown territories — at least unknown to the outer consciousness. Spirit challenges us and pushes us, making us at times

53

comfortable and at other times uncomfortable, and presents us with many conflicts. But, by doing our work, we can find fulfillment, peace, and Love in the process. Sometimes it seems that the fulfillment and love are a long way off, and Spirit is only showing us one step at a time. We learn to develop patience, have faith in the process, and know that somehow, some way, we will get there.

# The Freedom Journey

That's the journey — exciting, and sometimes tough. In my meditation, Spirit has often called it a freedom journey. Freedom means nothing more than being able to sit in your heart in peace and quiet, and be who you are in your God-given grace. Freedom and peace are both *inner* states of being, not outer. Peace is not the absence of conflict, but rather our *response* to conflict. Being free and at peace means knowing without doubt that no matter what is happening around you, nothing can harm you at your center.

Many of my Friday evenings are spent leading Spirit Circles — intimate gatherings for meditation, teachings, and messages from Spirit. The evening always begins with a meditation guided by Spirit. In one Circle, Spirit chose to speak about the freedom journey and its difficulties:

*The days as they come to you, one by one, seem to get really difficult at times. The tasks that come your way, the lessons, the opportunities for change, growth, and understanding get really hard. And we in Spirit keep coming to you and telling you that it is so simple. We want to help you understand that we are not at all making light of your earth-plane journey. The day-to-day activity and the day-to-day lessons, the hour-to-hour, minute-to-minute activity of your life may be at times filled with joy, ease, love, happiness, and laughter, and in the next moment be filled with challenge, dissension, and conflict. And we recognize that difficulty. What we want to help you understand is that* while the concepts of living are very simple, living the concepts is not always so simple. *You are in a physical-plane life, living in a realm where every bit of your physical being is connected to ego. And ego is essential. Don't try to get rid of it. Just remember that the balance between ego and soul is what the journey is all about.*

*We speak about the freedom journey. And what is freedom? Freedom is knowing who you are, and being willing and able to sit in who you are; being able to sit in your truth, with no more conflict at your center. There may be conflict going on all around you, but that conflict all around you is the way you come to find the peace at your center. Conflict in your life, challenge in your life, difficulty, questioning, doubting, on some levels, may never cease. The physical plane offers ample opportunity for dealing with all of these issues. However, the freedom journey is about learning to just sit in this deep place within you, your place of peace, in spite of the conflict or doubt. It's about knowing that there is a place deep inside your heart and soul where nothing but God can touch you, and that it is very possible to live your life from that place. No experience that you have, nothing that happens to you or through you, nothing that anyone says to you can hurt you when you are in that place. We are talking about the core of you, the essence of your being, your soul — it cannot be touched. However, from the first layer out from that core of soul, ego takes quite a beating. And as ego takes the beating, it hardens, creates an armor, and begins to fight back, which makes the challenge even greater. As the armor is solidified, it becomes almost impossible to get to soul. The freedom journey is about learning to take off the armor, enter into the place of peace, and* live *there — not just come for a visit every now and then. So the journey is tough. The lessons are tough. And the concepts are so easy, so simple.*

*Why is it so hard to be so simple? Everything in both the physical and spiritual planes is made up of some configuration of energy, some energy pattern. Habits are also energy patterns. Therefore, to put it simply, each of you has woven a web throughout and around your energy systems of habit — the way you live your life, the way you deal with conflict, with dissension, with joy and happiness and love, the way you deal with anything that comes your way. Reactions all come out of habit. They all come out of the patterns that make up the swirls of energy around your soul kernel. The soul kernel is pure Love. Everything beyond the soul kernel is ego. We speak to you in such simple terms of the lessons and the concepts and the guides of living. However, the ego energy patterns get very thick, very heavy, very slowed-down.*

*An easy way for you to understand this is that in your intellect you can easily comprehend how to do a particular task, such as swimming, in just a few minutes. But it takes you much longer to get the muscles to be fully coordinated to the point of becoming a champion swimmer. It is the same with these lessons and concepts. The guidelines for living are so simple. You can understand them as intellectual concepts in a moment. But your physical energy patterns are vibrating at a much slower rate than the thought process energy patterns holding the guideline. Therefore, it takes much longer to make the shift in physical form, in the ego form. And that's okay. What's important is that you are aware of your journey, aware of your energy patterns, aware of the places where you get trapped. That's all that's necessary, because through your awareness, energy shifts begin to happen.*

*As we give you such simple guidelines for living, at times it seems as though we are saying, "Look, you know, if you would just do this, everything would be fine." Well, it is just as simple as that. If you would just do "this" everything would be fine. And it is as hard as, "How can I possibly do that? From where I sit in this moment, I can't even imagine how to get there." It's okay. It's okay to be wherever you are. Honor wherever you are in your journey. And by honoring it and accepting it, you can begin to work with it. You can work with the energy pattern that makes up the being that you are in this instant, and begin to shift that energy pattern so that you get closer to being able to live in your heart center, not just visit there from time to time. Honor where you are. And as we keep nudging you along, pushing you further and further, encouraging you as you go through the journey, and saying, "If you would only do this," know that we are also honoring where you are. And know that even when we give such simple directives that seem so impossible to follow, we even honor that impossibility. As you can gently soften the ego armoring, we can begin to help you see the possibilities. Every day the journey is so easy, and it is so hard, and it's okay. Honor where you are. Accept it. Understand it as just part of the flow. When you can let go of your attachment to the difficulty, you can float. You can soften the edges. You can honor where you are, and then you can begin to fly.*

The journey toward spiritual awareness demands self-knowledge. It is a journey toward firmly establishing a clear personal relationship with the fullness of you and with your sense of the God-force. It is a path of self-truth and self-understanding. What we are talking about is not religion, or at least not what religion has come to mean in our modern language. This mystical journey is, however, about what religion meant in its original form — binding back to God. It is a journey to finding your own personal religion, which may or may not be a part of any established religious or spiritual tradition. It is a journey made up of ordinary daily experience as well as extraordinary insights and revelations. Your particular journey will be unique to you, and will belong to you alone.

Find your own way, led by your personal relationship to Spirit. Don't get locked into someone else's pathway, including mine. Throughout this book you will encounter many tools to pioneer your way through your self. As you make your way to your own soul essence, you begin to know who you really are. And then you begin to know God.

The following exercise will help you begin to identify where you are on your path right now. It is also an exercise that you may wish to come back to from time to time as a point of reference.

# Exercise #2
# Who am I right now?

Take a few moments to go back to Exercise #1 and come once again to your point of stillness. When you have reached your calm, quiet center, ask the question, "Who am

I right now in this moment?" Allow the response to come as thoughts, words, feelings, images, colors, or sounds. Make no judgment on what comes to you, and try not to have a preconceived notion of what the experience will or should be. Just sit in your point of stillness and allow yourself whatever comes. Afterwards, go to your journal to record your impressions and experience.

# 3

# Touching the Soul — Opening from Within

Too often we are encouraged to seek answers to questions outside of ourselves rather than explore our inner beings. We are taught to find the expert, to read a book, to seek advice. But the mystic's journey is one of opening from the inside out, learning to look inside for answers — to go deep into our hearts and souls where we can connect with the universal wisdom and receive guidance for our lives. There are times when it might be important to seek outside sources, but even then we must process that information through our own higher wisdom. God is found inside our hearts, not outside in a book, in a class, or in an institution. When we open from the inside, we allow God to live and breathe within us, giving us access to our own inner wisdom. Universal wisdom is revealed to us when we can open our hearts and receive.

Over the years I have studied with many wonderful teachers and learned from many inspired authors. However, the most profound teachings and understanding have come through my own meditation — through opening to, sinking into, and awakening to Love. In order to further facilitate that process for you, here are two guided meditations. They are designed so that, if you are relatively new to this form of meditation, you can work with them as two separate exercises. If you are quite comfortable with the process, you can continue from one to the next.

# Exercise #3
# The Light of the Soul I

Once again sit quietly with your eyes closed, back straight, feet flat on the floor or legs folded in a lotus position, and your hands resting comfortably on your lap. Take a few deep breaths, allowing your body to relax, and let your breath find its own natural, relaxed, easy rhythm. Bring your attention to your breath passing through your nostrils, and keep your attention focused there for a few moments. This will help you sink into a deeper level of consciousness.

. . .

As you continue to breathe, on the inhalation feel as though the floor of your current layer of conscious awareness opens. Then on the exhalation allow yourself to float down to the next deeper, quieter level. Continue this process until you are approaching a place of absolute quiet and stillness. Just keep breathing and floating down to deeper and deeper layers.

. . .

As you go deeper and deeper in your consciousness, you come closer and closer to your point of stillness. Even though at this point you may not feel that you are all the way there, imagine now that you can peer deep inside to the core of your being — to the very center of you. At this center you see a very beautiful light. It may be a small flame or it may be a huge bonfire — it doesn't matter. Just let this light appear to you in whatever form it does.

As you continue breathing, let your awareness move closer and closer to that light. Go deeper inside of you until you have reached this light. As you get closer to this beautiful inner light, you may feel warmer, you may feel vulnerable, tears may come to your eyes, or you may feel a gentle ache in the center of your chest at your heart center. This light is your soul, your essence, the truth of your being.

Take a few moments now just to bask in this light — to feel the energy that comes from it. That energy may be powerful or gentle, vibrant or calm, or some magical combination of all those things. Take your time to be with this soul light and feel its essence.

. . .

When you are ready, step into the light now, consciously entering into your soul. Step into the essence of you, and breathe. Breathe into the fullness of who you are as a soul essence. You may find that particular feelings or emotions come to the surface. That's fine. Just let them pass on through you. As you experience a feeling coming into your awareness, do not feel that you have to do anything with it. Just acknowledge it, and stay in the light.

Take all the time you need with this exercise, and then when you are ready, open your eyes and come back to this space. As you re-enter outer conscious awareness, you will notice that your body feels different. Your physical feelings and sensations are more "alive," and you are more aware of feeling your "insides." Take time to write in your journal about this experience before you move on.

# Exercise #4
# The Light of the Soul II

Take your time to return to your point of stillness and the light of your soul. Once there, spend a few moments once again just bathing in this essence of you.

. . .

As you sit deep within the heart of your being, begin to become aware of a beautiful golden white light shining down on you like a spotlight, and surrounding your physical body. This golden white light seems even more powerful and more gentle than the light deep within you. It is the light of Spirit, the light of Love, the light of God. As you stand in the

61

center of your own soul light and become aware of this outer golden white light, you realize that these two lights are coming together. In fact, you begin to realize that they are really the same. That golden white light of Love that surrounds you is also the light of your soul. Your soul is one with Spirit, with Love, with God. And you know deep inside your essence that this light is your home. This light is the place of wisdom and knowledge and peace within you. When you sit in your soul light and know your oneness with the divine, you can find the answers to your deepest questions, and receive guidance for your most important life decisions.

See in front of you now a pathway. Let it appear to you in any form, whether that be a path through the woods or a jet stream on which to ride. This pathway can symbolize your life journey. Feeling your oneness with Spirit, enter the pathway and begin this journey of conscious awareness. Feel the power and the strength, the gentleness and peacefulness of your soul, and, while standing firmly in your essence, begin the journey. Standing firmly in your soul, and knowing your oneness with Spirit, you feel a tremendous sense of assuredness and safety. Nothing can harm you here, for you are in your divine essence.

Take your time to explore your soul pathway now. Whenever you feel that you are stepping out of your deep inner light, take a few deep breaths and give yourself time to drop back in. Know that any challenge or obstacle you encounter in your life journey can be addressed in peace and calm from your deep inner light. Here you are one with Spirit, one with Love. And in Love, all things are possible.

. . .

With each inhalation, feel the Love that is your soul. And with each exhalation, feel that Love shining out of you to the world. Take your time to rest in your soul and your Love. And when you are ready, open your eyes and come back into this space.

# 4

# Creating
# A Language of Love

Part of the mystic's journey toward self-truth and self-understanding is opening new lines of communication with self, with others, and with Spirit. In my meditation over the years, Spirit has referred to this communication as a new language of Love. The prologue of this book is a dialogue with Spirit that introduces this concept. The language of Love is really the essence of the journey of the 21st-century mystic. In this chapter, we will begin to work with meditation as a tool, a study guide for opening to the language of Love, Spirit, and self.

In my classes, workshops, and counseling sessions, so many people express a yearning for a deeper connection with people in their lives and with God. They often find that there are no words to express their feelings and experiences fully. This yearning is a cry from the soul. Our souls yearn to share love, to experience in the physical dimension the oneness with all that they know from the spiritual dimension. Our souls are pushing us to find a new language, a new method of communication with one another, that can facilitate that sharing of love. The soul knows nothing of race, religion, social status, educational background, career success. The soul only knows its desire to communicate directly with other souls. In response to this yearning, Spirit offers the language of Love.

The language of Love often has no words. It is actually an underlying energy, an intention behind words or action. The language of Love is spoken through the way we look at others, the way we touch, listen, take care and nurture them. It is simply an energy that flows through us. The soul is the channel for that energy flow. Our job is to allow the soul to speak its Love language freely, to re-commit to Love as our intention in all communication.

Our first challenge is to speak the Love language with ourselves. We must be gentle and loving with ourselves as we make the journey toward self-awareness. This means looking deep inside to uncover all of the parts of us that make up the whole — the parts we like and the parts we don't like, the aspects that we're comfortable with and the aspects whose simple existence frightens us, the strong and the vulnerable dimensions of self, the loving and the unloving. As all of these aspects come into our conscious awareness, we have the opportunity to embrace and accept them — in fact, even to honor them as parts of the totality of our beingness. By honoring all of who we are, we can more easily speak this Love language with ourselves, and then with others and with Spirit.

The Buddhist tradition offers us a beautiful meditation exercise for exploring and experiencing the Love language. It is known as the "Loving Kindness Meditation."

# Exercise # 5
# Loving Kindness Meditation

Close your eyes, and begin by saying as a mantra over and over again, "May I dwell in my heart. May I be free from suffering. May I be healed. May I be at peace." After a while, move to someone quite close to you, like a spouse or lover or very close friend, and insert that person's name, saying, "May [name] dwell in her heart. May [name] be free from suffering. May [name] be healed. May [name] be at peace." Again, after a time, then move on to someone you are not so close to, but who is definitely a part of your life, inserting their name in the exercise. Continue with someone who is in your life on a regular basis, but whose name you do not know, then a complete stranger, and finally the world.

You can create as many variations on this exercise as you wish. It will help you understand your oneness with all of creaturekind, and open your heart to speak its Love language.

# The Power of Words

One important part of self-awareness is noticing the words and habitual phrases we use in our everyday language. In his book, *The Drummer's Path — Moving the Spirit with Ritual and Traditional Drumming*, Sule Greg Wilson addresses performing artists about their responsibilities to the audience. His words are a powerful teaching for us all, regardless of our roles in life.

> Whether it is acknowledged by the culture at large or not, artists affect people with much more than technique and training. They do it with who they are, with their emotions, with their life experiences, with their thoughts. One's state of Spirit molds the music and the art that is made, and it affects the people it comes in contact with. Your words, your thoughts, your work are charged with your cumulative and instantaneous Being. That's why in some African societies it is against the law to 'talk bad 'bout somebody.' Understand this truth. Because what you think and feel becomes your world.[1]

Whenever we have a thought, we have immediately given energy to the manifestation of that thought. When the thought is translated into words and spoken, we have given even more energy to its manifestation. Thoughts and words become things, circumstances, happenings. When our words and phrases are positive, flowing out of Love, we create positive energy in our lives, but when the literal meaning of the words is less than positive, or not what we wish to create in our lives, then we need to make changes in our habitual speech patterns.

A very common example of negative speech patterns is the prevalent use of sarcasm in popular culture today. Another is the use of slang, whose words, when considered literally, often have very negative connotations. Our speech patterns easily become habitual, so that we don't even notice the words we use. We may have no conscious negative intention with those words, but they carry with them powerful energy. As you become sensitive to the energy of language and "clean up" your own speech patterns, you will notice the jarring effects of negative speech in others. If we want to reach a higher consciousness, addressing our speech patterns must be one of the first steps, so that the Love language is our constant method of communication. We need to be very clear in the words we speak, making sure that our words convey the true essence of our message. In other words, be sure you *really* mean what you say, or don't say it.

The following exercise is a playful way to facilitate changing habitual speech patterns in order to direct your creative energy in a positive way.

# Exercise #6
# Monitoring Your Words and Thoughts

For a few weeks, create a game with yourself of paying attention to the literal meaning of your words and thoughts. Just have fun with it and notice how some of your habitual phrases and thoughts can be very productive in your life, and others are really creating "negative programming." What are your words really saying? How are your thoughts creating your reality? Even such simple statements as, "I'll never be able to do that," or "I'll try it, but I'm sure it won't work," or "She and I always disagree on everything," are reinforcing negative belief patterns and energy systems. An important part of raising awareness is clearing ourselves of that negative programming and of destructive habits. Words and thoughts are powerful creative tools. Use them for your benefit. Have fun with this game, and you will quickly transform your speech and thought patterns into constructive and positive creative energies.

After working with this exercise for several weeks, one student said, "Making mental pictures of my words has been great. I realized how I invite negativity into my life and prevent positive energy from coming in simply by what comes out of my mouth. When I began monitoring my words and thoughts, and began replacing negative thoughts and speech patterns with positive ones, so much changed — my attitude, my finances, and the people and clients I was attracting."

# Gifts and Talents

An important part of the 21st-century mystic's journey is recognizing gifts and talents, for they are a primary way through which the Love Language is spoken. We each have many gifts and talents — aspects of who we are that make us unique, aspects of us that cannot be reproduced in exactly the same way in any other being. Agnes de Mille, famous choreographer, tells of a conversation with another very famous dancer and choreographer, Martha Graham, that speaks so clearly of gifts and talents and to the journey of the 21st-century mystic.

> . . . Martha said to me, very quietly, "There is a vitality, a life force, an energy, a quickening that is translated through you into action, and because there is only one of you in all of time, this expression is unique. And if you block it, it will never exist through any other medium and it will be lost. The world will not have it. It is not your business to determine how good it is nor how valuable nor how it compares with other expressions. It is your business to keep it yours clearly and directly, to keep the channel open. You do not even have to believe in yourself or your work. You have to keep yourself open and aware to the urges that motivate you. Keep the channel open." . . .
>
> "But," I said, "when I see my work I take for granted what other people value in it. I see only its ineptitude, inorganic flaws, and crudities. I am not pleased or satisfied."
>
> "No artist is pleased."

"But then there is no satisfaction?"

"No satisfaction whatever at any time," she cried out passionately. "There is only a queer divine dissatisfaction, a blessed unrest that keeps us marching and makes us more alive than the others."[2]

A more expansive definition of gift or talent might read "any way that we allow Love to flow through us into action." The gifts might be singing, playing a musical instrument, painting, cooking, caring for children, organization, or public relations. Or the gift may also be of listening, caring, or compassion. Everyone has talents and gifts. Don't get stuck in how to label them or in the gift being some tangible thing that the world can so easily see. Many gifts are simply a state of being. What is important is the Love that flows through the activity or state of being.

Our gifts and talents are expressions of the soul, and, as such, yearn to be expressed. Yet they are often the source of great frustration because we are not always able to identify them and express them. Many people will say, "I don't really know what I am good at. I can't seem to find my niche." Our daily lives provide the opportunities to discover these hidden aspects of ourselves. We consciously or unconsciously create particular roles to play in our lives. We choose to be parents, teachers, counselors, plumbers, performers, volunteer workers, ministers, secretaries, maintenance workers, doctors, factory workers. We may even choose several roles to play at once. These roles are the pathways for our spiritual journeys on the Earth. Through them we uncover our gifts and talents and begin to develop them. We choose these roles for many different reasons. Sometimes we feel they are chosen for us, and are not really the roles that we wish to play. However, even if this is the case, by becoming aware of this situation, you are being given the challenge and the opportunity to make change, to make other choices, to break the molds in which you have been living, and create new ones. This may be a huge undertaking, and seem to be an impossible task, but the more you learn to respond to the yearnings of the soul, the more you uncover your true talents and gifts, begin to develop them, and advance in your mystical journey.

Gifts and talents, roles that we play, and choices that we make offer lessons for our learning and growth. They may manifest as wonderful, pleasant experiences, or they may appear as challenges. Gifts and talents and their corresponding roles are simply vehicles through which learning occurs. This is an important concept to understand. We get very caught up in ideas of success and failure, and lose sight of the fact that the *journey* is what is important. As I say to my singing students, "In the larger scheme of things, it doesn't matter at all whether or not you get to the stage of the Metropolitan Opera or Broadway. What is important is what you learn along the way." This is something we all know on some level, but it is easy to forget. Those who really embrace this concept and live it, find their career pursuits much more fulfilling. Our responsibility is simply to be open to our experiences along the way, both wonderful and challenging, so that the lessons can be learned and the journey continues to progress. Our gifts and talents are not just pretty packages to unwrap, set on the shelf, and admire from a safe distance. They are given to us to use, to explore, and through which to learn. Being good stewards of our gifts and talents means developing them to their full potential — taking on the corresponding role and being the best we possibly can be.

# Sharing the Gifts — Sharing the Love

By fully exploring our talents and abilities, and being willing to face each challenge and accept each opportunity that comes our way, we open our awareness to the deeper spiritual essence of the gift and talent. Developing the talent involves becoming highly proficient in whatever technical skills may be involved, but also opening to our higher creative force, Love or the God-force, inviting that energy to move through us. The degree to which we are able to invite Love to flow through us is the degree to which we find the full expression of our gifts and talents. The two processes actually work hand in hand, developing simultaneously. As we are willing to surrender to the flow of Love through our beings, and to actively work with Spirit in our creative endeavors, our gifts and talents become clear. At the same time, through exploring and developing these gifts, we learn to allow the Love to flow even more freely. By doing this we not only help ourselves, but we help all those around us. Through our gifts and talents we give to others. We all recognize how we enjoy being in the presence of certain people simply because it "feels good" to be with them. We may not even know the individual well, but something draws us to be near them. Although we may not be consciously aware of what is happening, on some level of awareness we recognize a certain quality of Love that flows through them.

I must emphasize one important factor, however. Giving to or helping others does not occur simply through our action. It is action that is driven and fueled by Love that enables us to give to others. When actions in and of themselves become important, and we realize that at some level, we are seeking recognition for that action, that is ego-action. This is sometimes a hard thing for us to recognize fully and admit, for we all like to think that our intentions are pure. However, when we can strip away the ego layers and allow our actions to come directly from soul, we are realizing our highest potential — action flowing out of Love. This brings us back to the language of Love, and the intention behind every word and action being Love. When Love flows, actions simply happen.

During one of my periods of inner struggle with my work, Spirit spoke in my meditation:

*Every life is about service. Everyone takes their journey and learns their lessons in different ways, but the ultimate lesson is service. And service to what? Service to Love. Are you serving Love, or are you serving ego? Are you serving the Higher Plan, or are you serving ego's desires? Human desires are there within you, as they are for everyone, and, in and of themselves, they are fine. Let them be, however, in service to Love rather than in service to immediate gratification. When you are serving your immediate gratification, you are not serving Love. In fact, you are blocking Love's flow. When you walk every step in service to Love, you are making the world a better place. When every breath and every thought has as its intention service to Love, you are on the path of truly serving the world, and having a profound impact on all around you.*

*Your work is very important. You are very important. But then so is everyone. The problem is that not everyone recognizes how important they are and their work is in the service of the world, in the service of Love. Your job is not to tell others how important they are. Your job is to know how important you are and to live your life, every moment, every breath, every action, in service to Love. Others will begin to see and know and understand and learn of their own importance as Love-servers as they are in your presence.*

*The doors are open. Heaven awaits. Enter into the gates of Love and make this your home. Make the House of Love, Heaven, your central office, from where you do the work of your life. The famous passage says, "Rejoice and be exceedingly glad, for great are your rewards in heaven." We say to you, when you live in Love, you live in Heaven on Earth, and your life will be full of great rewards.*

Alan: But how do we get to the place where we are always acting in service to Love?

*You take your journey. Every day, every activity, every interaction, is a part of your journey. Take advantage of every experience. But please don't judge them, because you will have many experiences in which you realize that you are not in service to Love. This is the only way to learn. You must take each experience, each feeling, each emotion, and learn from it. As your inner "issues" arise, work with them. Work through them. And then when you think you have it all done, go dig some more.*

*The treasures of Love are to be found through the process of growth and unfoldment of you. Yes, the growth and unfoldment of you. Ultimately, Love is not to be found outside of your own experience. You can observe someone else's experience of Love-flow, and participate vicariously, but wouldn't you like to have your own? It is there for the asking. Doesn't that sound simple? Well, as we have said before, the concept is very simple, but living the concept is sometimes very difficult. You have to work at becoming good at it — at least most humans do. As you dig in the "dirt" of your life and yourself, you find the rocks, the mud, the gnarled roots of dead trees, but you also find miraculous seeds ready to burst forth into new life if only given water and light and nurturing. You find the treasures of your soul buried deep beneath all of the rocks and the mud and the gnarled roots. Dig deeply, and take out each rock and examine it, embrace it, love it, and learn from it why it made your digging difficult. Strain the mud through a sieve and see what makes up its slimy substance — what is its essence that slows you down or keeps you caught or trapped? And gently and lovingly remove the gnarled roots of dead trees, look them over carefully, and study them, listen to them — for they are the artifacts of parts of you that were once active and may still haunt you.*

*This is the way to Love. This is the way to God. You dig down to a certain depth, clearing away the rocks and the mud and the roots, and you find a treasure of your soul. And you thank God for that treasure and bask in its beauty for awhile. Then you go back to your digging and go deeper, excavating more rocks, mud, and gnarled roots, until you find another treasure. After basking in this newfound beauty for awhile, you once again go back to digging, and so it goes for your entire life, and lifetime after lifetime. And through the excavation you uncover Love.*

*The more you uncover this Love, the more it shines through you. The more you uncover this Love, the more your life becomes dedicated only to uncovering Love. Everything else is just a result of uncovering the Love. Let the Love live through you, guiding you in your words and actions. Love has its own agenda through you. The deeper you dig, the more rocks and mud and gnarled roots that you heal and release, the more you are able to let Love lead you.*

# The Gifts of Conflict

Love is the healer — it creates opportunities for growth and transformation in our lives. Sometimes, as a part of that process, Love brings conflict or enormous challenges, many of which take time and tremendous effort to resolve. One of our current challenges is that we live in a bottom-line and "immediate gratification" society. We are overly eager to act, to know, to have, to fix, to end tension. Because we tend to want to have control over our lives, and for everything to run "smoothly," we experience great anxiety when all is not well. Most of us will just "do whatever it takes" to bring a quick resolution, often denying or ignoring the real issues, just so life can return to the status quo. But if we take a closer look, we find that the tension, the conflict, the problem, the question, the lack, is often a sign of something inside us that needs to be addressed, and is therefore a great opportunity or gift for learning and growing. The situation presents itself so that we might work through the process toward its solution or resolution.

When approached as an opportunity, the conflict can become that "divine dissatisfaction," to use Martha Graham's words — a feeling inside that keeps us pushing us past our "comfort zones" and into true resolution within ourselves as well as resolution of the situation. The "divine dissatisfaction" keeps gnawing or prodding us to dig deeper, to understand more fully, to work out the conflict, or to find a way for a complete and satisfying solution. The process is much more important than the ultimate resolution, because within the process are found the gifts and lessons.

Together, as we explore our gifts and talents, work through our conflicts, and come to know our Love, we become catalysts for one another's growth. No one *teaches* another anything. Everyone is simply, through their degree of openness to Love, a catalyst to help another in their own process of self-discovery. When Love is flowing with no blocks, then all knowledge, wisdom, and understanding is there. Too often, our culture's concept of teaching is one individual imparting knowledge to another. However, no one really teaches another anything. Real teaching is simply guiding the student to a place where they can learn. The true teacher does not pass out knowledge, but rather leads the student to the well of knowledge within.

# 5

# Intuitive Awareness

Intuitive awareness is a gift of Love to each of us — a talent that everyone has to some degree, which can be developed to guide and direct our lives in powerful and transformative ways. Just as we develop our other gifts and talents for use in our daily lives, it is our responsibility to develop our intuitive gifts to their fullest potential, as well, in order to be a true partner with Spirit in the co-creation of our lives.

Intuition is spiritual energy, not psychic energy. Psychic energy is purely mental energy, and limited to mental energy, while spiritual energy embraces the totality of the universe. Spiritual energy acknowledges that there is tremendous knowledge and wisdom available to us when we can become one with Spirit or the universal consciousness. Purely psychic energy is more an energy of the ego. Spiritual energy engages the soul. Through exploration and understanding of the soul energy, intuitive gifts make themselves known and can be developed. Spiritual energy encompasses psychic energy, but is not at all limited to it. The person who works with purely psychic energy may feel that *they* have the power to see, hear, know. The person who comes from a spiritual approach will tell you that they tap into a higher realm of energy, a higher knowledge to gather their information. They may feel that they work with spirit guides or teachers, or, simply become one with the universal consciousness. But, whatever their method, they acknowledge that they do not have the power by themselves. The are tapping into Love, into the universe, into the God-force, for their power.

The practice of working with this spiritual energy could, in a sense, be called the oldest religion in the world. In ancient times, it was used through shamanism and animism, the belief that every physical object is infused with spirit. Spiritual energy was spoken of quite freely in the ancient mystical traditions of all the major world religions, including Judaism and Christianity. In the late 1800s there was even a religion established called spiritualism. Surviving today as a very small organized religious practice, their beliefs are based on Christianity, but include belief in communication with the dead. Old-time spiritualism focused on mediumship, the ability to contact specific spirits and open up communication between the living and the dead. There are still gifted mediums today who are helping people come to peace with unresolved issues with those who have passed back to the spirit realm.

A broader approach, however, and the focus of our work through this book, is becoming one with Spirit or universal wisdom and receiving guidance and teaching for living. When working in this way, Spirit addresses issues in our lives, giving us deeper clarity of understanding of our soul journeys and experiences.

One of our first tasks in developing intuitive awareness, in learning the language of Love, and in discovering gifts and talents, is to become aware of the energy of Spirit as it is around us and moves through our lives. As we become aware of this energy, we can begin to work with it and get to know it. In doing this work, awareness is everything. Awareness is not something that you do. It is a state of being. To be aware is to be open to receive and participate in the magical dance that is going on all around and within us. To be aware is to know the self. Our understanding of God and of the universe grows with our own self-evolvement. The more we know ourselves, the more we know God.

Awareness simply means living life consciously. When we live our lives unconsciously, we begin to take on the attributes of whatever is around us, both positive and negative, being easily swayed by the forces and opinions of others. We somewhat mindlessly move through the motions of our lives, just following the patterns and footsteps of parents or teachers or friends — anyone who might be there to show us the way. However, when we live mindfully, with full attention given to each and every moment and activity in our lives, we begin to glow in our own personal light and truth. We come to know who we are. We begin to step into our own power and strength, and develop as individuals with unique gifts and talents.

In the Buddhist tradition there is actually a practice called mindfulness. This practice is a logical next step after working with speech and thought patterns. Mindfulness is simply focusing your attention on wherever you are and whatever you are doing in each moment. It is a state of becoming fully awake to who you are, what you think and feel, what the present moment is about, and clearly seeing your view of the world. Mindfulness brings with it a heightened state of awareness, opening you to the full spectrum of possibilities. It brings you back in touch with your own inner wisdom and your relationship to it. Mindfulness is becoming aware of each thought and feeling that you experience, mentally, spiritually, emotionally, and physically, as you experience it. When practicing mindfulness, there is an immediacy to your life. You begin to respond to stimuli immediately, knowing in each moment what you think and feel.

This practice of mindfulness or conscious living is an important step towards opening intuitive awareness. The more we can focus our full attention on wherever we are and whatever we are doing in any given moment, the more we become fully aware of all that is there for us in that moment. Our lives tend to get very unfocussed as we try to accomplish so many things at once, or in too little time. Try the following exercise.

# Exercise #7
# Mindfulness

For several days, put all of your attention towards doing only one thing at a time. Take all the time that each task demands, and only when it is finished, move on to the next task. This means that when you are preparing your food, your concentration is only on preparing your food, with no other distractions. When you are eating your meal, you are focusing your attention on the tastes and textures of the food and the nourishment the food provides for your body, and not watching television or reading while you eat. When you are going from place to place, you are focusing your attention on the method of transportation and on your experiences as you travel, rather than dulling your senses with the radio or walkman. When you are engaged in conversation with someone, you are totally present with them, knowing and experiencing your immediate thoughts and feelings as the conversation progresses, not thinking about where you need to go next or someplace else you might rather be. All of your attention is focused on the one activity of that moment.

If you really commit to mindful living for a couple of weeks, you will experience a tremendous shift in your perception and experience. Your food will taste better. Your conversations will go deeper and be more fulfilling. Colors and sounds will become much sharper. Even in cleaning your house, you will find a renewed energy for the process by allowing yourself to really be with the activity. Heightening your awareness to the world around you and your full experience in it is an important step in developing your intuitive gifts.

# The Intuitive Mind

As you move through your spiritual journey and increase your awareness, you will have many experiences that make perfect sense to your creative and intuitive mind, but may be difficult to explain in the rational mind. Students in class often say that if their experiences were not so clear and full of revelation for their lives, they might think that they were going crazy. They experience so many thoughts and feelings at once. This is very common when you first begin opening awareness, for it is like opening up the dam in a river. So much information comes cascading through you at once that you don't know what to make of it all. So it is my suggestion that you do not even try to make sense of it, at least not for now. When working in the intuitive mind, you are actively functioning on many levels of

78

awareness at once. The rational mind, on the other hand, functions only on one level of awareness at once. Therefore, experiences of the intuitive mind are very confusing to the rational mind. The experience of becoming one with Spirit and functioning with the intuitive mind is very much like a dream state where people and places all become one or come together in combinations that are not reality in waking consciousness. In dreams we often move quickly from one emotion to another and one experience to another. However, we accept this as natural because it is a dream. When working with the intuitive mind, you have access to a tremendous amount of information at once. Know your own experience, trust it, and don't be in such a hurry to find a rational explanation.

As you recognize kindred spirits among your friends and acquaintances, cultivate those relationships so that you have people with whom you can share your experiences. This is very important to your journey. You will want to exchange ideas with others, and you will find that your time together stimulates and challenges each of you to pursue your thoughts and feelings even further. You will also gain great clarity about your own feelings and experiences by listening to others share their experiences. This is one reason why a group setting for doing this work is so helpful. In my classes, I find that very strong bonds form between students during the time together, and many friendships continue long after the class has ended. This is simply because together we create a setting for a supportive and loving sharing of experiences and ideas — a setting where soul can be free to meet soul.

At the same time, it is important not to take on others' doubts and fears as your own. The only way to truly know your own experiences and feelings is to sit in your heart, that place of peace and quiet and stillness. Each person has their own truth. When listening to another's words, listen from your heart as well as your mind to know how their words resonate with you. Don't just accept another's truth because of who they might be. Trust yourself and your feelings. Their truth is theirs and very valid for them, but not necessarily for you. This is an important part of becoming self-aware.

Before going on to Part II, you may want to go back to the Point of Stillness meditation, the first exercise of this book, just to see how you are doing in your journey to the still, quiet place of your essence.

Do you find that since doing the work of these first five chapters you are able to get past the surface chatter more quickly and get to your point of stillness? Or do you find that you are even farther away from the point of stillness — a sign that perhaps there is some significant inner resistance that needs to be addressed. Again, make no judgment about what you find. Just accept the message of the exercise.

# Part II

# Spiritual Self-Discovery and Transformation

The greatest tool we have for knowing God is ourselves. Our bodies and souls are in constant evolution as a part of the ongoing creation of the universe, and the manifestation of the divine in human form. Seeking God through introspection and knowledge of the deepest self is not a new path. It is a path that has been pursued by mystics and mystery schools throughout human history. Through knowing ourselves, the essence of who we are as divine human beings, we find our way to God.

# 6

# Universal Life Force
# and the Human Aura

Through the first part of this book, we have discussed many spiritual principles in preparation for the more concrete inner exploration we are about to undertake. This exploration will be done through the chakras, energy centers in the body that are powerful tools for self-discovery, transformation, and awakening spiritual awareness. ("Chakra" is a Sanskrit word meaning "wheel of light." We begin our in-depth discussion of the chakras in Chapter 7.)

As an introduction to the chakra work, these next two chapters provide an overview of the chakra system, the human energy field or aura, and the universal life force which feeds that system. We will define these terms, look briefly at how these energies and concepts have been addressed historically, and give you some tangible experience with these energies. These two chapters contain a great deal of information, some of it more technical in nature. I have tried to present this material in a clear and straightforward way so as not to overwhelm you with facts and explanations. I encourage you to take your time so that you can grasp these basic technical concepts. They will lay a foundation for the more experiential work in the chapters that follow.

We begin with a guided meditation to allow you to have a tangible experience of energy moving in your body.

# Exercise #8
# Becoming Aware of Your Body as Vibrating Energy

Make yourself comfortable, sitting with your back straight either in a chair or on the floor, hands resting comfortably on your lap, and take deep and full breaths. Allow your breath to find its own natural steady and even flow, so that its gentle regularity can carry you into a deep meditative state.

. . .

As you continue to sink into deeper and deeper states of consciousness, allow yourself to continue taking deep and full breaths. As you are taking these breaths, feel as though you are breathing into every part of your body. Notice any place in your body that seems to resist the breath. When you find a spot that is resisting the breath, allow yourself to breathe into that area, and fill it with love. Massage it, caress it, kiss it gently, in your mind. Notice that slowly it becomes softer and gentler, and then releases, and you are able to breathe fully and easily into that place. Continue for a few moments, breathing into your body, finding any place where there is resistance, loving and gently massaging and nurturing this part of your body into ease, into softness. Then, when you are ready, continue with this meditation.

. . .

Begin humming quietly and gently now on any pitch that you feel comfortable. (Keep your teeth apart, and imagine saying "Ah" inside your mouth while your lips close to a hum.) Take a breath whenever you need to do so, and then return to the hum. The purpose of this is to feel the vibration of the humming move throughout your body.

As you continue your humming, slowly move through these next three steps:

1) Place your hands on various parts of your head and continue to feel the vibration.
2) Place your hands on various parts of your torso and feel the vibration.
3) Move your hands down to your legs and feel the vibration.

By now your entire body is vibrating with the hum. If there is any part of your body in which you do not feel the vibration, simply take note of it and allow that part of your body to relax and accept the vibration.

Become aware now of the vibration as it extends beyond your physical body into the space around you. This vibrating space around your physical body is called your aura. It is the energy field that surrounds your physical body, and is an active component of your being at all times. Continue humming, and feel this vibration of energy throughout not only your physical body, but also your aura. Notice any place in your aura that seems to resist the breath. Love that place, nurture it, caress it, hum into it, and you will notice that it gently softens and releases and clears, so that the breath may also fill that spot. Take a moment now to breathe into the energy field around your body, releasing any places that may resist the breath. Stop the humming when you feel that the energy is now cleared all around you.

As you continue breathing, you begin to feel your wholeness. You begin to feel and understand how the two energies, physical and non-physical, come together as one. You begin to understand that the center of the energy field that is around your body is actually somewhere in the core of your physical body — that the energy that surrounds your physical body actually comes from deep inside the physical body and extends way beyond it.

Slowly and gently bring yourself back into your full awake consciousness. Give yourself time to readjust to the room or your space. Record your impressions from this meditation exercise in your journal.

# Universal Life Force

Universal life force is the energy that moves through all time and space, creating and sustaining all things in the universe. Without it, nothing could exist. Scientists, philosophers, and mystics from all cultures have been talking about it for thousands of years, calling it different names. The ancient Hindu tradition, over 5,000 years old, calls it *prana*, the basic constituent and source of all life. This is the energy that is accessed through yoga breathing techniques (*pranayama*), meditation, and physical postures, to reach altered states of consciousness. As early as the 3rd millennium BCE, the Chinese called this energy *qi*. They believe that all matter, animate and inanimate, is composed of this energy. The Japanese refer to this same energy as *ki*. The Kabbalists, mystics of the classical Jewish tradition, referred to it as astral light. In the 6th century BCE, Pythagoras conceived of the universe as a living being, brought to life by a great Soul and filled with Intelligence. He referred to God as the Monad, the Supreme Mind. In other philosophical writings throughout history, Hippocrates spoke of the *Vis Medicatrix Naturae*, Hermes Trismegistus of the *Telesma*, alchemist Robert Fludd of *spiritus*, Franz Anton Mesmer of magnetic fluid, psychiatrist Wilhelm Reich of orgone energy, and more recent Eastern European scientists of bioenergy — all terms to describe the universal life force.[1]

This universal life force provides the fundamental drive for our individual energy systems. We each respond to this force in a unique way. It is our response to this energy, the amount of it that we allow to flow through our systems, that determines our individual vibratory frequency. That frequency determines the characteristics that make us each individual and unique. At a fundamental level, it is through our individual frequencies that we communicate with the world around us. This underlying vibration runs through our conversations, our touch, our smile, the look in our eyes, coloring every aspect of our being. We tend to draw to us energy systems similar to our own. This means, in simple terms, "like attracts like." Whatever our individual vibratory frequency, we will attract other people, animals, and situations, of a similar frequency and nature. If we want to change our relationships, our behavior, or our life situations, we first must go inside and see how we must change ourselves so that we can draw to us relationships and situations that we desire. We change our individual vibratory frequencies through meditation, addressing emotional issues, and bringing our spiritual journeys to full consciousness. The concentrated practice of raising energy frequencies (commonly known as "raising your energy") enables us to attract a higher level of relationship or situation, as well as access the higher vibratory rates of the universal consciousness for guidance and wisdom.

# The Aura

The term "aura" refers to the field of energy that surrounds all matter. It is a dynamic electromagnetic field created by the flow of the universal life force through individual chakras. Each of the chakras has a particular vibrational frequency. These frequencies combine to create the electromagnetic field of the aura. Its magnitude is determined by the amount of universal life force that is flowing. The aura is outside the range of normal vision, but within the realm of intuitive sight and feeling. Almost everyone is at least unconsciously aware of this energy field whether or not they can see it. In our common language, we call it our "space," and we feel uncomfortable when someone we do not know or trust steps too forcefully into our "space." The aura is our sensing mechanism to our environment. Through this energy field, we are able to sense another's presence nearby, we have a sense of liking or disliking a place right away, we feel the warmth and love emanating from someone who is dear to us, or we become aware of approaching danger on a dark street at night.

Just as with the universal life force, there is a long history of acknowledgment and study of the aura. As early as the 12th century CE, scholars Boirac and Liebeault were studying the effects that one person could have upon another simply by their presence. Early Christian paintings portray Jesus and other spiritual figures surrounded by fields of light. Many early Christian mystics and Hermetics wrote and spoke of this life-force energy that makes up the aura. Jesus was one of the greatest mystics to have lived, and the Bible contains many stories of his "energy" work, known as the miracles of Jesus. But Jesus also said, "the one who believes in me will also do all that I do and, in fact, will do even greater works than these,"[2] implying that this universal life force and auric energy can be accessed and utilized by all. Hildegard von Bingen, a 12th-century Christian mystic, was widely known and respected during her life for her study of healing through energy. Paracelsus, an army physician in the early 1500s, became a great alchemist and Hermetic philosopher, and was committed to reforming the practice of medicine. He practiced holism, believing that the mind and body affect each other. He referred to the aura as the "vital body" and a "fiery globe," and believed that the depletion of this vital body was the cause of illness. In the 1700s mathematician J. B. van Hellmont theorized that there was a universal fluid that flowed through all bodies, and that it could be used to influence the minds and bodies of others at will. Franz Anton Mesmer developed his theory of "animal magnetism," which he defined as an electromagnetic force that could be transmitted from one person to another and cause healing. The 18th-century clairvoyant Emanuel Swedenborg wrote in his *Spiritual Diary* about a spiritual sphere that surrounded everyone.[3]

At the beginning of the 20th century, many physicians became involved in investigating and developing theories about the aura. In 1911, Dr. Walter J. Kilner published *The Human Aura*, in which he wrote of seeing three misty layers of the human aura which changed considerably from person to person relative to age, mental and emotional status, and health conditions. He developed an apparatus through which you could see the aura, and by 1919 had developed a method of auric diagnosis of illness. Dr. George De La Warr and Dr. Ruth Drown developed Radionics, a system of using the aura to detect, diagnose, and treat illness. Psychiatrist Wilhelm Reich studied the relationship between the flow of universal energy through the body and physical/psychological illness. He integrated Freudian analytic techniques with massage and other bodywork techniques for releasing blocks in the universal energy flow as it moved through the body, thereby clearing negative mental and emotional states.[4]

Concepts of the aura and mysticism were reintroduced to the modern Western philosophical world in the second half of the 19th century through the work of Madame Helen Blavatsky, the founder of the Theosophical Society. From her travels and studies in India, she borrowed the Sanskrit term, *akasha*, to represent the universal life force. She said that *akasha* is the basic constituent of the *anima mundi*, or the world soul, which in turn constitutes the soul and higher spirit of humankind. Around the turn of the century, a group of early British theosophists, led by Alice Bailey, traveled to India, met many spiritual teachers, felt that they experienced enlightenment, and came back with the concepts of chakras and energy fields. Other important Western philosophers and writers in this field were Rudolph Steiner, Annie Besant, and Rev. Charles Leadbeater.[5]

The vibrational frequencies of the chakras determine the colors and sounds within the aura, and how far the aura extends from the physical body. The aura is an aspect of the mind, not in the intellectual sense, but rather the mind that embraces all consciousness — physical, emotional, spiritual, and intellectual. We tend to think of the mind as a thought machine, or an intellectual faculty located in the brain, that controls our lives in every way. This "bodymind," however, is not in the brain, but rather surrounds and pervades the physical body. It is in every cell of the physical body and extends as far beyond the body as the aura extends. Here, we are talking about the mind as an aspect of us that is connected to all consciousness. While the brain regulates and controls our bodily functions and intellectual processes, the bodymind is where *life* exists. Every thought, feeling, emotion, and experience registers in the bodymind and begins to affect our lives on some level. If this idea seems confusing to you now, you will understand it much more clearly as you begin to work in the aura and the chakras.

# Drawing in the Universal Life Force

Our level of conscious awareness is raised by increasing the rate of vibrational frequency within our energy systems. This can be done through the breath and meditation. Simultaneously, breath enters the body through the nose, while universal life force energy enters through the root chakra from the ground. In the normal course of daily breathing, we inhale, drawing breath and life force into the body, and then exhale, letting breath out and life force drain back down into the ground. In electrical terms, this could be called alternating current, in that the direction of the energy flow moves up your body on the inhalation, and then turns around and runs back down the body during exhalation. Breathing in this way maintains the level of energy and vibration that you are experiencing at that time. However, if you wish to raise your energy and vibrational frequency, you must create a direct current, feeling the energy rise in your body with the inhalation, and continuing the upward flow of energy throughout exhalation.[6]

I experience this direct current as a spin of energy, and often liken it to the spin of a football as it travels through the air when thrown by a good football player. As I inhale, I feel as if my body is hollow, and I am filling every corner and crevice of it with air, especially in the lower abdomen and legs — even filling my aura with air, but not in a forced way. With the inhalation, I feel my body open and the "football" of energy spin faster and faster up my body. Then, as I exhale, I feel my body continue opening and releasing any tensions or blocks, creating a clear and open channel for the "football" to keep spinning through, the spin getting faster and faster. It is important to remember that, in this process, you are opening to the universal life force and channeling it through your body. *You* are not creating this energy, nor should you try. Your responsibility in this process is to open the channel and invite the energy in. Take a few moments to do the following exercise to begin experiencing higher vibratory frequencies in your body.

# Exercise #9
# Breathing in the Universal Life Force

(Warning: This exercise can tend to increase blood pressure, so if you are pregnant or are challenged by high blood pressure, you may not want to do this exercise.)

Close your eyes and begin humming once again as you

were in the previous meditation. Take a few moments to really feel the energy vibrating.

. . .

Now as you inhale draw energy up from the ground through the bottom of your body. Feel this energy spin up your body, like the football spin. Take note of how far up your body the energy is able to come. Then as you exhale, allow the energy spin to slow down and run back out of the bottom of the body. Continue breathing in this way and experimenting with the energy for a few moments.

. . .

As you continue breathing, feel the energy spin up your body on the inhalation, but as you exhale, try to keep the energy flow going up your body and out of the top of your head. Do not allow the energy to run back down your body as you exhale. Continue this energy play for a few moments.

. . .

Finally, feel the energy spin up your body on the inhalation, and keep the energy flowing up your body throughout exhalation. However, feel as though you have on a cap that holds the energy in your body, not allowing it to flow out the top of your head. You will feel the pressure of the energy build in your body. Experiment with this for a few moments, and then remove the "cap" and resume normal breathing.


Through the breath we can begin to increase the flow of universal life force energy through our bodies, building stamina and physical muscle tone. The more often we work with this energy, and the more energy we are able to draw through, the greater our stamina and muscle tone, leading to an ability to raise our vibratory frequencies higher and higher. The muscle tone must be strong and firm and alive in order to run high levels of energy through our bodies, thereby increasing our individual vibratory rates. When this direct current energy, sometimes also referred to as kundalini (Chapter 8), is moving fast enough to carry you out of your present state of consciousness, you are projected into an altered state of consciousness through which you can access higher states of awareness.

To be in an altered state does not mean that you are unconscious or in a deep trance state. It simply means that all of your internal processes are accelerated and expanded. You have shifted to a state of being where the perceptions of the inner senses are brought to full conscious awareness. You actually enter an altered state of consciousness when daydreaming, or when you become engrossed in a movie or a good book, or when time seems to "stand still" in very intimate or profound moments of your life.

Altered states of consciousness are a very natural and normal part of our everyday life. When entered with intention, they allow access to information not usually available in a normal conscious state. We can access thoughts, feelings, and memories that are buried deep in our subconscious, and expand our awareness to merge with the universal consciousness, thereby functioning on many levels of awareness at once. We are able to solve problems, understand situations, and gain greater perspectives that can only be accomplished by moving into this altered state. Meditation, yoga breathing exercises, and hypnotherapy help carry us into this altered state experience. We are able to solve issues quickly that would have taken much longer to "talk out" in traditional therapy. This is simply because the act of talking brings us back into a single layer of consciousness and awareness, where we can only access and report from one level of awareness at a time. However, entering this expanded consciousness allows us to experience many levels at once, helping us understand the "bigger picture," the greater dynamics of the situation. It is as if you can be in many places, physically and emotionally, at the same time and see how all of the experiences and feelings are related.

As we have said, the mind is not just in the brain. It flows in, through, and around the body. The bodymind stores thoughts, feelings, and memories all over our bodies, deep within physical tissues. Opening to the larger bodymind allows our awareness to scan our entire physical body and energy field for thoughts, feelings, and memories. In addition, this altered state opens our awareness, through the bodymind, to the environment around us — words, images, emotions — all steps toward opening our awareness to Spirit.

# Experiencing the Human Aura

Below is a series of short exercises for beginning to feel and see the human aura. It is helpful to have a partner for these exercises, so if you are not working in a group, find an adventurous and open-minded friend who would like to experiment with you. Give yourselves permission to see and feel whatever you do, including, at first, perhaps nothing. The more you can relax into the exercises, the easier it will be for you to begin perceiving the energy. When you first begin looking at the aura, your first glimpses may be through your inner vision, not your outer vision. I still see auras principally through my inner vision, which feels a lot like imagination at first. So, what you see at first may feel like your imagination. That's all right. It might be, but chances are it is not. Just go with whatever you perceive. As you do these exercises, you are beginning to build up your perceptive and intuitive muscles. You have probably not used these muscles for a long time, if ever, so they may need some warming up. Just be patient and, famous last words, don't try too hard! You have to relax into this activity. So settle back, take a few deep breaths, and allow yourself to play!

# Exercise #10
# Perceiving the Human Aura

Step 1

Hold your hands several inches apart, with the palms facing each other. You will begin to feel a sensation of energy between them. It may feel like heat, or an electrical current, or a magnetic force. It will seem as though your palms and perhaps your fingertips have "come alive." (There are actually minor chakras in the palms of the hands which make your hands very sensitive to this energy.) Move your hands closer together and then farther apart, playing with this energy. Continue for a few minutes so that the energy builds up between your hands. You may experience this

93

energy as a ball or a balloon, or a stretching feeling similar to pulling taffy.

Step 2

Sit with your partner face to face, putting your hands up to each other so that your palms are touching your partner's, and your fingers extended straight up. Let yourselves begin to feel the universal life force as it is moving through your bodies by letting the energy flow naturally between you. Does it flow more naturally from one of you to the other, or does it feel like an even flow?

. . .

Now each of you pull energy in from your partner through the left hand and push out to your partner through the right hand. How does this feel?

. . .

Now reverse this flow — out through the left hand and in through the right hand. Is this a different feeling?

. . .

Stop the flow of energy for a moment. Then, one of you push energy out through both hands into the partner, as the partner pulls the energy in. Then reverse the flow between you. Take a few moments to play with this back and forth flow of energy. How does it feel?[7]

Step 3

Drop your hands from your partner's, and shake them out a little bit to neutralize the energy in them. Then put your hands back up, but this time 2-5 inches apart from your partner's hands. Begin to feel a ball of energy forming between your hands. As you feel the ball of energy, begin to play with it. Pull your hands farther away from your partner's, but no farther than you can still feel the ball of energy. Move closer and farther away, as if you are pulling taffy with your partner, and feel the energy stretch out between you. Then see how far you can move your hands apart from one another and still feel the energy. Now you are feeling the aura![8]

94

Step 4

Now that your hands are really "awake," hold your hands over various parts of your body and feel the energy coming out of them. Try this with your partner. Have your partner close their eyes and see if they can tell where your hands are over their body. Then let them do the same with you. Can you feel it? Open your mind and your awareness to all possibilities.

Step 5

You can do this exercise by yourself. Point the index finger of your dominant hand at the palm of your nondominant hand. The end of your finger should be about two inches from your palm. Begin to draw circles on your palm with your forefinger. Feel the energy that is projected from your finger onto your palm. Continue with drawing other designs and see what you feel. Then slowly pull your finger farther and farther away from your palm and see how far you can go while still feeling the "drawing."[9]

Step 6

This exercise is most easily done in a room with white walls or ceiling and dim lighting. Using the white wall or ceiling as a background, hold your hands out at arm's length in front of your face, palms facing you. Point the fingers of your hands towards each other, the fingertips of each hand about an inch apart. As you stare at your fingers, allow your gaze to soften, and look just past your fingers. You will begin to see a faint mist or haze around your fingers. It may be gray or whitish-gray, or you may see other colors. Remember the more you can relax your vision and the less you "try," the easier it will be to see. Also, allow your inner vision, or what feels like your imagination to awaken. You are now beginning to see the human aura. As you continue, notice that there are lines of energy connecting the corresponding fingers of your two hands. If you move your hands up and down in opposite directions, you will see that the corresponding fingers of opposite hands remain connected. Play with this vision and the auric energy, seeing the energy around your fingers, then around your hand.[10]

## Step 6

If you are working with a partner, ask your partner to stand against the white wall, and begin to look at their aura. Again, allow your gaze to soften and look just past their physical body. You will begin to see a haze or mist around their head, and then perhaps around their entire body. It is easiest to perceive the energy around the head region, so you might want to focus your attention there first. You may begin to see colors in their aura, and to perceive its general shape and feeling or texture. You may also begin to hear sounds within your inner hearing. Just take your time with this exercise, and, again, open to all possibilities. After a while, exchange places with your partner and let them look at your aura.

## Step 7

Another way to play with the auric energy is to stand at some distance from your partner and embrace one another in a hug with your auras. Then see how far apart you can get from one another and still feel the embrace.


Now that you have begun to feel and see the aura, we can continue with another exercise to help you use your aura as a sensing mechanism for gathering information. This exercise is a game that you can play alone or with another anywhere you are. The more you consciously use your "sensors" to gather information, the more aware you become of your surroundings in every moment of your life. Remember, the key to intuitive development is awareness.

We begin this exercise with very simple observations, and then as your skill develops, you can move on to more complicated ones.

# Exercise #11
# Developing the Auric Sensors

Take a small and simple object, like a penny, a pencil, or a matchstick, and hold it in your hand. Begin observing it with all of your observation powers — inner and outer vision, feeling, hearing, smelling, tasting. Spend a full 5 minutes just observing the object, finding out everything you possibly can about it. Stay focused on the object with no other distractions. After at least 5 minutes of observation, put the object away and write down your impressions. Describe the object as fully and in as great detail as you possibly can. Then take the object back out and verify what you wrote. Did you forget any detail? Did you get any details mixed up?[11]

Do the first part of this exercise every day for a week with a different object each day. This will greatly increase your observation skills, a very important step in opening awareness. After doing the exercise for a week you are ready to move on to more advanced objects.

Wherever you are, pick out an object that is some distance from you and begin to use your aura to feel it, sense it, know everything you can possibly know about it. Not only see the object, but use your aura to reach out to it and feel its textures, smell it, taste it, listen to it. Push beyond your sensory limits to stretch and increase your ability to perceive in new ways. Ask yourself questions about the object, such as, is its surface rough or smooth, hot or cold, and let your auric sensors perceive the answers. This is a great exercise to do outside your home or work environment because it offers a wonderful sense of discovery of unknown places.

# Grounding Your Energy
# Through a Meditation Altar

By now you are probably beginning to build up a great deal of energy in the space where you normally do your meditation work and your exercises. When working with such potent energy, it is good to have a point of focus to ground or center that energy. Therefore, you may want to consider creating a meditation altar in your home. The altar can be as simple or elaborate as you wish. On your altar you should place things that sustain you, that are important to you, that are sacred to you in some way. You may want to place a candle there (I suggest white, for it is the purest color energy), a picture of a spiritual figure who is important to you, flowers, crystals, rocks, symbols — anything that has significant spiritual meaning for you, and is comforting to you or brings you spiritual energy.

You may also wish to place things on your altar that represent problems or challenges you are currently facing in your life, inviting the sacred energy to bless that situation. Angela was having a major conflict with her adult daughter, and, at the time, they were not speaking. As she created her altar and invited Spirit to enter into her space, she placed photographs of her and her daughter on her altar, asking for guidance and blessing on their relationship in her meditation and prayer. Within several weeks the conflict began to resolve, and their relationship is now healing.

Since your altar is the place you have chosen to represent the presence of this sacred energy in your home, use it as a place to "give over" your concerns, your worries, your projects, your manifestation goals. Sometimes very simple acts of surrender pay off.

Be creative and have fun as you allow your altar to take form. It should be in a place where no one else will disturb it, for this is your meditation center, a focus for your personal spiritual energy. You will find your altar to be a great source of comfort and grounding as the energy builds around it. Then, as time goes on, "tend" to your altar, much as you would "tend" a garden. Keep it clean. Keep it alive by periodically adding things to it that represent where you are currently in your journey, and removing things whose significance may have passed. Remember that energy is a living and breathing thing, and, since your altar is to be the center of your spiritual energy in your home, it is also a living and breathing energy.

# 7

# The Journey
# of the Chakras

"Chakra" is a Sanskrit word meaning "wheel of light," referring to energy centers in the body through which we exchange information and energy with our environment and the universe. Although there are a variety of philosophies surrounding chakra energies, their number and placement, and color association, we will be working with the traditional ancient Hindu system that is most widely accepted.

We begin this introduction to the chakras with a meditation fantasy which will give you some tangible experience with these energy centers. You will begin to be aware of the color energies associated with the seven chakras and how they open the flow of the universal life force. It is not so important that you feel specific sensations in particular parts of your body at this point. What is important is that your conscious awareness is introduced to the energies of color.

## Exercise #12
## Chakra Meditation Fantasy

Make yourself comfortable and take deep and healthy breaths, allowing yourself to settle into a deep meditative state.

101

. . .

Imagine yourself in a beautiful green meadow surrounded by trees. In the middle of the meadow is an ancient stone pool fed with clear, sparkling water from an underground spring. Now feel yourself diving into the water and starting to swim. This may be the most refreshing experience you have ever had. You feel awake and alive and invigorated. And as you swim in gentle, easy strokes through the cool, sparkling water, allow any heaviness of your life to simply wash away. Feel yourself become lighter and lighter as the water supports you. Float on top of the water as it holds you so gently. And then go down and swim under the water and feel the water rush past you. As you do, all sorrows, all woes, all fears, all anger, any heaviness in your life can simply wash away.

Step up onto the stone walk surrounding this beautiful pool. Feel the warmth of the sun. It quickly dries you and bathes you in light. The warmth of the sun reminds you that the Divine Spirit is indeed inside of you and is connecting your inner light, the light of your soul, to the Light of the Universe. As you stand and take in the majesty of your surroundings, the beautiful trees, meadows, and flowers, and you hear the birds singing, feel the strength of Mother Earth pouring up into your body. Feel it come up your legs and through your hips and into your torso and out of the top of your head. Feel this bright red earth energy, this great life-force energy surge through your body and know that you are a part of Mother Earth's kingdom.

. . .

Feel the bright orange light of the sun, the brilliance of this color. Feel it pulse through your body, as your creativity is opened and inspired, truly connected to the great High Source. In this moment, let your sexuality be open and freely expressed. Feel your primal passions for life open and pulse.

. . .

The warm and embracing yellow light of the sun now penetrates your skin so that you know you are safe, secure, happy, and loved. This warm, yellow color emanates through all of your body and shines out for others to feel. You know that you can claim your place in the world with confidence, now being your own drummer instead of always having to march to someone else's beat. You can acknowledge the light and dark parts of self and let them balance peacefully. Feel your ambition and desire and realize that these are healthy feelings when ego and soul are balanced.

. . .

Look once again at the beautiful green rolling meadows, the lush green of the trees, and feel yourself be healed as the brilliant green washes through all of your senses. Feel yourself enveloped in the green color. You may even want to lie down in the grass, feeling the cool earth and grass embracing you. Know that you are loved.

. . .

While lying in this rich, thick grass, look at the beautiful bright blue sky. Float up into the beautiful celestial blue heavens and know that you are free to be, free to say and sing; that no longer must feeling and emotion be trapped inside. Feel your throat open as never before and issue forth glorious sound. Feel the God-spirit pouring through you and out of you through your sound.

. . .

And now float gently back to the earth, having felt and claimed as your own the freedom that comes through opening to the celestial realms. Peer into the deep blue waters of the pool. Look into the deep blue and allow yourself to be lost in it. Let yourself see reflections, any connections to ancient times, pictures, anything that comes to you through the water. See it, bless it, and know that God comes to you through your opening to see and hear and feel.

. . .

Look once more toward the heavens and you see beautiful violet rays of the sun coming through scattered, white, billowy clouds. Jump onto one of these rays and let it carry you back up into the heavens. Feel the top of your head open and the Blessed Spirit enter in. Hear Spirit's voice above your head. It may sound like your voice or the voice of someone familiar to you, or it may be a completely new voice to you. Open to Spirit to speak, and just listen. You may hear specific sounds or words, or you may simply experience thought transference. Just open and let be whatever is. Here you open to Spirit to speak to you and through you and live through you. Remain here for a few moments and commune with the Blessed Spirit.

. . .

In a moment you will come back to this space. But before you open your eyes, take a moment to remember the swim in the pool; remember the red, life-force from Mother Earth; remember the bright orange from the sun; the yellow embrace of the sun; the deep healing in the green grass and trees; remember the blue sky; the deep blue waters; and the violet sun rays. Feel all of these energies intermingling within you and know that you are Love.

. . .

And, as you are ready, open your eyes and come back to this space.

In the traditional chakra system, there are seven primary chakras in the human body and many secondary ones. In our journey, we will work with the seven primary chakras. Usually described as being located along the spine (see illustration on page 105), they provide gateways to understanding the many aspects of soul and ego. They represent aspects of who we are, how and what we think and feel, and our ability to change, grow, and transform. Each chakra reflects an aspect of consciousness that is essential to our lives. In her book, *Wheels of Life*, Anodea Judith writes, "The body is a vehicle of consciousness. Chakras are the wheels of life that carry this vehicle about — through its trials, tribulations, and transformations."[1] Through the chakras, we gain a deeper understanding about how we experience life, and why we experience it the way we do, how we perceive reality and why, and how we relate to ourselves, others, and society.

# The Seven Chakras

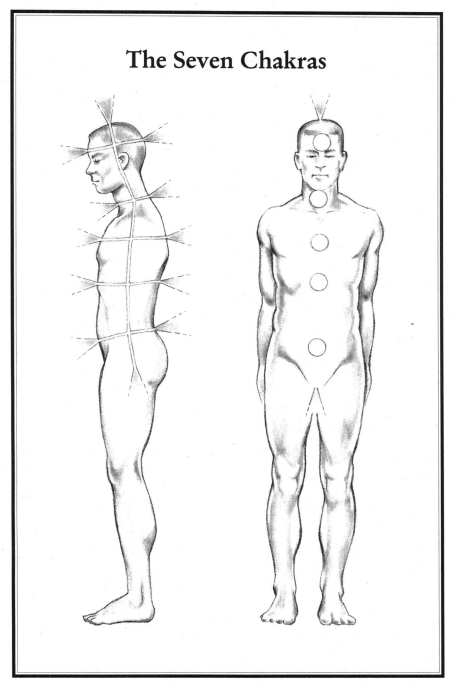

The chakras are powerful tools for self-discovery. They hold the keys to our deepest feelings, our deepest sense of who we are and how we fit into the greater consciousness of creation. In yoga philosophy, the chakras are considered to be the focal point for transforming the universal life force into the body's energy system.

Each chakra has characteristics that are discernible by the intuitive senses — distinct color, size and shape, rotation or spin, and intensity. These characteristics reflect its state of health and balance, and functionally affect the aura. When a chakra is "frozen," there is a complete block of energy flow. This is the most dangerous condition of the chakra because it has completely shut down, leaving you no access to the important energy of that chakra and those aspects of yourself. The shape may also appear distorted.

I "see" the chakras as spinning cones of energy, the small end of the cone being at the body, opening out away from the body. My friend, Edward, sees them as spinning wagon wheels. You may see them in another way. Or, you may not see them at all, but instead feel them or sense them in some other way. It may also be that you do not have any sense of them at all at the moment. Just keep playing with the energies, and you will begin to develop your own ways of perceiving them.

When the chakras are balanced and healthy, the colors are clear and shining. The rotation of the chakra is clockwise (as the clairvoyant looks at the person) and smooth, and they appear as perfectly shaped cones or wheels. We refer to this as an "open" chakra. In a clockwise spin, the chakra draws energy up from the one below and into the body from the environment. When the chakra is out of balance, it may be spinning counterclockwise, or be "frozen" in place. We refer to this as a "closed" chakra. A counterclockwise spin drains the chakra and body of its energy, and dissipates the upward flow of universal life force as it moves up through the chakra system. You could think of a counterclockwise spin as a leak somewhere in the plumbing system of your house which causes greatly reduced water pressure everywhere else.

Intensity refers to the degree of "openness" of the chakra, the velocity of the spin or frequency of vibration, and therefore the amount of energy actually produced by that chakra or allowed to move through it. A chakra produces its own electromagnetic field.

106

The combined energy fields of all the chakras create the aura and determines the predominant colors in the aura.

Each chakra also has a corresponding color vibration. The color is created by the vibrational frequency generated by the spin of the chakra. The aura is generated out of the combined energies of the chakras. If one particular chakra is stronger than the others, that color will dominate the auric field. For instance, if someone is in a highly intellectual state of being, associated with the third chakra, their aura might be primarily yellow, the color of that chakra.

The direction of the spin, the shape, and the quality of color in the chakra indicate the state of health of both the emotional qualities of that chakra, and its corresponding physical organs. In a healthy state, all of the chakras will be essentially the same size and shape, and all seven colors will be present in the aura.

The more universal life force we can allow to flow through us, the healthier we are. A lack of flow eventually leads to disease, distorts our perceptions, and dampens our feelings, thus interfering with a smooth experience of full life. We generally think of energy entering the body through the root chakra and working its way up through the energy system. The chakra energies build upon one another in a sort of stair-step fashion. The lower three chakras are more related to the physical realm and are denser energies, moving at slower vibratory rates. The upper three chakras are more related to the spiritual realm, and are less dense energies, moving at a faster vibratory rate. The heart is the meeting ground for the physical and spiritual worlds, a great alchemical pot where heaven and earth come together. Each chakra is also related to a basic element, and the elements get less dense as you ascend the ladder of the chakras, as well.

Root chakra — earth
Sacral chakra — water
Solar plexus chakra — fire
Heart chakra — air
Throat chakra — sound
Brow chakra — light
Crown chakra — thought, pure awareness[2]

Moving up the ladder in this way is known in the Hindu tradition as the *shakti* flow of energy. This is the liberating current that flows from bottom to top, more dense to less dense, slow-moving to fast-moving.

# The Seven Chakras

| Chakra | Location | Color | Attributes |
|---|---|---|---|
| 1) Root | under the bottom of the torso, at the perineum | red | life-force energy, survival instincts, fight or flight syndrome, physical aspects of sexuality, physical sensation, root of masculine energy |
| 2) Sacral | just below the navel, in the pelvic region | orange | emotional life and feelings, emotional aspects of sexuality, creativity, root of feminine energy |
| 3) Solar Plexus | just below the base of the sternum, in the arch of the rib cage | yellow | mental life, intellectual activity, judgment, personal power and strength, manipulation and control, security |
| 4) Heart | center of the chest | green | love for humanity, unconditional love, dreams |

| 5) Throat | base of the neck | light blue | expression of creativity and truth, letting go of aspects of your personality and your life that no longer serve you |
|---|---|---|---|
| 6) Brow | in the middle of the head, behind the eyes and between the ears | indigo | clairvoyance, visualization, imagination, access to your future |
| 7) Crown | crown of the head | violet | opening to higher consciousness, integration of spirituality into life |

The lower three chakras are more related to "earth" energies and physical life, while the upper three chakras are more related to "heaven" energies and spiritual life. The heart chakra is the bridge, uniting the physical with the spiritual.

You may notice that the chakra colors are the colors of the rainbow spectrum. You can remember them easily by the acronym, Roy G. Biv — red, orange, yellow, green, blue, indigo, violet.

This current is the journey of opening to higher consciousness, moving from the limitations of the physical world to the boundless freedom of the spiritual world, and is fueled by the life-force energy that flows in through the root chakra.

It is equally important, however, to work with the *shiva* flow of energy, which comes in through the top of the head and moves down toward the root chakra and the earth for grounding. Anodea Judith defines grounding as "a process of dynamic contact with the Earth, with its edges, boundaries, and limitations."[3] Grounding means feeling solid, real, present in the moment — feeling physically alive with the invigorating energy that comes from the lower chakras. It means really feeling your feet and legs as they touch the ground and carry you; becoming aware of gravity and feeling it hold you to the earth. Without grounding we lose our focus, our ability to concentrate or hold our attention in one place. We cannot manifest our thoughts or ideas in the physical plane of existence — our thoughts and ideas remain just that, thoughts and ideas with no physical form. The *shiva* energy is the manifesting current as opposed to *shakti*'s liberating current. As the *shiva* energy comes in through the top of the head and begins to travel down through the chakras, ideas gain in density, transmuting from thought to imagination, to verbalized expression, to a clear plan of action, to physical form. What was vague awareness gradually becomes more specific. Our physical needs are met. Manifestation requires focusing the thought process in order to bring it into physical form. This process requires grounding. Liberation without grounding leaves you scattered and confused. Grounding without liberation is stifling and boring. Both currents are required for full conscious living, and all of the chakras must be fully activated for this complete flow.

As each individual progresses through his spiritual journey, so does all of humanity. Each generation is usually able to sustain higher vibrations than the last, so that humanity moves in its evolutionary plan toward higher vibrations and expanded realities. To that end, each chakra has a purpose, a mind of its own, a journey of its own that is related to the larger journey of the individual. If one particular chakra becomes predominant in an individual, the issues of that chakra tend to control their life, influencing their values, assumptions, and judgments. The same is true for an organization or a culture. If either one gets locked in the issues of one particular chakra, its philosophies can become single-minded or dogmatic.

Each chakra and its development represents the evolution of psychological patterns in your life. In unpleasant experiences we often block our feelings, stopping a great deal of the natural energy flow through our bodies. This affects the development and maturation process of the chakras. For example, a child who is rejected many times when seeking love from parents may suppress his inner feelings of love out of what he feels is self-preservation. In order to do this, he stops the flow of energy through the heart chakra, which then slows its development. Or another person experiences sexual abuse as a child and therefore chooses to deny any feelings in the lower part of the body. In time, these issues will have to be addressed in order for the individuals to reach full emotional maturity.

The chakras offer another tool for use in our process of growth, understanding and healing. Through the chakra work in classes and private counseling, I have seen many people experience great revelations about their lives, their challenges, and difficulties. They were often able to resolve these issues quickly once they had recognized what was happening in their energy system. In serious emotional issues, more traditional forms of psychotherapy may be recommended. However, the process of traditional models can often be greatly accelerated by using the chakras as a tool for healing.

Each chakra holds keys to understanding who we are, why we think the way we do, why we have certain feelings, even why we look the way we do. When our memories or feelings around issues of a particular chakra are unpleasant, we often attempt to suppress them. However, these memories are imprinted in our energy system. They can never be eliminated. Therefore, when we encounter a closed chakra, it is important to be gentle and loving with the opening process. Opening chakras can be like opening a floodgate — the raging river comes pouring through, and we can feel overrun by all that we feel if the opening happens too quickly.

When the floodgate does open, it can be overwhelming at first. But try to let the feelings and emotions pour through. Most of us have experienced this at one time or another. Sometimes there is just nothing like a good cry, or some other form of healthy "venting." Then when the waters are calm once again, there is a wonderful

111

feeling of relief and peace. Go slowly and gently, giving yourself permission to experience whatever comes up along the way. Then continue to the next chakra as you feel you are ready.

# How do I work with a chakra?

So the question arises, "How do I work with a chakra? How do I open a closed chakra, or balance the energies within a chakra?" There are several ways to approach working with a chakra, and probably the most effective is a combination of all of them. You can visualize, meditate on, and wear the color of that chakra, with the intention of bringing that particular color energy into your consciousness in every way you can. Sleeping with the color is a great method. In your sleep, you open to deep unconscious levels, and are very receptive to energy. Therefore, sleeping with a towel, sheet, or sleepwear of that color can have a profound effect.

Because you are so "open" during sleep, where and with whom you sleep is very important. You are open to taking on whatever energies are around you. Be sure you want the energies of that space and/or person. A similar energy transference happens when you are eating. When you eat, your energy system is in "acceptance" or "receiving" mode. Therefore, you are also, on some level, taking in the energy of what is around you when you eat. Watching television, especially the news, or engaging in heated discussions over dinner, are very disruptive to your energy system. Your body absorbs the negativity. Mealtime, as well as sleeptime, should be accompanied by soothing surroundings.

Another way to work with a chakra is to visualize it spinning healthily and freely in your meditation. If you realize that the chakra is stuck or spinning backwards, create a visualization or imagination exercise to enable you to get it unstuck and spinning in the right direction.

Each chakra chapter includes at least one major meditation exercise for working with that particular chakra. Ultimately, in working with any chakra blockage, we have to fully address and walk through the emotional issue that is creating the block. As you go through the chakra chapters, the concepts and attributes discussed will trigger reactions and responses within you, both physically and emotionally. The most important thing you can do is to be aware of those responses and step fully into them, explore them, let them speak to you. Be willing to go as far as you need to go, and give as much time as is necessary to fully resolve and heal whatever issues arise. This is the only way to effect a lasting change within that chakra.

You will also find some issues discussed in more than one chakra. Any issue may arise in any chakra. Each chakra represents a particular aspect of that issue. For example, issues of self-confidence and humility arise often in both the first and third chakras. Personal truth is recognized and acknowledged in the third chakra, but expressed through the fifth. These are simplified examples, but they illustrate the complexity of the chakra system and of your personal make-up.

In some chakras, you will feel very comfortable, experiencing no serious inner conflicts. In others you may feel overwhelmed with emotion, fear, resistance. It's okay. That's normal in this process. Be gentle but firm with yourself. Give yourself the time you need. Don't force an issue. Simply maintain a loving persistence until the issue is resolved.

The chakras are living energy centers in a constant state of flux. A chakra may be open one moment and closed the next due to your life circumstances. However, certain chakras will be open most of the time and others closed as your habitual pattern. It is the chakras that are habitually closed that you will need to give the most attention. Once you have gone through all seven chakras and done your work in each one, take a little rest, and start over again on a deeper level. As you become more and more attuned to your energy system, you will be aware of particular chakras that are calling you to work, and you will let your awareness guide you through the life-long, ongoing process of clearing, balancing, and healing.

There is a lot of introductory information presented in this chapter. However, after you have explored several chakras and experienced some of these energies for yourself, feel free to come back to read this chapter again. You will find that what is confusing now will be clearer for you then.

# 8

# Chakra One: Life-Force

The Root Chakra
Color: red
Location: under the bottom of the body
at the perineum

We begin our in-depth chakra work with the first one, known as the "root" or "base" chakra. It is the first rung in the ladder, the first step in the staircase that makes up the seven-chakra system. The root chakra is located under the bottom of the body, between the anus and the genitals. To sense where it is, we can do a quick exercise.

## Exercise #13
## Feeling the Root Chakra Grounding

Stand with your feet directly under your shoulders and absolutely parallel to one another. You may feel a little "pigeon-toed" at first, but focus your attention on the feelings in the area of your body between the anus and the genitals. This part of your body will feel "open." You will feel a connection to the floor or to the ground.

115

Now, to contrast this feeling, turn your toes outward so that your feet are pointing away from each other. You will notice that this space under the bottom of your body "closes." You may even feel "lighter" on your feet, or not as stable in your stance. When you pull your feet back into absolutely parallel alignment, the space opens once again. You are now feeling the root chakra open and close.

Continue going back and forth between these positions a few more times, and you will begin to be able to feel energy moving in through the open chakra. You may also notice that the energy flow feels stuck here when the chakra is closed. How does this feel to you? How do you experience the open and closed chakra? If at first you do not experience tangible sensations of energy movement or being blocked here, do not get discouraged. Just give yourself time, and use your imagination a little if you have to in order to get started. Continue to play with this exercise for a few days until you have clear sensations of an open and closed root chakra.

As you are getting attuned to the energy, start paying attention to the alignment of your feet as you walk. Keep them absolutely parallel, and you will notice an increase of physical energy as you walk. Turning your feet out, on the other hand, drains your body of energy and vitality.

This is a very simple exercise to manipulate the chakra open and closed. There are many more factors that we will discuss which affect its state of being, but the physical aspect is certainly an important one. As we begin to move ahead with our work in this chakra, and as you spend time on your own working with the issues and characteristics of this chakra, pay attention to your feet and the energetic opening under the bottom of your body. Notice the position of your feet and this opening as you stand, walk, and sit, and become aware of when you open and close this first energy center. You will learn a great deal about how you invite the life-force energy of the universe into your body and energy system, and, perhaps more importantly, you'll begin to notice the circumstances under which you close this center.

116

# Survival

The chief purpose of the root chakra is to maintain physical life. Through this chakra we experience physical reality in our own unique and individual ways. The quantity and quality of life-force energy to which we open determines the quantity and quality of physical energy we experience and our will to live. The root chakra feeds basic life-force energy to all other parts of the body and their respective physical functions. Therefore, we find our basic instincts for survival here. The "fight or flight" syndrome is a root chakra response, and our fears of a life-threatening nature register here. It is through the root chakra that we become aware of any impending danger or threat to our physical well-being.

Anger and fear around survival issues are two powerful forces often found in the root chakra. We all have yearnings deep inside for love, acceptance, safety, and security. Sometimes we feel inadequacies in our lives around some of these issues, and react by becoming overprotective of possessions or boundaries, "acting out" in various ways, or manipulating people or situations or finding ourselves in codependent situations (also involving the solar plexus chakra). But, underneath any of those reactions are simply fears of not having enough love or acceptance, or of whatever we need to survive. When this yearning and fear turns to desperation and hopelessness, it can lead to anger and violence. The survival self of the root chakra is kicking in and saying, "I have to have this now or I will die," and will therefore do whatever it takes in that moment to get that thing or that feeling. When we walk into the fears and work with them, we can begin to diffuse the anger and potential violent explosion. (We will work more directly with anger and fear in Chapter 11.)

# Mother Earth

The root chakra is our physical connection to the earth, and to the universal life force energy that flows through all living things. In our Western mode of thinking, we tend to look upon things of an "earthly" nature as being less pure or less spiritual than those of a "heavenly" nature. We are often uncomfortable even talking about the lower parts of the body and their functions. Sexuality and its expression have been considered only from their primitive, physical drive perspectives. The sacred creative and healing power that is released through sexual expression is often overlooked. This pure, primitive, physical desire energy feeds us our basic life-giving essence. Indigenous cultures, on the other hand, have always recognized these aspects of the root chakra, and will tell us that the earth energies are not only divine in nature, but essential to completing the full human and spiritual experience. "Mother Earth" and "Father Sky" simply are two aspects of the same universal life force energy. We receive the physical aspect of that life-force energy through the Earth, and the spiritual aspect from the Heavens.

When I was growing up, our next-door neighbor was a wise and wonderful elderly woman whom we called Cousin Lucy. I spent every afternoon after school with her, helped her with various projects, and listened as she shared her wisdom about life. One of Cousin Lucy's many hobbies was ceramics. Her brother had made her a potter's wheel out of an old farm wagon tire and axle. She would go to the country to her family farm and dig the clay out of the earth, bring it home, and process it herself through sieves and cheesecloth until she had pure clay to work on her potter's wheel. As we worked side by side, she would say over and over, "such good, clean dirt. God has given us such pure clean earth, and that earth can give us everything we need." Cousin Lucy recognized the sacredness of Mother Earth, made beautiful things from Her, and always expressed deep gratitude for Her many gifts. The root chakra is our connection to Mother Earth.

Through Mother Earth and the first chakra, we find our sense of groundedness. The more we extend ourselves in exploring the higher dimensions, the more rooted or grounded we must be. A good analogy for the necessity of grounding is a roller coaster. Because the cars are firmly connected to the tracks (grounding), the roller coaster train can travel at lightning speeds in all kinds of configurations. If, however, the cars were not attached to the track, they would go flying off into the air at the first turn. The same is true for us. In the root chakra we begin this journey of raising our energy to higher and

118

higher vibratory rates. As long as we are grounded, we can raise our vibrations to create and manifest wondrous things in our lives and for the world. But without solid grounding, we easily "fly off the track," becoming distracted or unable to bring our dreams and goals to reality.

Unfortunately, our Western culture has so emphasized intellectual development that it is very easy to lose our connection to Mother Earth. Or, sometimes people can become so focused on their "spiritual journeys" and the upper chakras that they forget about the root chakra and its essential contribution to life. One of my voice teachers, so thoroughly grounded in the old Italian school of singing, used to say to me, "The highest trees have the deepest roots," referring to the singer's need to stay rooted in the floor when singing high notes. The same axiom applies so clearly to our lives. The higher we wish to fly, whether in career success, academic or intellectual studies, or personal and spiritual development, the more grounded we must be. An open root chakra helps us remain firmly anchored in this physical dimension and in our present reality. It keeps us fully in touch with and open to receiving the life-giving energies of the Earth.

# Physical Sensation

Through the root chakra, we first become aware of our physical feelings and sensations. Physical touch, and the ways in which we are touched, bring powerful messages to our awareness. When someone close to you caresses you in a tender way, you recognize a physical sensation of warmth and love. But when someone touches you roughly or in an inappropriate manner, this sends very different signals to your conscious awareness. These are just two simple examples of how we become aware of our feelings or sensations through the tactile senses of the root chakra. When we cut ourselves off from physical stimulation, we cut off the life-giving energies of the root chakra. Over a long period of time, this denial of the root chakra can lead to physical and/or emotional dysfunction. We will talk more about this later in the chapter when we discuss the kundalini energy which is awakened from the root chakra.

Because all physical and tactile sensations come into our awareness through the root chakra, this is also where we first become aware of all memories related to any physical experience, both pleasurable and painful. Pleasurable memories help us remain open in this chakra to receive the full life-giving essence of its energy. Painful memories, on the other hand, of trauma, sexual abuse, physical injury, or other such experiences, can easily encourage us to close this chakra, suppressing the painful memory. This, unfortunately, also robs us of the life-force energy that we need for fully satisfying, healthy living.

# Cosmology

Author and teacher Matthew Fox speaks of the first chakra in terms of vibration and cosmology. He says that it is through the root chakra that we connect at a primal level with all of the cosmos. Through the root chakra we feel, usually at an unconscious level, the sensation of our personal vibration, through which we connect to the vibrations and sounds of the universe. Every being and every object in the universe has its own unique sound because it is a unique vibration. Opening the root chakra allows us to vibrate in harmony with all of creation, allowing us to flow in cycle with the universe.[1] When the chakra is closed, on the other hand, we pull back into our own private world, become unaware that there is anything or anyone else outside of our little private world. We begin to function in disharmony with the world. Deepak Chopra speaks of "entrainment with the universe" in addressing this same concept. He defines Love as unity consciousness.[2] The base chakra is where we find that unity conciousness, from a primal sensation level, because the base chakra is where we first open to the physical sensations of Love — the recognition that we "feel" a certain way, physically, when we experience the flow of Love through our beings.

120

# Addictions

Although they can be found in all chakras, addictions usually have their root in the first chakra. Addictions are caused by an overpowering need to feel something other than what we are feeling. They have the paradoxical effect of making us feel one thing while we are deadening another feeling. They create a distraction to keep us from having to face the true feeling and its resulting sensation that is inside us. Addictions become a "mask" to wear in order to avoid having to see the "real face." They give the illusion of protecting us from our pain, and of keeping others from knowing of our pain. The addiction closes the root chakra and gives the individual the sense that they are receiving their life-force energy from the addictive substance. This, of course, is complete illusion, but a very comfortable illusion to the addictive personality. The more the root chakra is closed, the easier it is for the individual to be taken in by illusion. In order to experience healing, the addictive personality must first be willing to stop the addictive behavior long enough to be out from under the "mask" of illusion. Then begins the process of facing the underlying pain, fear, and anxiety, and working through these issues to come to a peaceful resolution.

# Personal Potential

The root chakra has hidden within it all the potential for our lives. You might say that the root chakra is the opening to all possibilities of the physical world, and the crown chakra is the opening to all possibilities of the spiritual world. Through the root chakra we find the seeds of our lives that have been planted deep in the soil, but must now be watered, nurtured, loved, and nourished in order to break through the ground, grow, blossom, and bear fruit. These possibilities are just waiting for us to pull them up and begin to let them move up through the chakras so that they may develop to their fullest potential. Meister Eckhart expressed this concept by saying, "The seed of God is in us. A fig seed grows into a fig tree, a

121

hazelnut seed a hazelnut tree, so should not the seed of God grow into God!" Our divine potential lies buried deep in the root chakra. Through opening this chakra and fully exploring all that is there for us, we can find our divine seeds and begin to nurture them to their fullness and maturity.

# Charisma

The root chakra is the source of a basic charisma or animal magnetism within an individual. In the ancient world, a person who exhibited this animal magnetism or charisma was considered to be a very powerful person. This quality has nothing to do with physical attractiveness, but rather to do with how the person carries themselves, speaking with self-confidence and a sense of authority, and ability to command the attention of others. Author and healer Rosalyn Bruyere speaks of this charisma and its duality with humility. There is certainly a direct relationship between charisma and awakened kundalini or life-force energy — the more awakened the kundalini, the more animal magnetism is present. However, without humility, the charisma can become arrogance or dominance. Humility is important to keep the charisma in balance.[3]

This is not to confuse humility with retreating from your power. On the contrary, humility means embracing the root chakra power, recognizing its proper use and purpose, and honoring it without flaunting it. The fully alive base chakra brings power and humility into perfect balance. Embracing the power and humility of the root chakra and using it brings us both strength and flexibility. However, if we do not humbly embrace the power, too often it is either abused or completely suppressed, both of which rob us of valuable life-giving energy.

Any kind of service to the world or to individuals requires this full embrace of power and strength, balanced with humility. This balance leads to service with integrity, rather than a false service motivated by an inner need to be fed. If you are serving in order to fill your own need, you might want to look at your root chakra issues to see where you have a need to balance. Once you have addressed your own issues, you can step into service clear in your desire to help others.

Another important aspect of service is developing the ability to call upon the universal life-force energy to support us in that service. Through the root chakra, we can learn to become channels of the universal life force rather than drawing on our own limited life force.

# Characteristics of an Open Root Chakra

When the root chakra is open and balanced, the body feels calm, relaxed, without tension. You feel a physical flexibility and comfort in your body. There is a powerful energy present that helps you to master your life. You enjoy the challenges and opportunities of your work rather than being overwhelmed with responsibilities or obstacles. You experience material sustenance in your life. You recognize that you always have what you need for a comfortable life. There is a strong sense of "I am here now" — a power and vitality that helps you be well-grounded in your physical reality. You do not feel "spacy" or "flighty," but rather secure in your physical world.

The freedom journey that we spoke of earlier in Chapter 2 begins with balance in the root chakra. This gives a sense of freedom without limitation. When this chakra is open and balanced, there is a sense of freedom without limitation. There are no entrapments, no boundaries in which you feel you are enclosed. With the root chakra opened, you feel as if the world is yours to explore, to experience, to learn from, and to share in. There is an exhilaration about life and all that it has to offer. Your exploration is fed by your abundant physical energy.

# Characteristics of a Closed Root Chakra

On the other hand, when the root chakra is closed, you may experience a resistance to life-force energy. You may avoid any strenuous physical activity and be low in physical energy, often resulting in illness or a significant lack in physical strength and power.

There may be a tendency to cling to the tasks of everyday life, for they give you a false sense of groundedness or purpose, or a false sense of energy. This can be another aspect of an addictive personality. You may become fanatical about your work, while at the same time the creative power of your work is blocked. In a state of quiet you perhaps feel numb or depressed, not feeling anything, because you are not able to access the vibrant life-giving universal energy. Therefore, you keep yourself very busy doing many activities because that gives you a feeling of aliveness. There are often fears over not having enough in the material world. The lack of groundedness can result in making you very impressionable, easily swayed by others' thoughts, ideas, and opinions.

Dysfunction in the root chakra can also cause you to be in a constant state of reaction rather than response. Response comes from a clear, calm, and level-headed state of being. Reaction comes out of confusion, anxiety, and stress. When you are fully grounded and comfortable in your surroundings, you will be able to respond appropriately to situations and circumstances. However, without that firm grounding and confidence (also associated with the solar plexus chakra), you may tend to live in a constant state of reaction, a constant state of defensiveness, desperately trying to hold on to some kind of reality that will allow you to feel safe.

Lack of balance here can create aggressiveness or belligerent behavior. You may act impulsively and recklessly, often craving excitement, not acknowledging the inappropriateness of your actions. Hyperactivity is also often associated with a closed root chakra, as is obsessive sexual behavior. These are all symptoms of the root chakra calling out for attention and healing.

When a person is stuck in the root chakra, they may also tend to be possessive of belongings and people, and very territorial. We see this in the developmental process of small children. They go through a period in which they are very possessive, not wanting to share anything. It is important to allow them this process so that they learn to feel safe in their physical world. Once they have realized that they are safe, they grow past this possessiveness, and are eager to share their possessions and their energies with others. However, if children are forced past this possessive stage before they are ready to move on in their development, or if an individual experiences repeated losses in life, they may become closed in the root chakra, holding on tightly to everything they have because of such great fear of loss.

# Kundalini

Within the root chakra is the basic release of life-force energy through the body. We will refer to this energy as kundalini (from the Hindu tradition) or life-force, but it is also known by many other names, such as *qi* or *ki*, in various traditions. This life-force essence is released from the root chakra and travels up the spine, awakening all of the other chakras. At the same time, a grounding-force energy moves down the sciatic nerve from the root chakra through the feet and into the ground. This opposite force energy is similar to the action and energy of a rocket. When a rocket takes off, there is a tremendous thrust of energy downward which shoots the rocket high into space. This is the force of the root chakra. When this chakra is fully enlivened, there is a thrust of energy down the legs into the ground, giving you a feeling of tremendous stability and solidity. At the same time, a rush of energy shoots up the spine and out the top of the head, giving you the feeling of flying. This energy experience is the gateway to experiencing many levels of awareness at once. You are firmly grounded in your physical reality, yet you are traversing many higher levels of awareness at the same time, fully aware of the energies at each of those levels.

The chief purpose of the kundalini energy is conscious awareness — an awareness of the self and the way the universal life force moves through us, as well as an awareness of our personal connection to the universal life force as it creates and maintains all that exists in the universe. We access the kundalini through the first chakra.

The kundalini energy allows us to be aware of our experiences and feelings. In simple terms, you could consider that there are two systems that join together to create the whole you: the physical/emotional system, and the mental/intellectual system. The kundalini carries the experience through the physical/emotional system (beginning in the first two chakras) on to the mental/intellectual system (third chakra) to register it in conscious awareness. This process begins with the physical sensation of the experience being recorded in the root chakra. Then the kundalini carries this awareness on up to the second chakra where we have a corresponding emotional sensation, and begin to associate emotional feelings with physical sensations. From here the awareness travels on up to the third chakra where it is acknowledged and recorded as conscious memory. The experience is now a part of our conscious awareness.

Therefore, if the kundalini energy is flowing, we are aware of sensations and emotions, and they are registered in our conscious memory. However, if the kundalini is not flowing, there is no acknowledgment of sensation or feeling, no registration of the memory in conscious awareness, and the experience remains locked in the body. We have no conscious recall or memory that this experience ever occurred. Therefore, just as the root chakra and kundalini energies allow us to acknowledge and register an experience in our conscious awareness, the shutting off of the kundalini flow allows us to deny that an experience has occurred. This becomes a strong defense mechanism, for when there is no conscious registration of the experience, we do not have to deal with it or the feelings it stirs within us. Over time this can lead to disease or some form of physical, emotional, or spiritual dysfunction.

Kundalini is essential for the spiritual journey. Only when the kundalini is flowing freely throughout our energy systems can we be fully aware of our experiences and the lessons or opportunities for growth that are being presented to us. When the kundalini is weak, we have no energy for our spiritual journey. We have no recognition of our gifts and lessons as they come to us, and their spiritual significance. The flow of kundalini determines how easily we can recognize the essence of our situation, circumstance, or experience, learn from it, and facilitate the necessary changes in our lives in order to move on through the experience. With weak kundalini, we are moving very slowly through our soul's evolutionary path. With strong kundalini, however, we have a heightened awareness of all that is around us and within us, we can be in touch with Spirit on profound levels, and we can move along expeditiously in our soul's journey.

When we have painful or traumatic experiences, we may tend to block the kundalini from flowing so that the feeling and memory of that experience is blocked from our conscious awareness. The kundalini does not carry the record of the experience up through our systems to register it in consciousness, so it becomes stuck in a particular place in the body. When memories remain trapped in the body and are not brought to conscious awareness, they are holding us hostage, in a sense. We remain stuck in our development in some way, because the kundalini is not flowing through that memory for its healing. Therefore we are still "held back" in some way in our growth and development. Wherever the kundalini stops in our bodies, this becomes our level of conscious awareness.

When the flow of kundalini to any particular chakra is weak, there are significant effects on the areas of life associated with that chakra. In the root chakra, weak kundalini flow manifests as a very limited sexual drive and limited energy for day-to-day living. There is a limited sense of touch and tactile feeling. There is very little awareness of feeling in the body, very little sense of or response to sensual stimulation, physical pleasure or pain. You cannot "hear" the powerful messages that the body is constantly sending you for your health and well-being.

Because the second chakra is related to our emotional life and our initial connection with others, if the kundalini does not reach here, there is a limited ability to know our own feelings or to sense what others are feeling. Our ability to perceive others and relate to them empathically is greatly compromised.

When the kundalini does not reach the third chakra, our intellect and memory are affected. The more energy enters the third chakra, the more information we can assimilate on a mental level. Remember the mind is really an energy field all through and around your body. Information and memories are stored throughout the cells of the body. The flow of kundalini must be strong enough to reach all parts of the body to find the necessary information and bring it to conscious awareness. Lack of kundalini to this chakra also weakens our self-confidence and sense of power and strength.

The heart chakra is the center for universal love. You might say it is the seat of the soul. When the kundalini does not reach the heart, there is a lack of sense of the soul and of the divine within us. It is difficult to reach a sense of inner peace and rest because we do not know our "inner home," our essence, and therefore difficult to tap into our inner wisdom and guidance. Because the heart chakra is also related to the circulatory and respiratory systems, these physical systems may be greatly compromised.

The lower three chakras are related more to the physical aspects of life, while the upper three chakras relate to the spiritual aspects. The heart chakra brings the physical and spiritual together. Moving on up to the throat chakra, we find the first of the spiritual chakras. It is, in a sense, the "root chakra" of the spiritual energy centers. If the kundalini does not reach the throat, there is limited energy feeding the spiritual life. The throat chakra is also related to speaking your truth and expressing your creativity. With limited energy here, you are not able to fully speak your truth.

When the kundalini does not reach the brow chakra there is little imagination or ability to visualize. Therefore there is a lack of creativity because you are lacking the ability to see what you wish to create, and then project it into manifestation. Another symptom of a lack of kundalini flow to the brow chakra is anxiety. Anxiety is caused by not being able to see any other possibility than your current situation. Since the brow chakra affects your ability to consider the future or imagine other possibilities in your life, a lack of kundalini flow here can lead to periods of anxiety.

Finally, if the kundalini does not reach the crown chakra, you have a limited ability to move into altered states of consciousness, including sleep or trance.[4]

A law of science says "nature abhors a vacuum." When the kundalini is not flowing through the body's energy system, a kind of vacuum is created. Nature, not wanting an empty space, will automatically fill the empty space with whatever energies are nearby. Therefore, a person whose energy is very low is susceptible to the effects of their surroundings. It is virtually impossible to keep ourselves in such an insulated or protected life that we never encounter negative energies, whether in the form of fearful people, a situation filled with anger, or a person overcome with sadness. Therefore, in order to maintain our own sense of balance, and to recognize our feelings as our own and not someone else's, our kundalini energy must be flowing freely. This allows us to be fully aware of all that is happening within and around us, and able to respond appropriately.

Some authors say that the element associated with the root chakra is fire, while others feel it is earth. I can easily feel both elements at work here. For me, however, earth is the stronger element in the root chakra, while fire is the element of the solar plexus. Earth corresponds much more to the deep sense of groundedness. At the same time, there is a kind of "purifying fire" energy inherent in the root chakra. When that rocket-like energy is thrust down into the ground and shoots up the spine, there is a clearing away of blocks, and powerful purification can occur. You can work with these two elements to see which belongs to the root and which to the solar plexus within you.

Depression is caused by a lack of flow of kundalini. Depression means literally the absence of feeling. By moving the kundalini energy through the chakras, we certainly begin to feel again. We may not like what we feel, but at least we have come alive once again and can begin to work with the issues at hand in a productive way. The first step, therefore, in dealing with depression is activating the root chakra and getting the kundalini energy moving.

Having discussed the issues of the root chakra and kundalini, now it is time for you to work with this energy center in an experiential way. With each chakra we have a meditation to work with the breath, color, sound, and trigger words, in order to further facilitate your exploration, self-discovery, balancing and healing. There are specific instructions for each chakra.

As we have already discussed, each chakra has a corresponding color. You may want to wear that color for the meditation, or wrap yourself in a towel, sheet, or large piece of fabric in that color. For chakra work in classes and with clients, I have large pieces of light-weight, silky-feeling, inexpensive fabric in each of the chakra colors. The fabric can be wrapped around the area of the body of the particular chakra, or spread out on the floor to create a sea of that color into which you can peer.

Each chakra also has a corresponding pitch vibration. Although the precise pitches actually come from the ancient Indian musical scale, in the interest of practicality, we will use our western diatonic musical scale. The pitches will still be very close to the ancient Indian scale. You can use an inexpensive pitch pipe (found in your local music store), or other musical instrument you may have, to find the proper pitch for each chakra. Both seeing the color and singing the pitch will help facilitate the opening and balancing of the chakra.

Finally, each meditation includes a series of trigger words. These words represent aspects both of an open and closed chakra. Some of the words will mean nothing to you, while others will spark strong responses or reactions. When you experience a reaction or response to a word, stay there for awhile and explore this feeling. Then continue with the next word when you are ready.

These instructions are repeated within each meditation so that you can relax and get the most out of your experience. Again, allow yourself to move at your own pace, and to feel whatever you feel with the meditation. Some chakras will feel joyful or peaceful, while others will not be so comfortable. If you are in a group, everyone's experience within a particular chakra will be unique, so don't feel that yours should be like anyone else's. We all have issues in our lives, but they manifest in different ways and in different chakras for each of us. So, be patient, and honor your own feelings and experience.

# Exercise #14
# The Root Chakra

Allow yourself to move into a meditative state. Breathe deeply and let your body relax. Concentrate your breathing in the area of the root chakra, pausing after the exhalation to encourage the energy to move down the spine. Visualize a bright red light moving all through this region of the body. Feel the bottom of your body become warm and relaxed as you continue breathing. Concentrate on your physical feelings in that area of the body. You may also experience emotional feelings. Just allow them to come to your awareness, without feeling that you must do anything about them. Allow the vibrations of the red color to move through you so that you may experience this color through all of your senses.

In order to heighten your experience, you may wish to

130

tone on the vowel sound, "oo," on the pitch C. Vocalize the vowel for as long as you wish, taking breaths whenever you need, and then continue. You will find that the sound vibration opens this chakra even more. The sound of your own voice is your most potent personal healing force.

. . .

In order to continue facilitating your process of self-discovery, as you continue to work with the color, your breath, and the root chakra region, begin to move through the list of trigger words below. The words represent aspects both of an open and closed chakra. Some of the words will have no meaning to you at all, and some of them will spark strong, and perhaps even profound reactions. When you experience any reaction to a trigger word, allow yourself to remain there for a while and explore your feelings. Then, continue with the list when you are ready. As you explore this chakra, you may find other words that you wish to add to this list. Feel free to explore here in any way that you feel is right for you. Take as much time as you need.

| | | |
|---|---|---|
| power | source | fire |
| Holy Spirit | purifying fire | primal |
| earth | dancing | nature |
| life-force | strength | excitement |
| energy | red | uncovered |
| serpent | desire | temptation |
| me | self-preservation | memories |
| physical | earth mother | grounding |
| physical mastery | pride | materialism |
| physical pleasure | physical pain | vitality |
| passion | matter | survival |
| the body | food | beginning |
| rage | blood | shame |
| revenge | release | union |
| charisma | humility | awareness |
| sensation | freedom | |

Take your time now as you continue to work in your

131

meditation with whatever has come to your awareness. When you are ready, go to your journal to record any impressions, thoughts, or experiences that you had in this meditation.

# 9

# Chakra Two:  Creation

Sacral Chakra
Color:  orange
Location:  pelvic region, just below the navel

As we move from the root chakra to the second chakra, known as the sacral chakra or the sexual-creative chakra, we move from the tactile to the emotional. We also move from a consciousness that says that the whole world exists just for you and your personal needs to a somewhat higher awareness that recognizes that there are others in the world with whom to relate. In the second chakra we become aware of having physical/emotional feelings for others, and physical/emotional relationships with others. I say physical/emotional because the emotions associated with the second chakra are still of a somewhat primal and physical nature. As we move on up the chakras, the feelings become more sophisticated. In the second chakra, we recognize our basic needs to be touched in loving ways and to establish emotional relationships with others. The second chakra is also where we find our ability to and interest in empathizing with others — to feel what they are feeling. In the root chakra consciousness, we are only interested in what *we* are feeling.

The following partner exercise will help facilitate this transition from the root chakra to the second chakra. If you are working through this book in a group, choose a partner. If you are on your own, invite your adventurous friend to join you again.

133

# Exercise #15
# Communication Through Touch

Choose a spot for this exercise where you can feel free to move around slightly within your seated position. The floor is an excellent place because there are no restrictions of furniture.

Sit face to face with your partner and begin the exercise by placing your hands palm-to-palm with your partner's, as in the beginning aura exercises. Then close your eyes. Allow the energy to begin to moving between you through your touching hands. Allow there to be a "push-pull" or "give-take" exchange as you begin communicating with one another through your hands. Begin to explore your relationship together through this sense of touch.

As you each sense permission from the other, allow your hands to begin moving past this initial position, so that you explore one another further through touch. Your hands may move to your partner's arms, shoulders, neck, or head. Again, it is important that you sense your partner's permission before you take each new step. Establishing safety and trust together is essential. As you feel the trust building between you, continue your exploration with one another as far as you are both comfortable. The only rules here are that your eyes remain closed, you do not speak, and that you maintain physical contact in some way.

As you explore and communicate with one another through touch, you will begin to feel your partner's energy and learn something about your partner. But you will also learn a great deal about yourself and your level of openness, as well as sense your own blocks and fears at this physical level. As you explore and discover your partner and yourself, just observe what you feel, making no judgments about your feelings or about your partner. Just learn from and through one another.

After about ten minutes (or longer if both you and your partner seem to want to continue), say your farewells to your partner through your touch. Go to your journals to write about your experience before you talk about it with your partner. This will help you be clear about your own experience, and not be influenced by your partner's. Consider how you felt in "giving" to your partner, and how you felt in "receiving" from your partner. Then, when you have both finished writing, talk with one another and share your experience together. If you are in a group, after talking in partner pairings, open the discussion to the group and share your discoveries, revelations, and experiences with one another.

# Sexuality and Creativity

In the second chakra we find the primary energy for our passions and desires — our passions for living. Sexuality and the soul's yearning to create are two of our strongest passions. Spirit spoke very clearly about these issues.

*Let us move into the sexual-creative chakra. Sexual and creative: these are important words and concepts. You are a sexual being — all humans are. It is up to you to determine how free or how stifled you will be as a sexual being, but you are a sexual being. This sexuality is the core of your creative process, for it is the core of YOU. Sexuality is the deepest part of self-identity, for it is how you relate to Self and how you relate to others.*

*We speak of sexuality here not as an act, but rather as a state of being. Sexual energy is an energy of attraction and opposition. A "chemistry" of some kind exists between any two people when they first meet. Therefore, the first bands of energy that form between any two people occur at the sexual-creative chakra. This is regardless of the kind of relationship that will be established between them. As the relationship develops, the bands will grow out from this chakra to the higher centers, and the relationship will begin to take on more shape and dimension.*

135

*This second chakra is "we," while the first chakra is "me." Here you first become aware of others as beings with whom to relate. Sexuality must be clear and free in order to allow "we" to happen freely on any level. You recognize this in yourself in that when you feel very open in the sacral chakra, you are very comfortable socially. But, when you close here, you move back down into number one and only want to deal with "me." Here is the issue of sexuality — being open so that the initial "chemistry" with another can occur. Step into yourself — the deepest part of Self, and let the energies flow, both from earth and heaven. Release the past and future here, and be at peace with the beautiful sexual being that you are. Remember that sexuality is the essence of you because it is your primal energy. You can make choices about sexual behavior or expression, but in order to become a truly realized being, the sexual energy itself must be allowed to flow freely in an uninhibited manner.*

*Now we move to "creative." When the sexuality is open, released, and flowing freely, creativity begins to flow. You will find your relationships moving into much more interesting realms. You will no longer be so quick to put a label on your relationships or allow them to become stuck within a certain framework. You will be more willing to let them flow and find their own way, not necessarily having to fit into any particular mold. Releasing your sexuality releases creativity. Creativity enhances relationships. Relationships enhance LIFE. For creativity is about "we," not about "me." As you open to the world and to relationships with other beings, you open communication and creativity. You create as a form of expression and communication. We aren't speaking here of creativity as limited to "the arts," but rather creativity as it flows through your life, allowing you to create what you wish within your life. This is why the second chakra must be opened and developed to its full potential. In the root chakra is life-force energy. In the sacral chakra is the first step of how to use that energy. In all staircases there must be a first step, or the entire staircase comes tumbling down. Build your foundation. Allow this wheel to spin freely, and, as it spins, it will clear and purify, bringing its many gifts to your full awareness.*

When the sacral chakra is open, we feel a sense of freedom in our lives — a freedom that comes with being comfortable with our sexuality and our primal essence. We are comfortable being with other people, feeling free to simply be ourselves. An open second chakra gives us confidence in knowing that we are lovable just the way we are — that there is no need to create a facade in order to be accepted by others. We find our creative juices flowing, and are able to work creatively with others, even when their ideas or perspectives are different from ours. We don't feel threatened by the differences, but rather can find ways to complement one another.

Issues of love and acceptance of our physical bodies are associated with the sacral chakra. When this chakra is closed, we may find ourselves using our sexual energy as a way of getting attention or gaining approval or acceptance. Sexual "acting out" is often a cry from the second chakra for attention or recognition, a cry for affection and acceptance. Deep inside, there are usually feelings of inadequacy, or feelings of not ever receiving enough love and affection. This can lead to sexual addiction in some form. When we address these emotional issues, however, and take steps to begin the healing process, the acting out begins to disappear.

When this chakra has been closed due to emotional or physical trauma, the results can also be a complete shutdown of sexual energy, resulting in a lack of physical vitality. Other symptoms of a closed sacral chakra are worrying about what others think, an inability to get along with others, and a general mistrust of others.

The second through the sixth chakras each open out both the front and the back of the body. The front side of each chakra is its expressive side, the feeling or feminine energy aspect. The back side of the chakra is the will aspect of the energy, the male aspect. The two sides of the chakra must be balanced to one another in order to have the balance of expression and will, of the creative aspect and the assertive force to give this aspect a voice in your life.

The front side of the sacral chakra affects the quality of love for the sexual partner, and the giving and receiving of physical, mental, and spiritual pleasure. The back side affects the quantity of sexual energy. When it is open, we feel our sexual power, but when it is closed, our sexual power is greatly diminished. We may even tend to avoid sexual activity, claiming that it is not important in our lives. By doing this, however, we are stopping the flow of the kundalini energy at the second chakra, cutting off its flow to the higher energy centers.

Because of the strong sexual and emotional energies associated with this chakra, we have a responsibility to use these energies appropriately. Sexual energy can be extremely powerful in certain circumstances. Author John Nelson says body sexuality is God's way of calling us into communication with one another.[1] It can either be transmuted into creative energy that is an expression of Love, using the sexual energy for the greatest good, or it can become a manipulative force, used to gain power over others. When the latter occurs, again we have stopped the kundalini energy in the second chakra, not allowing our consciousness to develop beyond that point.

One of our greatest challenges today is that we live in a culture where sexuality is either exploited or completely denied. A healthily balanced attitude toward sexuality, sexual expression, sexual intimacy, and sexual energy is more the exception than the rule. We either tend to have solid barriers put up around all aspects of sexuality, being completely closed in this area of our lives, or have no boundaries at all, with sexual energies running rampant with no focus. Balancing this chakra means addressing all issues of sexuality. It means opening this potent force of energy and channeling its power into appropriate and responsible outlets. Each person must decide for themselves what is appropriate for them. There are no hard and fast rules for all. But when you act from a sense of integrity and self-truth, you find your own path with the energies of the sacral chakra. (We will discuss sexual expression and relationships in Chapter 12.)

# Feminine Wisdom

While the first chakra is the root of masculine energy, the second chakra is the root of the feminine. Both energies are present in every person, and must be balanced to one another for optimal living. In the root chakra we find assertiveness and action, while in the second chakra we find tenderness and expressiveness. Here lies our feminine wisdom, the emotional aspect of our being, our ability to identify our feelings and fully experience them. The feminine is the creative impulse, through which the masculine energy pulses, carrying the impulse to manifestation.

Clairsentience or "clear feeling or knowing" is connected to the sacral chakra and the solar plexus chakra. In the sacral chakra we find our abilities to empathize with another, and to "know" things through our feelings. In the solar plexus we find our "gut feelings," our deep inner sense about which decisions to make and how things are going to resolve.

# Giving and Receiving

In the second chakra we also find our abilities to give and receive, to nurture others and to be nurtured. When this chakra is in balance, we are able to give and receive freely and comfortably. However, when this chakra is out of balance, people find themselves comfortable either with one or the other, but not both. They find it easy to give and give and give, but do not feel worthy of or comfortable with receiving from others. Other individuals gladly accept all that others wish to give them, but are very reluctant to give anything of themselves.

# Go with the Flow

The element associated with the second chakra is water. It is the element of flow, change, transformation. The second chakra affects our abilities to experience change and transformation in our lives. When this chakra is closed, we become inflexible. Any change is uncomfortable, and, at times, even paralyzing. However, when this chakra is open, we are able to "go with the flow," as it were. We can accept life's twists and turns and take it all in stride.

Before we go into the second chakra meditation, we have an exercise for recognizing and acknowledging feelings and emotions. Choose a time when you can be relaxed and not worry about the next activity of your day, and enter into a deeply relaxed state.

# Exercise #16
# Recognizing and Acknowledging Your Feelings

Take your time to go into a relaxed, meditative state. Then ask yourself what you are experiencing in your feelings right now. Distinguish between what you are thinking and what you are feeling, and work with the feelings. Are you feeling peaceful, excited, anxious, sad, angry, joyful, frustrated, guilty, lonely, fulfilled, serious, playful . . .? Go into your feeling and give it a voice. Ask it to talk to you and tell you what the experience really is. Hear it and listen to its point of view. If it helps you to write, then write. Just give it a voice. Stay with this exercise until you feel a sense of completion for now.

Having completed the above exercise, you are now ready to move on into the full meditation exploration of the second chakra. The following meditation will lead you deeper into your awareness of the issues that you might have to work out in this energy center. I suggest you do this exercise when you are not pressed for time, so that you can take as long as you wish for this exploration.

# Exercise #17
# The Sacral Chakra

Allow yourself to move into a meditative state. Breathe deeply and let your body relax. Concentrate your breathing in the area of the sacral chakra, pausing between the exhalation and the inhalation encouraging the energy to move down your spine. Visualize a bright orange light moving all through this region of your body. Feel the second chakra region become warm and relaxed as you continue breathing. Concentrate on your physical feelings in that area of the body. You may also experience emotional feelings. Just allow them to come to your awareness, without feeling that you must do anything about them. Allow the vibrations of the orange color to move through you so that you may experience this color through all of your senses.

In order to heighten your experience, you may wish to tone on the vowel sound, "oh," on the pitch D. Vocalize the vowel for as long as you wish, taking breaths whenever you need, and then continue. You will find that the sound vibration opens this chakra even more. The sound of your own voice is your most potent personal healing force.

. . .

In order to continue facilitating your process of self-discovery, as you continue to work with the color, your breath, and the sacral chakra, begin to move through the list of trigger words below. The words represent aspects both of an open and closed chakra. Some of the words will have no meaning to you at all, and some of them will spark strong, and perhaps even profound reactions. When you experience any reaction to a trigger word, allow yourself to remain there for a while and explore your feelings. Then, continue with the list when you are ready. As you explore this chakra, you may find other words that you wish to add to this list. Feel free to explore here in any way that you feel is right for you. Take as much time as you need.

| | | |
|---|---|---|
| sex | creation | orange |
| fire | desire | passion |
| physical expression | sexual love | opposite sex |
| same sex | relationship | surrender |
| challenge | society | power |
| responsibility | orgasm | barriers |
| spiritual communion | vitality | intercourse |
| separation | primal | earth |
| give | receive | intimacy |
| unconditional | conditional | cooperation |
| self-love | we | you and me |

| change | opposites | movement |
| pleasure | emotions | nurturing |
| water | clairsentience | sensuality |
| socialization | shame | creation |
| independence | sexual addiction | touch |

Take your time now as you continue to work in your meditation with whatever has come to your awareness. When you are ready, go to your journal to record any impressions, thoughts, or experiences that you had in this meditation.

The feminine core of the second chakra energy is the source of our creative urges and power. While still working in this fertile area, continue with the next exercise to invite the Creative Energy of the Universe to move through you. Explore this energy within your meditation, so that you come to clearer and clearer understanding of your creative role in the world. This will prepare you to continue your journey on to the solar plexus chakra.

# Exercise #18
# Meditation for Creation

Allow yourself to enter a meditative state. After you have reached a deep state of consciousness, invite the Creative Energy of the Universe to manifest in some form behind you. Take your time, and let the images, feelings, or sounds of its manifestation take form. How does this Creative Energy come to you?

As you become comfortable with this energy, begin a dialogue with it. Ask this Creative Energy of the Universe what it has to say to you. How does it wish to move through you? How does it wish to help you in creating your life? Is there a larger plan for your life than you have been aware of up to this point in your life? Work with the Creative Energy

142

of the Universe for guidance and direction in further opening your second chakra and your creative process. You may want to write in your journal as you go along with this exercise, or complete the exercise in a meditative state and then record your impressions in your journal afterwards.

# 10

# Chakra Three:
# Personal Power

Solar Plexus Chakra
Color: yellow
Location: just under the base of the sternum
in the arch of rib cage

The solar plexus chakra is an incredibly complex energy center. In this chakra we work with issues ranging from self-esteem and confidence to co-dependence, fear, judgment, pain, compassion, and a host of others. However, all of these issues center around our ability to step fully into our personal power.

Before we dive head-first into this potent energy center, take some time to do the following exercise. It will help you know more clearly your personal relationship to the concept of power.

## Exercise #19
## Power

Take several blank sheets of paper. On the top of the first one write the word "power." Then, on that page, write every word or phrase that comes into your mind from the word "power." Don't think about it. Just free associate, and write whatever comes to you. When you have finished making your list of words or phrases, turn to a clean sheet of paper and write whatever comes to you in paragraph form. Again, don't think about this. Just write whatever is coming to you. Let Spirit and/or your deepest self speak freely to help you discover your true feelings and associations with the word and concept of "power."

# The Rebel Within

In the psychological developmental process, we might say that the first two chakras are much more affected by our childhood and young adult environment and situations or aspects of our lives over which we do not seem to have active conscious control. However, in the solar plexus, we first assert our own will to create our lives as we want them to be. We take the strong creative energy of the second chakra and begin to act on it. Having recognized and acknowledged our passions and feelings in the second chakra, we begin to hear and feel the beat of our own drum in the solar plexus chakra, rather than just following along to someone else's or society's beat. It is often where we find the rebel within, for in the solar plexus chakra we find the strength to take a stand against something that we believe is not right or fair. We begin to act on the urges inside to create our own lives rather than to live under someone else's authority. When we can hear our own drum clearly and know its rhythms, then we begin to find our place in the world, to know our purpose, to set goals and make plans, and begin to take clear and appropriate steps to move ahead. In essence, we begin to discover and employ our personal power.

# The Mental Chakra

The solar plexus chakra is also often referred to as a mental chakra. It is the center of the bodymind. The degree to which this chakra is open and spinning determines our ability to integrate intellect with emotion, to move beyond the mind as a computer full of information and move that information into every cell of our bodies. Here we have our "gut" feelings, those instinctive feelings that tell us how we really feel down deep inside. This is the mind to which we must ultimately listen, for it combines intellect with experience and feeling. In the solar plexus lies your "conscience," your integrity. We all know that unsettled feeling in the pit of the stomach when all is not well. This is the solar plexus chakra sending warning signals that there is something to which we need to pay attention.

An open solar plexus chakra also facilitates our ability to integrate technology and technical information into our lives. This chakra is associated with industry, with intellectual activity, with mechanical concepts. We can look at human evolution as a climb up the ladder of the chakras. During the Stone Age, the human consciousness was focused in the first chakra. The only concerns in life were survival and meeting immediate physical needs. As humanity evolved into the second chakra, there began to be an awareness of others, the establishment of family and community, and the desire to provide for the immediate physical needs of one another. This was the Agricultural Age. During the 1800s we moved into the Industrial Age, with the development of mechanical systems, factories, mass production, and the more recent technological age. We began to have a much broader awareness of the world, moving beyond the local community or country. This was a move into the third chakra.

# Self-Confidence

In the solar plexus, we face our issues of self-confidence and self-esteem. If we have dealt with and cleared our emotional issues in the first two chakras, then the more we explore in the third chakra and find our pathways into the larger community and world, the more we gain in confidence. This is the chakra of expansiveness. The solar plexus is the sun in our bodies. The energy of an open and clear third chakra is captured by the image on The Sun card in the major arcana of a traditional tarot deck, a child riding a horse in the blazing sun, free and open to all life's possibilities. Because of the sense of self-confidence and freedom that comes with a healthy solar plexus chakra, there is a sense of safety and security in life. There is a sense of fulfillment in your emotional life. When this chakra is closed, there may be a feeling of being overwhelmed by emotions, or of being emotionally distraught.

At one point when I was really grappling with issues of self-confidence, and trust and faith in the processes of my life, Spirit had this to say:

> *Confidence and humility go hand in hand. For when one is truly confident, one can be humble. There is nothing boastful about it, for you are secure in yourself and therefore have nothing to prove to anyone. You also recognize, when confident and humble, that your gifts and successes come from a higher source.*
>
> *When, however, you feel a need to receive praise or to be supported from outside of yourself, you are stepping out of soul and into ego. You are not confident and therefore ego jumps up in defense. Just now you experience this as you doubt your ability to communicate clearly with us. Doubt is an element of ego. Pride is an element of ego. Praise and adulation, when received by ego, build armor and walls of separation. Praise and admiration, when received by soul, flow through your beingness through the soul's recognition and acknowledgment of a higher power.*
>
> *Confidence is important — essential to the healthily balanced individual. You can only be confident when ego is doing its part. But with humility, soul is still the overseer. Let yourself be in both confidence and humility. Then you are allowing the journey of the soul. You will find that the soul is, by nature, quite confident, in a quiet and peaceful and humble way. Let it speak. Let it live.*

# Energy Exchange

Through the solar plexus chakra we exchange energy with the world around us. When we feel we are being challenged or attacked in some way, we may tend to harden or build an armor around this energy center in protection. Even just crossing your arms across your chest or abdomen blocks this powerful energy center. The solar plexus is our "soft underbelly," our most vulnerable spot, physically. If we get hit here, the wind is knocked out of us. So, our animal instinct tells us to protect this spot. However, when tightening or creating an armor over this spot, we not only keep out the negative energies, but we cheat ourselves out of all of the positive energy around us as well. When we close ourselves off from the world, no communication can happen, and therefore no resolution can come to any situation.

When we are comfortable in the solar plexus chakra, we can have a sense of humor about life. Healthy self-esteem and self-confidence bring us a positive sense of humor about ourselves and others, where a blocked third chakra will tend to bring self-deprecating humor, and usually a more sarcastic sense of humor toward others.

# Judgment vs. Discernment

When plumbing the depths of the solar plexus, we are confronted with our beliefs, our judgments, and our prejudices. Here we can begin to recognize the difference between judgment and discernment. Discernment is an important skill to cultivate — the ability to recognize whether or not something is right for us, personally, without making a judgment about the thing itself. However, when we step over into judgment, we are creating separation within ourselves, and between ourselves and others, by labeling things as universally good or bad, right or wrong, better or worse. The healthy solar plexus is a place of merging energies, not of separating them. The solar plexus is the place where we know in our "guts" what is right or wrong for ourselves. It is where we recognize our sense of values. It is very important that we listen to these feelings and trust our instinctive knowledge about what we should do. But as soon as we begin to turn to judgment over others or to feel that we know what is best for another person, and advise them without their request, we have allowed ego to come to power. This actually creates an armor over the solar plexus chakra, or tightens its spin, polarizing the discerning soul from the judging ego, and creating more separation between ourselves and the other person.

# Compassion

Work in the solar plexus begins to develop our sense of compassion, for here we begin to experience our connectedness with one another and the roles we play in one another's lives. We begin to experience empathy for another's situations and feelings when this chakra is open. Compassion literally means "with passion;" its Greek root means "bowels turned over." When we can constantly "turn over" and give a voice to our inner feelings, we can begin to hear and feel the inner yearnings, pains, and sorrows of others. We will do two exercises related to these inner feelings a little later in this chapter.

# Fire in the Belly

The solar plexus chakra holds the fire in the belly. Here we get the "fire-power" necessary to change our ways, to step into our strength and power, and ultimately to speak our truth (which is related to the throat chakra). When this chakra is closed, we find ourselves just "dealing with" our issues in order to get them over with and out of the way quickly. However, in an open third chakra, we really live out our issues, work through them, and find lasting resolution, rather than just "patching them up." Work in the solar plexus means getting to the root of the issue, not just treating a symptom. When we are willing to walk all the way into the issues of our lives, the fire of the solar plexus demands that we face them and sit with them until they are healed. As we are able to release our judgments of others and recognize on a higher level our interconnectedness with all beings, we open the door into the heart where we can begin to love unconditionally.

# Moral and Ethical Values

In the solar plexus we encounter our moral and ethical passions, and our attachments to our feelings and beliefs. In the root chakra we dealt with physical passions, and in the second chakra with emotional passions, but in the solar plexus we explore our beliefs and our integrity, and the passions that we feel surrounding these issues. In our culture we tend to be very cut off from our passions. We are taught that the expression of any full-blown passion, feeling, or emotion is not appropriate. This causes us to suppress our feelings, often leading to bitterness. Over a long period of time, if the suppressed feelings are not given appropriate release, the dam holding them back can finally burst, leading to violence or other destructive or harmful behaviors. We are taught to keep our passions and our needs for personal empowerment in check, rather than to *live* our passions and fully express our personal power and strength in healthy and creative ways. In the solar plexus we come face to face with these issues and work through them to find balance and healing — we begin to find out who we are at a gut level. We find the strength and courage to "do what we know we have to do." Our intellect may be guiding us in one direction, but the inner wisdom of our deeper truth and integrity guides us somewhere else.

# Finding Your Place in the World

While the root chakra is based on individual survival consciousness, and the second chakra on a basic emotional and creative consciousness, still within a small community circle, the solar plexus chakra takes us into a consciousness of relating to the larger world community. Here we begin to recognize that there is a much larger world than just our home environment. We begin to open our awareness to that larger world and see how we fit in. We begin to take on particular roles, recognize our talents and our passions, and become willing to step into them and develop them, "coming into our own."

# Healing – Facing the Unknown

The third chakra is associated with our healing and our ability to merge energies in our lives. Here we come to our "edge," face the unknown within ourselves, and begin to deal with our sense of personal potential and power. We are dealing with a much larger concept of healing than that of having an illness, going to the doctor, taking medication, and getting well. Healing in its broader sense means becoming whole. It means coming into alignment with the self and with the universe. Healing means self-realization — recognizing the wholeness of the soul, and letting the body and ego come into balance with the soul. Healing is ending the separation between aspects of ourselves and of our lives, thus ending the separation between ego and soul. In an Omega Institute conference, Stephen Levine defined healing as "entering with intention and awareness that which we have avoided and run away from." He went on to say, "Healing is the growth that each person seeks. Healing is what happens when we come to our edge, to the unexplored territory of mind and body."[1] Through the energies of the solar plexus chakra we begin to find the courage and strength to step into the unknown, to explore the depths of self.

Spirit had a few words to share here:

*There is a lot of talk these days about healing — about how you need to heal. But what does that mean? Healing means returning to your in-born wholeness, finding your truth, allowing an open exchange of energy between self and the Universe, knowing your oneness with All.*

*How do you heal yourselves mentally, physically,*

*spiritually, emotionally? The first step is to realize that the healing is happening all the time. It has been happening all along. It may be hard to see when the times are tough, when you feel trapped in circumstances that appear to be beyond your control, when you are in any kind of pain, when there is abuse on any level. But if you can step into much higher levels from there, you can recognize that every place that you are is perfect for you in your journey, and that every being with whom you are encountering time and space is perfect for accomplishing the lesson at hand.*

*For many people, healing, or "going through their stuff," is what they do with their therapist. That may be one very important aspect of going through your stuff. But moving through your stuff happens in every activity in every minute of every day. Healing, like Love, demands surrender. Healing means coming back to Love — surrendering to Love flowing through your entire being. Healing means uncovering your truth and living it. Every moment is healing. You just may not be aware of the healing. But as you become aware of every situation as a gift for healing, as a gift for the journey, as a gift for moving through your stuff, then you facilitate the healing process, and the pain dissipates, and the circumstances begin to change.*

*You are healing in every moment of your life. Don't worry so much about how to heal. Rather, open your awareness to the fact that it is already happening, and see where that leads you.*

# The Shadow Self

It is often in the solar plexus that we begin to recognize our dark sides, the shadow aspects of our personality. When we are willing to look honestly within, we find the ways in which we have succeeded or failed in fulfilling our dreams and goals. Our western society is strongly built on concepts of success and failure. However, a major part of the healing that occurs in the solar plexus is the realization that success and failure only have to do with ego. The soul is busy taking a

ON BECOMING A 21ST-CENTURY MYSTIC

journey and having experiences from which it will learn. It knows nothing of success and failure. The soul only knows truth, honesty, and integrity. As long as we live our lives from a place of truth and integrity, allowing Love to flow through our beings, then we are following a pathway toward our healing. With these realizations, we are able to let go of our attachments to success, and simply take the journey.

# Desire, Need, and Attachment

Attachment is a big issue of the solar plexus. Through attachment, whether it be to a person, a job, a situation, a problem, or an idea or belief, we feel some kind of control or security. There are literally bands of energy that form between the solar plexus chakra and the object of our attachment. Energy bands form from the second chakra through emotional sexual attachment, and from the heart chakra in love attachments, but from the solar plexus we find the energy bands that form out of control and security issues. In balancing this chakra, we learn to let go of our attachment to the outcome of a situation, to a job, or to a lover, no longer depending on the object of our attachment to give us an identity or a reason for being. As we let go of the attachment, we experience healing, because we begin to find our wholeness within ourselves.

Here we also address our issues of desire and need. When ego and soul are in balance, desire is a healthy feeling, leading you forward in your journey of development. However, when ego begins to reign, desire becomes need, and as the energy becomes more and more distorted, need becomes greed. Martha began working for a large bank in an entry level position with a great desire to advance. She was very bright and learned quickly, earning several promotions in rapid succession. However, as she kept being promoted, she became somewhat obsessed with climbing the corporate ladder. She basked in her new-found status and power over other people's career paths, and began to thrive on those feelings. She became willing to do anything necessary to insure her continued promotion and increased power. What was once healthy ambition had become desperate need, leading

154

to aggression and manipulation. Her ego craved more and more power at the expense of others. Only when she was faced with a life-threatening illness did she realize that she had alienated her closest friends, family members, and colleagues. Desire, need, and attachment to outcome are important issues to address so that we can be aware of the important inner balance, and always follow the direction of the soul as we continue the journey.

Another aspect of this issue is genuine need becoming neediness. This is a sign of tremendous weakness, not only in the solar plexus, but in the lower chakras in general. When a person becomes needy they tend to suck energy from everyone else around them, refusing to step firmly into their own power, strength and life-force in order to find their own sustenance. Rather than addressing their own issues and learning to provide both the physical and emotional nurturing that they need, they will seek out others who will take care of them.

# Personal Power

One of the most difficult aspects of the solar plexus for many people is the issue of power. We have all, either in this or other lifetimes, been both the perpetrator and the victim of abuse of power. There are two kinds of power. The first is power over something or someone, as in a person of authority who likes to give orders to their subordinates. The second is simply the power to be — to be who we are in our truth and strength. This is the person who is confident in their abilities and strengths, and quietly goes about doing their work, feeling no need to exercise that power over someone else. In the journey of the solar plexus we come to understand our true power and strength, and know how to simply *live* it rather than wield it. When we stand firm in our power and our strength from a place of pure Love, there can be no misuse of power, because ego is in full and complete service to soul and to Love. This is the ultimate lesson of the solar plexus — that we learn to stand in the full splendor of our beings, opening to the world through our gifts and talents, and developing them to their fullest potential, living our strength. There is no need to *show* our strength to anyone. Others will recognize the beauty of our being through our living.

Because all relationships of any kind involve some kind of power play, there are very strong bands of energy that grow between the third chakras of individuals in any kind of relationship. The basic patterns or energy matrix that any individual tends to create here are established in the birth or early childhood family. These patterns become habit at an early age. As we grow and develop, these patterns mature with the development of awareness and of self, but those first fundamental patterns are very strong and difficult to change as life goes on. This is why we tend to see so many repeated patterns over the years in our various kinds of relationships. For example, if you had difficulty with your father's overbearing personality, you may see difficulties in any relationship where the other person represents a power figure or becomes a father figure to you. If you experienced fierce sibling rivalry as a child, you might feel extremely competitive with your colleagues as an adult. If you grew up in an abusive family, you may be more prone to be an abusive parent or spouse. It is certainly possible to change these patterns and create new habits and behaviors in relationships of all kinds, but we must work very consciously to do so. Otherwise, we simply fall back into the old habit.

A part of this power game is the interplay of attraction and manipulation. The power of this chakra is tremendous, and we all can become masters of manipulation of people and situations in our lives. Many books have been written on the subject of co-dependence, which is, in simplest terms, "I'll protect you from this if you'll protect me from that." Co-dependence is all about making "deals" — usually unspoken contracts between people to maintain a false feeling of safety, security, and power. Becoming aware of these tendencies is an essential step in balancing the solar plexus chakra energies. Letting go of our attachment to particular outcomes is the first step in being able to allow the energies to develop into healthy patterns. We will discuss this more in the chapter on relationships.

# Facing the Daily Challenges

Here in the third chakra we face the practical challenges and problems of our lives, and fight our daily battles. The deeper we go in our work here, the more we realize that the people in our lives are simply mirrors for us to see and know ourselves. The person who irritates us is often giving us the gift of showing us a part of ourselves that we don't particularly like. When we are standing in a place of less awareness, we tend to create battles and enemies outside ourselves, finding someone or some situation to fight against. That is the ego's way of coping with inner conflict. But when we come to the soul essence in the solar plexus, we realize that the outside battles are just the manifestation of what is happening inside, and that we must go inside to meet our own well-disguised dragons. That's where the real battle lies. Being rigid in our beliefs and harsh in our judgments only leads to inflexibility in life. This makes any kinds of adjustments to situations and conditions all the more difficult. When we can become more fully aware of our inner battles and stop projecting them outside of ourselves, we can more easily let go of ego judgments and prejudices, and come to a place of peace inside. Then we can more fully realize that a true state of peace does not necessarily mean the absence of conflict, but rather our own inner state. When we are in an inner state of peace, we can accept conflict around us and work through it in a gentle and nonjudgmental way, not getting tied up in our attachments to certain feelings or outcomes.

# Rude Awakenings

The solar plexus is also where we experience what my mother calls "rude awakenings" — times when we suddenly realize something about ourselves, our lives, or our world, that shakes us all the way down to the deepest part of ourselves. Rude awakenings confront us with things that must change, with unacknowledged aspects of ourselves, with realities of our world. They may manifest as tragedies, traumas, or catastrophes. But, if we will heed the call, we can recognize them as opportunities for growth and change. Unfortunately, we must sometimes be faced with very difficult times before we can turn around and take a new direction. Rude awakenings are opportunities for a shift in perception to help us move forward on our journeys, and to help us open more fully to Love.

When we find ourselves experiencing a "rude awakening," it is very easy to respond, "Why me?" This response comes from the ego aspects of the solar plexus chakra. However, when we are stuck in the "Why me?" we can never really get to the "Why?" We need to turn the question around to say, "How could it be that I was chosen for this miraculous gift? How was I chosen for this opportunity?" That would be the soul's response. I fully admit that to respond to rude awakenings in this way is usually a big challenge. But the ultimate challenge of the solar plexus is to be able to see everything that happens to us as a gift — every situation, every relationship, every circumstance. The solar plexus is where we consciously begin to work with these issues. When the circumstances seem devastating, which is when, of course, it is hardest to see the gift, the first step is to acknowledge and honor whatever we feel at that moment, and allow ourselves to sit in that feeling. Then, as we sit in the feeling, we can begin to sort out the differences between ego-reactions and soul truth. This is an important part of the journey toward healing, toward wholeness. In learning the difference between ego and soul, we open our awareness much further to our own essence. Finding the ego/soul balance, and then honoring what we are feeling in that moment leads us to our power, to our strength. From that place of balance, we can move on, making our journey toward the heart chakra. A "woe is me" response, on the other hand, is being stuck in ego-reaction, which does not even allow us the possibility of seeing the gift or opportunity. When we accept the challenge of working in the solar plexus, we have the opportunity to see and accept the gifts or opportunities in every moment of our lives, and ego comes into perfect balance with soul.

# Ego/Soul Balance

Along with the power theme that flows through all of the issues of the solar plexus, we also find ego. In order to move from the solar plexus to the heart chakra in the process of raising consciousness, we must bring ego into balance with soul. The solar plexus is a very difficult chakra for many people, because there is a kind of breakdown that occurs here — a breakdown of old defenses and armoring, so that the truth of who we are can move on to the heart. The "fire in the belly" of the solar plexus can burn off the excess garbage and help us get to our essence. If we move on to the heart still living our lives more from ego than from soul, then the rest of the developmental process will be distorted. The pure energy essence of the upper chakras will not be able to shine. This process is tremendously challenging for most people. The challenge of the solar plexus and of the ego is lifelong. The key to growth is constant awareness of these issues. The ego-soul balance is very delicate, one that requires a tremendous amount of day-to-day attention.

# Addictions and Compulsions

Addictions can be rooted in any chakra, but in the solar plexus we find the control issues of addictive or compulsive behavior patterns. Addictive or compulsive behavior of any kind is a call for Love, a cry from some part of us that is yearning for attention. These behaviors are often manifested in order to mask pain or other feelings, with the false assumption that the numbed state that comes from the addictive/compulsive behavior is better than whatever we might feel without that behavior. Addictions/compulsions therefore become control issues — grasping at any way we can find to control our feelings, and others' feelings and behaviors toward us. In addressing the issues of power, manipulation, and control, we can begin to get to the root of the addictive/compulsive behavior. There are many treatments and recommendations made to individuals for changing these behavior patterns, but, in order to be successful, they must ultimately address these control issues. They must be willing to sit down in the pain and fears and begin the process of healing.

# Courage to Face the Feeling

In the second chakra, we became aware of our feelings and emotions. Now in the solar plexus, we summon the courage and strength to recognize them for what they are and to work with them. We learn to recognize the difference between feelings and emotions, responses and reactions, and find our inner truth. Whatever we feel at the deepest and purest level at any moment is our power and strength, because it is our truth. This is the second and third chakras working together. In the second chakra is the pure feeling itself; in the third, we bring the feeling up to full active consciousness. We begin recognizing the power that lies within the feelings, and then channel that energy into appropriate outlets. When we honor our feelings and are true to them, we live in integrity. The following exercise will help you begin to get in touch with what you are feeling in any given moment, and then begin to work with that feeling. Choose a time when you can be relaxed and not worry about the next activity of your day, and allow yourself to enter into a deeply relaxed state.

# Exercise #20
# Giving Your Feelings a Voice

We begin by repeating an exercise from the second chakra and then continuing the work into the realm of the third chakra.

In your relaxed state, ask yourself what you are experiencing in your feelings right now. Distinguish between what you are thinking and what you are feeling, and work with the feelings. Are you peaceful, excited, anxious, sad, angry, joyful, frustrated, guilty, lonely, fulfilled, serious, playful . . .? Go into your feeling and give it a voice. Ask it to talk to you and tell you what the experience really is. Hear it and listen to its point of view. If it helps you to write, then write. Just give it a voice. Take time to do this before you move ahead in this exercise.

. . .

Lie on the floor or the bed and make yourself comfortable. Put the feelings that you have just identified into your solar plexus and breathe. Let your body and your intuition help you know whether you are dealing with a real feeling or an emotional reaction. Make no judgment on whatever you discover. You are just collecting information. If your intuition tells you that this is a feeling that you want to keep, breathe it into your entire being as you inhale. If your intuition tells you that this is something that you need to release, then do so on the exhalation. Vocalize the sound of the feelings as you exhale. If you wish to release the feeling, the sound will help carry it out of your body. If it is a feeling that you wish to keep, let the sound vibrate and resonate the feeling throughout your entire being.

Your body can show you the way to peace. Do not be afraid to let sounds flow from your body loud and strong. Feel the release that comes from letting go of something you no longer want, or the release that comes from letting go of resistance and allowing a good feeling to overwhelm you. You may want to do this exercise regularly as a way of identifying what you are really feeling, and finding your own inner peace.


Having completed the above exercise, you are now ready to move on into the full meditation exploration of the third chakra. The following exercise will lead you deeper into your awareness of the issues that you might have to work out in this energy center. I suggest you do this exercise when you are not pressed for time, so that you can take as long as you wish for this exploration.

# Exercise #21
# The Solar Plexus Chakra

Allow yourself to move into a meditative state. Breathe deeply and let your body relax. Concentrate your breathing in the area of the solar plexus chakra, with no pause between inhalation and exhalation in the breathing cycle. Visualize a bright yellow light moving all through this region of the body. Feel the solar plexus region become warm and relaxed as you continue breathing. Concentrate on your physical feelings in that area of the body. You may also experience emotional feelings. Just allow them to come to your awareness, without feeling that you must do anything about them. Allow the vibrations of the yellow color to move through you so that you may experience this color through all of your senses.

In order to heighten your experience, you may wish to tone on the vowel sound, "awh," on the pitch E. Vocalize the vowel for as long as you wish, taking breaths whenever you need, and then continue. You will find that the sound vibration opens this chakra even more. The sound of your own voice is your most potent personal healing force.

. . .

In order to continue facilitating your process of self-discovery, as you work with the color, your breath, and the solar plexus region, begin to move through the list of trigger words below. The words represent aspects both of an open and closed chakra. Some of the words will have no meaning to you at all, and some of them will spark strong, and perhaps even profound reactions. When you experience any reaction to a trigger word, allow yourself to remain there for a while and explore your feelings. Then, continue with the list when you are ready. As you explore this chakra, you may find other words that you wish to add to this list. Feel free to explore here in any way that you feel is right for you. Take as much time as you need.

| | | |
|---|---|---|
| desire | rigid | connected |
| power | judgment | center |
| will | ambition | emotionally fulfilled |
| emotionally distraught | safety | mental |
| security | attraction | mother |
| healing | manipulation | pain |
| wholeness | need | social responsibility |
| the world | greed | shame |
| exchange | Spirit | hard knocks |
| society | heavy lessons | success |
| relationships | path to the heart | guilt |
| darkness | expansiveness | inner space |
| fight | pleasure | sunshine |
| aggression | spiritual wisdom | suppression |
| peace | personal identity | self-love |
| challenge | energy | flexible |
| technology | addictions | fire |
| magic | bitterness | moral outrage |
| humor | initiation | dependence |
| violence | truth | |

Take your time now as you continue to work in your meditation with whatever has come to your awareness. When you are ready, go to your journal to record any impressions, thoughts, or experiences that you had in this meditation.

# Pain

There are three particularly challenging feelings or emotions that can be associated with the solar plexus chakra: anger, fear, and pain. As you are moving through each chakra, you may be already dealing with these issues as you come to realizations about your life. In Chapter 11 we will deal at a deeper level with anger and fear, but here in the solar plexus chapter we take a deeper look into how emotional pain may be impacting your life.

Pain is a powerful agent in our lives. We tend to treat it as the enemy. We are socialized mentally and psychologically to try to kill or deaden the pain. But pain can actually be one of our most valuable gifts, albeit challenging. It can bring great revelations to us. It can give us opportunities to see where we have closed off the flow of Love.

Pain is an energy pattern. Energy itself can never be destroyed, but any particular pattern can be transformed into other energy patterns. Our goal in working with pain is to transform it into peace. Ego is also an energy pattern, a fabric that surrounds the soul. The ego energy pattern consists of the body and the energy systems in our lives that facilitate physical existence. When we experience pain, whether emotional or physical, a rip has occurred somewhere in that energy pattern. The energetic "nerve endings" are raw, torn, exposed. The more we resist touching the tear in order to begin the healing process, to begin re-weaving the fabric, so to speak, the more we experience anguish and suffering. Anguish and suffering occur when we hold the pain at bay, refusing to enter into the issues that, if resolved, would allow the energy to flow.

When the tear first occurs, the pain may be excruciating. We feel that we cannot possibly go on. But it is important to recognize that the pain exists in the *ego* energy pattern, not in the soul. Soul remains untouched. Soul is Love. The healing process begins when we step into the tear, the gap, the wound in our ego energy system that is causing the pain. The wound or tear is an opening to Love, which lies underneath the ego covering. Love is the healer. When Love starts to flow, the anguish may at first be even more excruciating, because ego's attachments, which often mask themselves as love, are the cause of the pain in the first place. Therefore, ego will resist the Love salve. It is ego's resistance to the Love salve that causes the anguish. When we can allow the wound to remain open, letting it bleed to clean itself of the poisons, then the Love can flow through it so that the pain doesn't remain trapped inside.

Stepping fully into the pain, with both feet, and fully experiencing it, allows us to reclaim our power from the pain. When we can step fully into the pain, it begins to diminish, because in doing so, we make a strong statement that we are no longer afraid of it. We are ready and willing to face the issue square-on and move through it, working with that energy pattern to transform it to a new place. As

164

we move through this process, we move back to what caused the tear in the first place, and then begin to release the cause as we face it square-on.

Some of our wounds are very deep. A woman came to talk about her pain around the violent loss of her child. Although it had been many years since her daughter's death, she still felt so much pain. Together, as we worked with the issues, we came to understand that the pain will never go away; but it can transform to another state of energy. When you commit to working with your pain, it can eventually transform to tenderness, sadness, gentleness — a softness within. The event or circumstance that created the pain in the first place is now a part of the fabric of your life. That can never be changed. Although the gaping hole in the fabric weaves itself back together in time, the spot remains tender. That spot is a heart opening, an opening through the ego fabric for Love.

Helen came to talk about her 19-year-old son's recent tragic death in a freak camping accident. In the three hours that we spent together, she gave me one of the most powerful gifts I've ever received. She told me her story from the moment of receiving the telephone call informing her of his death, through her awareness of the constant presence of her son's spirit, and taking care of his friends and the rest of her family, to her stillness and reflection after it was all over. Where most people would be feeling tremendous anger and bitterness, she spoke of the man responsible for the accident, who was now in jail, with such compassion for him and the anguish he must be experiencing at his own carelessness. Many times during our conversation, I began to cry, not so much out of sadness, but from the powerful heart opening that I was experiencing. Helen was so willing to sit in the depths of her pain and devastation, and from there find her strength. She gave renewed meaning to Spirit's teaching that whatever you feel in your heart in any moment is your power and your strength because it is your truth. Helen is speaking and living her truth. And she is giving a tremendous gift to the people around her by showing that we can sit in the depths of our pain and it is safe there — that it is okay, and that, in fact, in our deepest pain, or our deepest feelings of any kind, is our strength.

Pain does not go away. But, through the full grieving process, over time, it heals. The fabric of our lives is re-woven. Rick Jarow, one of my teachers, speaks of this mourning and grieving process so beautifully:

> Within the wound is the foundation for great power, if we are willing first to grieve and then allow the healing processes to occur. To grieve means to let it bleed, to allow the flood of hurt, vulnerability, disappointment, and heartache to flow on its own course. We might fear what could happen if we remove our finger from the dike, but we have to ask ourselves if it is worth the energy expended trying to continually patch the make-shift wall we have constructed to meet the world . . . The 'blood' of the wound may flow and flow, but if we can allow ourselves to be nonjudgmental about what is happening, this grieving process will eventually take us to an entirely new place.[2]

The healing is our return to wholeness, accepting the experience and learning from the pain as a part of who we are. When pain is what you feel in the moment, step into it, because it is your truth in that moment. And in your truth is your strength to begin transforming the pain to peace.

Work in your meditation, starting from wherever you are right now. Allow yourself time. Honor your place in the journey, and the mourning and grieving process of pain and change. Do not try to make the entire journey in one meditation session. Do your work, taking one step at a time, and, as Spirit once again reminds me, *Rejoice, rejoice and be exceedingly glad, for great is your reward in Heaven.*

# Exercise #22
# Embracing Pain

Take yourself into a meditative state. See yourself in a great open space or void. At some distance away from you is your pain, appearing as a heavy fog. Slowly begin moving toward the fog, and take note of how far you must travel to

CHAKRA THREE: PERSONAL POWER

get to the pain. How far have you separated yourself from your pain? How do you react to seeing your pain over there? Continue moving toward the fog, and as you reach it, allow yourself to feel it from the outside.

Now slowly move into the fog and make your way to the center. As you go deeper and deeper, the pain may become more and more intense, but you will find that as it becomes very intense, it also releases. Go all the way to the center of the fog, where you can't see anything because the fog is so thick. Stand there in the center and take deep breaths, breathing into the pain. As you breathe, keep the pain flowing and releasing. DO NOT HOLD ONTO THE PAIN!! As you continue breathing and feeling the pain you notice that it is starting to diminish. The fog begins to lift and clear away. Finally, all is clear, and you are peaceful and calm.

Now see a few steps away from you a great white and golden Light. Move toward that Light as though it is a spotlight on a stage. You know that this Light is God, and you step fully into the Light, feeling as though now you have come home. The pain has eased. Bathe in this Light for awhile.

Remaining in this Light of God, come back into this space now, knowing that you are always in the Light of God. Healing is always available to you — all you have to do is walk in to the pain, let it move through you, and stand in the Light of God.

# Initiation — Surrender to Love

The lower three chakras represent our connection to the physical world. The upper three chakras represent our connection to the spiritual world. The heart chakra is the connector in the body between the physical and spiritual worlds. The solar plexus, therefore, has the highest vibratory rate of the physical chakras. It is, in a sense, a place of initiation. It is the gate through which we must pass in

167

order to move on into the heart and continue the mystical journey. However, in order to pass through the gate, we must work through our issues of the solar plexus and find the balance here between ego and soul. We must take our first steps toward our complete surrender to Love. Spirit has spoken with me quite clearly about this ultimate surrender.

*Love is the all-powerful force of the Universe, and everything exists as some manifestation of this force. Therefore, conflict is also Love, manifesting in a particular form to bring healing. Love is what brings the conflict to the surface so that the resolution can occur.*

*Love is not something into which you enter; it is an energy to which you surrender so that it might enter into and flow through you. Love is not a verb. You cannot "love" someone or something; you can only be a channel through which the Love flows. When you fully surrender to Love, you are simply letting this all-powerful force manifest through you. The master teacher, Jesus, said, "Love thy neighbor as thyself." But that first presumes that you can allow Love to flow through yourself. Therein is the real challenge of that teaching. Allowing Love to flow freely toward the neighbor is easy; indeed, it happens automatically when Love flows freely through yourself.*

*Conflict arises when ego decides it will claim ownership and creatorship of Love. No being creates or owns Love. It is far too great to be contained in any one physical form. Love is. Love is what creates and destroys. Love is what powers all aspects of existence. It is the divine energy that has created you. However, you live in a world where you are encouraged to believe that you alone have the power to create and destroy. This is yet another example of the separation of ego from soul. Soul would have you surrender to Love and be the vehicles through which creation occurs in the physical world, thereby encouraging a flow of energy and a flexibility within the body. When ego claims this power, however, it becomes muscle-hold rather than muscle-flexibility, and physical and emotional armoring begins. An ego façade is built. Living in ego, this armoring covers over the Love so that it cannot flow through your beings. Ego knows*

168

*that its creations are not real and therefore becomes very defensive in order to keep up the façade. Ego creations may be very beautiful, enticing, and seductive, but they are much like a stage set. They look beautiful from a distance and on the surface, but when you go over to the walls of a set and push a little bit, they fall over. They have no substance. Ego has no substance; but it will do all it can to convince you that it has great substance. Hence, ego is always living in fear that its secret will be discovered.*

*When you can live your lives surrendering to Love, you can be immediately aware of when ego armoring begins to take place. However, after years of ego armoring, the armor is no longer well-oiled and flexible. It has rusted and locked in place. The surrender to Love may at first be very painful because the "rusty joints" of the armoring must be broken down and released. Love is the oil. Once the Love oil begins to move through the joints, the armoring begins to release and can be easily and painlessly removed.*

*Keeping up a façade and putting on armor ultimately creates tremendous conflict — conflict within yourselves, which then often leads to conflict with others. Conflict is one way that soul has of helping you learn. Conflicts may appear to be with other people, but when you dig deeper into the issues, you will see that the struggle is really within yourselves. When there is a lack of flow of Love toward another, it is because there is a lack of flow of Love through self. Perhaps the easier teaching would be, "Love thyself as thy neighbor." Many people tend to find it easier to send love out to others than to allow that flow of Love through themselves.*

*Because the body is an aspect of ego, conflict or situations which demand your surrender may cause you physical distress. Ego has great fear of surrender, because it will then no longer be able to manipulate situations. The body enters into conflict because Love is crying out to you to surrender, and ego is desperately trying to remain in control.*

*Awareness is an equal partner with surrender, for you must be aware in order to know your level of surrender. The ego is a master at deception. It will have you believe you are completely*

169

*giving yourself over to Love. But look more closely. Don't be fooled by the disguise. Ego-love is only a form of manipulation. It is synonymous with co-dependence. Ego-love is a method of getting another to fit your mold. You must shed the ego-love and surrender to Love-flow in all aspects of life and relationships. Ego-love is simply a deep and thundering cry to self to surrender to Love.*

*The goal is to surrender to Love and be a vessel through which Love flows. Then you can begin to understand that nothing belongs to you — not even your bodies, not even your souls. You are all a part of the All, the great collective, the Universe. The ego is created to be the caretaker of body, soul, planet, etc., during physical incarnation. It must understand its role in the larger scheme of the Universe.*

We have called the solar plexus the "fire in the belly." This is a fire of initiation — burning off the unnecessary "stuff" in our lives. It is a fire of purification. It is surrender to Love, letting go of attachment, taking off the armor, seeing our conflicts, relationships, life experiences and situations for what they are as a part of the soul's journey, and as a part of the process of ego-soul balancing. We walk into the fire and let our very lives begin to burn. What burns away is that which is not essence, that which is not necessary. And then we are ready to pass through the gateway into the realms of the heart. This purification process is the journey of the solar plexus and heart together. For many people, it is a rough road. But the great reward is that the road leads on to the heart and unconditional love. Take your time with this chapter. You may even want to return to the exercise on power at the beginning of the chapter and see how your thoughts and feelings here might have changed. Allow yourself to work with whatever comes up, and be patient and gentle with yourself, while at the same time firm and honest. Then you will pass through the initiation to the heart.

# Lay Down Your Sword

Lay down your sword.

When your defenses are up,
    there will be many battles to fight.
When you can lay down your sword,
    the battles will disappear.
And then you will realize
    that there are no battles on the outside —
    that all of those battles
    which kept your sword at the ready
        are on the inside.
Put down your sword.
Take down your defenses.
And the outside battles will disappear.

Then you can address the inside battles.
This demands trust in yourself
    that you can find your own way,
        that you don't have to carve out
        your pathway with your sword.

The first step is to lay down the sword,
    enter the Heart,
        and begin to live there.

# 11

# Walking into the Anger, Facing the Fears

We take a short break here in our chakra journey to look at some areas that often need healing work in order for us to make the step from the solar plexus chakra to the heart. In this chapter we will work with anger and fear to uncover the ways in which they block us from experiencing love. Then in the next chapter we will discuss relationships as a pathway from the solar plexus to the heart.

The two basic feelings we experience are fear and love. Every other feeling or emotion that we experience comes out of a fundamental place of fear or love. Fear might manifest as anger, jealousy, envy, co-dependence, paranoia, manipulation of others, of any one of a host of emotions and behaviors. Love, on the other hand, might manifest as joy, elation, peace, serenity, high levels of creativity, or fulfillment.

A big part of the journey from the solar plexus to the heart is walking through our fears. Without making this journey, we can become caught, and our fears become our biggest stumbling blocks. We may cut off energy flow in some way in order to "protect" ourselves from imagined future experiences. However, as we discovered when working with pain, our fears can also show us where the energy of Love has stopped flowing. They are the stuff out of which our inner dragons are made, but they can also lead us to further understanding. One of my friends speaks of recognizing the dragons as they appear, and inviting them for tea. In a very civilized manner, she sits down with the dragons and talks through the issues. In doing this, she is disempowering the dragon, disempowering the fear. As the fear is disempowered, the blocks to the flow of Love begin to fall away, and you can move on in your freedom journey.

# Anger

One of the most powerful emotions that comes out of fear is anger. In our culture, we discourage the expression of anger in any straightforward way. We are rarely encouraged to invite the dragon of anger to tea and have a chat. This leads to the anger being buried deep inside, where it begins to fester and grow. As time goes on, we become like a pressure cooker inside, not being able to handle the inner churning of anger as it seeks an outlet. When we can allow the anger to have a voice, allowing the energy to flow once again, moving on through our energy systems and out, it does not get stuck and therefore hold us in its power. When anger is trapped inside us, we are literally held hostage by that emotion, because everything that we think, say, or do, is coming through a veil of anger.

Spirit offered these words on anger:

> Anger is a reaction to frustrations and fears that arise when Love has gotten stuck. As time goes along, and the Love remains blocked, the anger finally explodes. Often by the time the explosion occurs, the actual catalyst for the explosion has nothing to do with the real anger. It was just the storm that finally broke open the dam.
>
> When you experience anger, it is important to let it out as soon as possible. It is simply stuck energy — stuck Love. And some part of you is crying out to get back to the Love. Stand face-to-face, toe-to-toe with your anger, and ask it what it is really trying to say, down underneath all the fireworks. Let it speak to you, and you will learn much more about your own Love.
>
> As you work with your anger, you may finally come to a point where it has no name. This is a good sign. When you can name your anger or your fear or your anxiety, you are working

174

*with feelings that are closer to the surface. But when you come to a place where you can no longer name the anger, you are really getting deep inside. You are getting down to the core of the stuff. At that point you are getting to the anger that has been there perhaps for lifetimes. It doesn't have a name anymore, and it doesn't matter anymore where it came from. It just must be released, like a pressure cooker. Find ways to release the anger. Write. Yell into a pillow. Throw glasses against a rock wall — just not against living creatures! Let the flow of feeling come to an equilibrium. Everything that you feel is real to you in that moment. There is nothing wrong with it. You make choices as to how to express it, and when it involves another person, you make choices as to how to deal with it with that person. And then you go to work with the other person.*

*In your meditation, sit with the other person or the situation to know if your anger toward them is justified. If so, then find a rational and honest way of approaching the situation. However, the anger that you feel toward that person or situation may be reflecting a part of you that is unhappy. It could be that the other person or situation is serving as your mirror, showing you an aspect of you that you are having a hard time with. And that's why you have come together with them. This is a challenging concept to accept, especially in the heat of the moment. But when you can be calm and quiet, and reflect on what is really happening, you find your own fears and unhappiness.*

*Everything and every person is a gift, a blessing. Embrace your anger. Make love to it. Now there's a tough one! Make love to your anger. It will then diffuse very quickly. The anger won't know what to do. You will have acknowledged part of you that needs to have a voice. Make love to every aspect of yourself. It is all divine. It is all Love.*

By first working with anger, we can begin to work our way down to the underlying layer of fear. Working with these feelings and emotions is like peeling away the layers of an onion. We go step-by-step, working with each issue and emotion as it comes up. The roots of our angers and fears are usually lodged in the first three chakras, for in these chakras we live our physical lives. Therefore, in order to move on into the heart and the upper chakras with a clear path, we begin to address these issues at deeper levels.

# Exercise #23
# Releasing Blocked Anger

Take several pieces of unlined paper. At the top of the first sheet, write your name and address with your *non-dominant* hand.

. . .

Now with your *dominant* hand, write the question, "How does it feel to write with your non-dominant hand?" Then answer the question by writing with your *non-dominant* hand.

. . .

With your *dominant* hand, write, "Please tell me who I am." Respond by writing with your *non-dominant* hand.

. . .

With your *dominant* hand, write the question, "Is there something else you would like to say?" Answer by writing with your *non-dominant* hand.

. . .

With your *dominant* hand, write the question, "Is there something that I am angry about that is blocking me from the fullness and joy of life?" Once again, answer by writing with your *non-dominant* hand.

. . .

With your *dominant* hand, write the question, "What color is my anger?" Then answer by writing with your *non-dominant* hand.

. . .

When you are finished, put your pen and paper down. We now move on into a meditation to work with your anger. You will find that you have already begun to enter a meditative state through this exercise. Close your eyes and allow your breathing to find its own steady and even rhythm. Take a few moments to sink into a deeper state of consciousness.

. . .

Invite your anger to sit down and talk with you now. Ask it what it really means to say to you. Keep breathing, so that you keep energy flowing. Talk with your anger with your inner eyes and ears open, with your heart open, with courage flowing freely, and you can begin to see through it. You can begin to realize that your avoidance of anger or your reluctance to give it a voice gives it power. It can begin to control you or hold you hostage. However, when you sit with your anger and give it a voice, allow it to speak freely to you, it begins to dissipate. It no longer has a power over you because you have taken the power back. You have taken charge of the situation by inviting the dragon to sit and talk. You have brought the situation to your terms now, rather than being manipulated by the false power of the dragon. You have taken the initiative to say to the dragon, "I need to understand you." Simply by taking this step you have disarmed the dragon. You have taken your power back. Our desire is not at all to destroy the anger, for it is a very potent force — an energy that we want to harness and transmute into a positive force. Invite the anger to speak with you. You will come to know its nature and its underlying fears.

. . .

Quietly now allow your anger to move into all of your body. It's okay. You really can do this. Just keep breathing and let it come on in. Gently accept the anger and all that it means to you and bring it into every cell of your body. Accept it. Love it. And let the anger keep talking to you. Allow the anger to show itself in every part of your being.

. . .

Now notice the places in your body where the anger has attached itself, as if it were chains or shackles. Do not try to do anything with those chains and shackles — just feel where they are.

. . .

Now focus your awareness on one set of chains and shackles. Gently caress them, massage them, give them love. As you do this you will feel the shackles begin to soften and loosen their hold on you. Continue loving and caressing, and as the shackles begin to fall open, gently and lovingly remove them from your body. Then move on to the next set of chains and shackles. Go through this same process again. Caress them, massage them, give them love. You will feel the shackles begin to soften and loosen their hold on you. Continue loving and caressing, and as the shackles begin to fall open, gently and lovingly remove them from your body. Take as long as you need now to continue moving through any remaining sets of chains and shackles of anger in your body. Remember to always move in Love. When you have completed this process, then continue with this exercise.

. . .

Quietly and comfortably allow your breath to flow freely in and out. Let all tensions, thoughts, emotions dissolve into space. Visualize the color of your anger, and fill that color with White Light and Love. Breathe in this Light and let it wash through your entire being. Wrap yourself in this Light. Bathe yourself in it. Ask the Light what it has to say to you. And finally, see your anger dissolving into the Light. You have reached a new level of freedom from your anger. You have reclaimed some of your power. You have taken another step toward the heart.

Some of anger's chains and shackles may never return, and others may grip you again tomorrow. If that happens, just take the time to go through this exercise again. It may take a number of times to completely dislodge the anger from your body. If it has been locked deep inside for a long time, or if there are a lot of issues around this anger, it will not be released in one exercise. Those feelings took a long time to build up, and now will take some time to release. However, each time you work through the exercise, you will take another step in your journey toward the heart.

178

If you found that you had a lot to work with in the last exercise, you may actually want to spend several days working with it before continuing with this chapter. Then when you feel you are ready to work with the dragons of fear, move on.

# Fear

Just as our culture does not encourage a healthy expression of anger, we are also not encouraged to acknowledge and own our fears. Acknowledging fear is often viewed as a weakness, something to be ashamed of. But, I am reminded of Jorge Alfano's words again: "There is nothing wrong with fear. It's just a sign that you are crossing over into the unknown." Yes, crossing over into the unknown, the unsure, the untried, the unproven, the untested waters. Fear is often a natural response. Honoring it within ourselves and then walking into that fear in order to take the next step is an essential part of our spiritual and human journey.

Spirit spoke about fear:

> *Fear is an ego response. Soul does not understand or know fear; it is a completely foreign concept to the soul. Fear comes when you are not able, for whatever reason, to stay with soul guidance; not able to stay in each moment as it comes. It enters at any point that the flow of Love stops.*
>
> *Ego lives either in the past or the future, not in the present moment. To be in the moment means surrendering to Spirit or Higher Self. Ego, in its healthily balanced state with soul, is very necessary to allow you to see past and future. It allows you to see where you have been, and learn, grow, and benefit from those experiences. Ego allows you to look into the future to chart your course for fulfilling your physical-plane mission. However, when ego comes out of balance and begins to control soul, it will immediately seek to gather power and keep the individual locked in past or future in order to maintain its power or control. When you can focus your attention in the moment, soul can come back into its leadership role.*

*When ego takes control and holds you in past or future, it will also continually remind you of the "negatives" of those time frames. This is a way for ego to keep its control, and not allow you to be calm and still in the moment. Ego creates fear to keep you moving around anywhere except in this moment. It knows that in order to remain in control, it must keep you out of the present moment. When you can come back into the moment, soul begins to flourish once again, and the ego falls back into balance.*

*Staying with each moment as it comes is essential for surrendering to the Higher Self or to Spirit guidance. You must be able to focus your energies totally in the present; and then, through peace and calm and stillness, ego and soul can work together to help you see into the past for remembering where you have been and to look into the future to loosely plot your course. Making plans for the future is fine, but what is important is not to become attached to those plans. You must remain flexible so that at any moment you feel the direction of soul or Spirit leading you down a different pathway, you may respond. This is a different thing from being distracted off the course. When you stay in the moment, there are no distractions. There is only soul-ordained journey. When the ego-soul balance is perfect, you are in the moment and can see into the past and future, but you* do not go there to live. *This it the difference between ego-control and soul-freedom.*

In order to stay in the present moment, the fears which take you out of this moment must be addressed. And so, we move into the next exercise to work with fear.

# Exercise #24
# Facing Inner Fears

Once again, take several pieces of unlined paper. This time, with your *dominant* hand, write, "Hi. How are you doing?" Then allow your *non-dominant* hand to write its answer. (Allow yourself to really elaborate — not just say "Fine, thanks!")

. . .

With your *dominant* hand, write, "What have I learned about anger?" Answer by writing with your *non-dominant* hand.

. . .

With your *dominant* hand, write the question, "Is there something that I am afraid of that is blocking me from the fullness and joy of life?" Answer by writing with your *non-dominant* hand.

. . .

With your *dominant* hand, write the question, "What color is my fear?" Answer by writing with your *non-dominant* hand.

. . .

When you have finished, put your pen and paper down, and we move on into a meditation to work with your fear. You will find that you have already begun to enter a meditative state through this exercise. Close your eyes and allow your breathing to find its own steady and even rhythm. Take a few moments to sink into a deeper state of consciousness.

. . .

Invite your fear to sit down and talk with you now. Ask it what it really means to say to you. Keep breathing, so that you keep energy flowing. Talk with your fear with your inner eyes and ears open, with your heart open, with courage flowing freely, and you can begin to see through it. You can begin to realize that your avoidance of that which you fear or your reluctance to give it a voice gives it power. It can begin to control you or hold you hostage. Its power over you is only as strong as your refusal to walk into it. However, when you sit with your fear and give it a voice, allow it to speak freely to you, it begins to dissipate. It no longer has a power over you because you have taken the power back. You have taken charge of the situation by inviting the dragon of fear to sit and talk. You have brought the situation to your terms now, rather than being manipulated by the false power of the dragon. You have taken the initiative to say to the dragon, "I need to understand you." Simply by taking this step you have disarmed the dragon. You have taken your power back. Our desire is not at all to destroy the fear, but rather to understand its nature, honor it, and begin to fill it with Love. Invite your fear to speak with you.

. . .

Quietly now allow your fear to move into all of your body. It's okay. You really can do this. Just keep breathing and let it come on in. Gently accept the fear and all that it means to you and bring it into every cell of your body. Accept it. Love it. And let the fear keep talking to you. Allow the fear to show itself in every part of your being.

. . .

Now notice the places in your body where the fear has attached itself, as if it were chains and shackles. Do not try to do anything with those chains and shackles — just feel where they are.

. . .

Focus your awareness on one set of chains and shackles. Gently caress them, massage them, give them love. As you do this you will feel the shackles begin to soften and loosen their hold on you. Continue loving and caressing, and as the shackles begin to fall open, gently and lovingly remove them from your body. Then move on to the next set of chains and shackles. Go through this same process again. Caress them, massage them, give them love. You will feel the shackles begin to soften and loosen their hold on you. Continue loving and caressing, and as the shackles begin to fall open, gently and lovingly remove them from your body. Take as long as you need now to continue moving through any remaining sets of chains and shackles of fear in your body. Remember to always move in Love. When you have completed this process, then continue with this exercise.

. . .

Quietly and comfortably allow your breath to flow freely in and out. Let all tensions, thoughts, emotions dissolve into space. Visualize the color of your fear, and fill that color with White Light and Love. Breathe in this Light and let it wash through your entire being. Wrap yourself in this Light. Bathe yourself in it. Ask the Light what it has to say to you. And finally, see your fear dissolving into the Light. You have reached a new level of freedom from your fear. You have reclaimed some of your power. You have taken another step toward your own liberation from the traps of your fear.

Some of your fear's chains and shackles may never return, and others may grip you again tomorrow. If that happens, just take the time to go through this exercise again. It may take a number of times to completely dislodge the fear from your body. If it has been locked deep inside for a long time, or if there are a lot of issues around this fear, it will not be released in one exercise. Those feelings took a long time to build up, and now will take some time to release. However, each time you work through the exercise, you will have taken another step in your journey toward freedom.

As you continue to do the work of this chapter, you may certainly feel the presence of other dragons that are keeping you trapped in one way or another. They may be a need to control, co-dependence issues, emotional pain caused by a very hurtful experience, or any one of a thousand other possibilities. In this chapter we have worked specifically with anger and fear, but you can use these tools to work with any feeling, emotion, or issue that arises. I encourage you to be creative and imaginative as you consider the exercises here and how you might use them to address various issues in your life.

# 12

# Relationships — Pathways from the Solar Plexus to the Heart

As we climb up the ladder of the chakras, we continue to open and grow to new levels of awareness and sensitivity. We have talked about the passage from the solar plexus chakra to the heart chakra being an "initiation" into a higher level of consciousness. One of the principal ways through which we experience that initiation is relationship with others. Often, the word "relationship" is considered to mean a romantic involvement between two people, but I speak of it in this chapter as an involvement of any kind between two or more people. Relationships come in the form of parent-child, sibling, professional colleagues, social club associates, employer-employee, friends — the possibilities are endless. All of these relationships present gifts, challenges, and opportunities, often all at the same time! And, in the end, all the same guidelines apply, regardless of the label you attach to the relationship.

## Successful Relationships

When discussing relationships among our friends, we often talk about the work it takes to have a successful relationship. However, it is very easy to focus our attention on the outside work, getting caught

185

up in the logistics of the relationship rather than looking inside to see what is happening in our deepest feelings. It is easy to get caught up in creating a "successful" relationship. Success or failure implies that we had a particular goal in mind, and either accomplishing it or not. In terms of relationship, we tend to think of success meaning living happily ever after together in whatever context that relationship exists. However, I'd like to suggest that any relationship that comes together, fulfills its purpose or offers a learning experience, and then changes form when the purpose or experience has been completed, is a "successful" relationship.

Every relationship has an energy and an agenda of its own, and can be a great and powerful energy flowing between the individuals involved. When each individual can tune in to the highest and purest level of the relationship energy and let go of their own ego's perceived needs, then they can be aware of the opportunities, gifts, and lessons that they can learn walking side by side with the others involved. No one of us is here to teach another. We are in relationship with one another each to be a catalyst for self-learning and growth for the other. Love (as the creative force of the universe) flowing between two souls is very beautiful. The ultimate lesson of any relationship, and the ultimate lesson of life, is to allow Love to flow freely.

# Commitment

An enlightened form of commitment in relationships of any kind means commitment of one soul to another soul, not commitment of personality to personality, ego to ego, dependency to dependency. Enlightened commitment means committing yourself to the essence of another being, letting go of judgments of personality. It means committing to a constant flow of Love. The goal is to allow each to live life in its essence — soul energy — with no extra costumes or judgments.

# Enlightened Relationships

We enter into relationship with another playing particular roles, such as parent, child, sibling, lover, friend, employer, employee. These roles create the framework through which to begin our journeys together. However, the path to enlightened relationship carries us through and beyond that framework to a point where we are simply meeting soul to soul. In a soul-to-soul relationship there are no roles or labels. Labels imply a time/space realm of limitation and restriction. They are created by ego, and enforce limitation and separation — putting everything into neat boxes which can be carefully controlled and manipulated. Again, this is a part of the framework for initial exploration. But the real gift of the relationship is the journey through the framework — from ego meets ego, to soul meets soul. Soul knows no limitation. Soul only knows oneness with all. When we can meet soul to soul in relationships, we have moved beyond ego restrictions. Then, together we have entered into enlightened relationship.

As we move into a soul-ordained freedom journey, there will be individuals who do not understand the concepts of our journeys, and may begin to drop out of our lives. This does not necessarily mean that something or someone is wrong. It just may mean that the lessons between you are completed for this time. And so you move on. You shed layers of ego-clothing so that the real freedom-journey can continue. Freedom means no restrictions, no limitations, no boundaries. Freedom means ease of movement, no more pushing and shoving.

Spirit interjects here to say,

*Do not be overly concerned when at times you realize that you do not have your freedom. You have found yourself in that position in order to see clearly how to remove the chains that still bind you, and learn to step unencumbered into freedom. There will be many rivers to cross and chasms to leap. These are not obstacles to your goal or destination, but rather gifts to facilitate learning and growth. Move to the center of self and look out. Let the Love energy of all relationships guide you. See*

187

*how all of your relationships are a part of a larger plan for your journey onward. Sit in your soul, and gently remove any obstructions that might block your clear vision and your continued journey — a journey in Love.*

# The Inner Journey of Relationship

The journey, in its fullest sense, must be walked alone. Others come and go from our lives at different points, but the real journey happens inside each of us individually. We continue to open into the deeper parts of self in order to know our own wholeness. In our present-day culture, we talk a lot about need and co-dependency as if they were dirty words. But there is a place inside where we do need one another. And that is a very important place to find within our human condition. We are human, after all. Sometimes we forget that. A part of the human condition is a connection to other humans. And a part of the human condition in many parts of the journey is a connection to another special person. This is not the pathway for every person in every lifetime, but it is the pathway for many people.

Even within a pathway that includes another significant person, however, one must still at times walk on their own. Co-dependence comes in when we begin to feel like we need a partner to make us whole. Whatever it is that we feel that we need from another is actually what we need from ourselves. The partner is simply a mirror to show us what it is that we need to develop within ourselves, what we need to be able to depend on in ourselves. When we look to the other person and depend on them to fulfill that need, we are in effect losing a part of ourselves. We are keeping that part of ourselves from opening and developing to its full potential. Depending on the other person to fill that need is only a temporary solution, for when that person is no longer there, you are once again in need.

Spirit speaks once again:

*Any aspect of self is only alive for as long as you continue to keep it alive. The parts, characteristics, or aspects of you that you know are important in your life, important in what you give to yourselves, to the world, and to Spirit, can only get stronger through your use, and by coming to know that you can depend on them. When you come to depend on these aspects from someone else, those muscles atrophy within you. The longer they atrophy, the more difficult it is to get them going again. Don't be afraid to walk any part of the journey alone. Don't be afraid, within your relationships with others, to still maintain yourself, your independence, your wholeness, your dependence on you.*

*The partner in relationship is not there to simply "accompany" you on the journey. The partner is having their own journey. Neither can you "accompany" them. You mirror for each other. The journey may be walked side by side or hand in hand with another, but the journey is alone. The partner is just walking beside you at this point in their journey. Do not think that your agendas are the same, because they are not, no matter how similar the journeys may seem. You set yourself up for disappointment when you regard the partner's journey as the same as yours. A part of growth and development is learning to walk side by side with all creatures, recognizing, acknowledging, honoring the similarities and differences in your journeys, and continuing to hold your own agenda as they hold theirs. Do not try to take on someone else's agenda, and do not expect any one else to take on yours. Simply be together in Love and walk your pathways — each alone, side by side.*

*When you enter into any kind of significant relationship, you take the partner into your energy and embrace. Therefore, you are responsible for maintaining your integrity with them. Maintaining your integrity with another does not mean that you have to know for sure whether or not this partnership is for life before walking in. It simply means standing in your truth, as clearly as you are able to know it in that moment. Moving deeply into enlightened relationship, the two partners are encountering one another soul to soul. Soul only knows the present. To the soul, commitment means being fully present with one another in this moment. Soul only knows this moment, and its own pure and open and divine flow of Love. Soul moves from moment to moment to moment. When it is time for the relationship to be over, if that time comes, soul moves on. It is*

189

*ego that insists on having a lot of pain. Integrity in relationship means honoring your soul. By honoring your soul, you honor the partner's soul as well.*

# Finding the Right Partner

Many clients often ask, "How do I know if this is the right partner?" Spirit turns the question right back and asks,

*When you sit in your quietness, in your deepest self, and feel the energy that is at the core of your being, how does that energy resonate with the core of the partner's being? Once you have felt that resonance, the challenge then becomes to accept your impression, whether or not it is the impression you wanted. You must continue exploring together with the partner until you both feel that you have really met soul to soul. There is no hurry, because when you finally come to soul meeting soul, time means absolutely nothing. You will know the answer to your question when your souls meet face-to-face. Then you will know if you are meant to have this dance, and not be concerned with its duration.*

# Communication

Another issue that often comes up is, "I keep saying to my partner, won't you *please* listen to me? Won't you *please* talk to me?" Spirit responds,

*Look at the word "please." The first four letters make the word "plea." When you come to the place where you feel like you are pleading, when you are saying "pleeeeeeeease," you are in trouble. You are not sitting in Love. You are sitting in ego. You are sitting in your need, in the worst sense of the word. There is no one else who "needs" to hear you, and there is no one else who "needs" to talk to you. There is no one else with whom it has to happen. It is with you. Now there comes a point between any two people in any kind of relationship when there are conflicts and struggles. But all the pleading that you do with the other when they are not ready to hear or to talk is only going to chase them away. They can only be where they are and you where you are. Patience in this situation means being willing to wait until both of you have come to a place where you can hear one another.*

One of my teachers used to say that everybody has the same 100 lessons to learn — it's just that each learns them in a different order. So one person might be on number 97 and another might be on number 54, which makes it difficult for them to come together in that moment. When your partner can't hear you, first go inside and ask, "Can *I* hear me? Do I make any sense? And who's talking, my ego or my soul?" If it is your soul that's talking and you can clearly hear yourself, then perhaps the partner is somewhere else right now, or for their own reasons does not choose to hear. And that is okay. Love is taking you to different places at the moment. It might be for five minutes, or a day, or for two weeks, or for 50 years. It doesn't matter. There is no time in the Love realm, anyway. On the other hand, if you recognize that you are pleading from ego, then it is time to stop and reevaluate the whole situation.

There is a difference between ego desire and soul desire. Ego will trick you into thinking you want lots of things, and then you get them, or come close to getting them, and you realize you don't want them after all. Or, you lose them before you got them, and when you finally get some perspective on the situation, you look back and say, "Thank goodness I didn't get that. That wasn't right for me at all!"

Soul does not plead. Soul simply speaks truth. When you feel the need to plead, then you know that it is time to stop and have a look. When the partner is ready to hear, they will hear. But it doesn't mean they are in the wrong place, or that you are in the wrong place, when either of you can't hear. You are both simply following your journeys, and Love is carrying you down different pathways at the moment.

191

# Growth and Change within Relationship

Another frequent question centers around how to deal with fear, guilt, and emotional upheaval, when it seems that a relationship has ended or changed for one partner, but not the other.

*First let's go to the fear. You may think that you are afraid of hurting the partner, but the real fear may very well be of the hurt that you will experience in dealing with the partner. But why need there be hurt when there has been Love? The Love that you share may shift into another form, but it doesn't die. Your human love relationship is formed out of Love energy, which continues to move through you and through the partner. The Love energy is also the energy of the relationship, manifested in a particular form. So when you know that Love is doing the creating, what's the fear? The fear comes from ego because ego knows it can't control the relationship any longer.*

*As long as you are together within a defined relationship, ego can step in and control. You have put a label on the relationship and said, "This is what we are to one another." And ego loves labels. That's ego's realm — cut and dried, clearly marked and delineated. When the relationship starts to shift out of that place, ego doesn't know what to do, and there's your fear. And there's the guilt. You think you didn't love enough or care enough or something enough. But what's the guilt for? When you are living in your heart and letting love be Love, manifesting however it does, then no one is "at fault." No one "changed" or "fell out of love." You can't "fall out of love" anyway, if we want to get really technical about it, because Love is not a verb or a noun. It is an energy that is. And you are all made up of it. Love is you and the energy between each one of you. Love manifests in many different ways. When you are sitting in your heart, and being honest and true to who you are in the blessedness of the Spirit, then there is no fear and there is no guilt. There is just Love. And from that place in your heart, you can let Love manifest however it does, guiding you along the path. That's what relationships are all about — learning lessons, providing*

192

*mirrors, helping you to know who you really are. Many of you know that on an intellectual level, but it is sometimes hard to remember when you are in the middle of your turmoil.*

*It gets even more difficult when one partner thinks they have more awareness than the other. You cannot judge what the partner's experience is, because, although their ego pain might be unbearable for moments, days, or even weeks, you don't know what they are clearing out and what they are getting rid of, what they are working through on very deep or karmic levels. How is there guilt if you are letting Love do the work? Love is what is guiding you on this pathway. Not you. Not the partner. It is when you stay stuck in the label, saying, "I am this and you are that, and together we are this" — that's where ego is and that's where ego can control. And that's where ego is running the relationship. When you can surrender, you have an opportunity to come into a moment in your life when you can truly say I am Love, you are Love, what we feel between us is Love in some form, and that Love is now shifting from this form to another. Sharing your Love, you can then follow its direction. At that point, relationship becomes an opportunity for both partners to step to a higher level. When you can surrender, allowing the Love configuration to shift, to manifest in a different way, who's to say that the relationship is ending? It might get stronger. It might get deeper. You might completely separate for a while. And you might find yourselves back together at another time.*

*A relationship is an energy, an entity all its own. It has its own agenda. And it is an agenda that is blessed with the grace of Love. Surrender to it, and let it guide you.*

# Intimacy and Spiritual Communion

Spirit has also spoken about sexual intimacy and spiritual communion.

*In your current times, too often you first assume that a particular relationship can or should be sexual. My dear one,*

193

*very few relationships have as their true highest intention a sexual component. Sexual union is the highest form of communication between two beings. However, in making your fast assumptions, you make it one of the lowest forms. Sexual union is communion of spirit. It is the highest and most profound coming together. Sexual union can only happen when both individuals have let the energy rise to all chakras, not just the second or third. Sexual union means letting the sexual life-force energy (this IS the creative force of Love, after all) rise and meet the partner on every chakra level. You put so much pressure on yourselves to have sexual relations so quickly. But under that pressure, you have sex, not communion. Certainly, a relationship grows and develops through its sexual component. But the energy must be well above the second chakra in consciousness in order to ever expect to go beyond just sex and reach communion. Do not be in a hurry.*

*Many people will come into your life with whom you will experience "electricity." This electricity is your energy meeting and dancing. But not every dance is intended to lead to the bedroom. Let a relationship guide you. We have said this before. Let the relationship lead you to its highest intention. Some relationships have as their intention deep friendships, some teacher-student, some business adventures, and some the ultimate spiritual communion of sexual union. Please do not try to "figure it out," "second guess," or "jump the gun." Don't be so quick to apply a label. Just take the ride — see where the relationship itself leads you.*

# Taking Relationships to the Heart

We've talked about many aspects of relationship, but I still found myself saying to Spirit, "I understand all of these concepts now very well. But I still am not clear about how to really live these concepts." I could understand where I wanted to go, but I didn't really know how to get there. Then, one evening during a class session on the solar plexus chakra, Spirit said to me, *Relationships rarely get beyond the solar*

194

*plexus chakra. They touch into the heart chakra from time to time, but rarely do they live there. Relationships live mostly in the lower chakras, in your ego agendas of power, control, needs, desires, immediate gratification, co-dependence.* This challenged me to look at relationships in a new way — relationships of all types. It felt to me like a "wake-up" call from Spirit, saying "Things have to be different from now on!" At that point I began understanding much more clearly the development of our human relationships in the 21st century.

# Recognizing Our Many Selves

In the weeks that followed that class session, I continued to ask Spirit for more guidance about this "wake-up" call. Spirit began by talking about all the many "selves" within us that make up our larger "Self." I was given a list of some of the possible "selves," such as the survival self, lustful self, sexual self, creative self, emotional self, passionate self, power self, control self, doubts and fears self, confident self, co-dependent self, expectant self, attachment self, judgment self, and the unconditional love self. Spirit explained that while we would all like to think that we live in the unconditional love self of the heart, we in fact spend most of our time bouncing around between all of the other selves in the lower three chakras. Each of these selves has their own story, their own blocks and fears, their own dramas. Each has its own deep yearning for love, acceptance, and a sense of belonging. And each, at times, may have its own set of feelings of inadequacy that leads to different reactions — becoming overprotective of possessions or boundaries, "acting out" in various ways, manipulating people or situations, or a host of other possibilities.

Spirit helped me understand that in order to get to the unconditional love self of the heart, we have to be willing to spend time with all of those other selves and embrace them — embrace their fears, angers, sorrows, and pains. We must recognize and honor our own personal and very private yearnings for love, acceptance, and belonging. Through this we can see that our outer reactions to fears — manipulation, acting out, creating protective armoring or walls — are simply defenses created by those inner selves that are in some kind of

195

pain. Getting to the unconditional love self of the heart means first embracing the fears, angers, sorrows, and pains of these many selves, and nurturing them to healing. What I realized in this whole process was that, in the end, I was going to have to *experience* my own feelings, not just *mentalize* them.

Our difficulties with going to the heart and living there, lie in not being able to experience and embrace our own fears and pain. I think the keywords here are "not being able." It is the hardest thing in the world to walk into and embrace our fears and pain. Yet once we do, the heaviness of our lives begins to lift away, and we can begin making our way on to the unconditional love self of the heart. When we can each recognize how difficult it is to embrace our own fears and pain, we can begin to honor someone else's difficulty — even recognize from our own experience their feelings of hopelessness and despair that come out of feeling trapped in their painful and fearful situations. Ultimately, we acknowledge that our stories may be very different from one another on the outside, but deep down at their roots they are very similar if not the same. Honoring and embracing all of the selves within us, along with their fears, sorrows, and pain, we can more fully understand and embrace those selves in others. We begin to recognize that each person has all of the same selves that we have. We all have our issues in different places, but we all have them. These issues are aspects of the human condition — part of the learning and growth that we each experience.

# Keeping the Battle on the Outside

When we can accept these aspects of ourselves — our own dark sides, realizing that the dark sides simply come out of fear — we can more easily accept them in others. We often tend to judge these dark sides, these conflicts, these many selves in others, because they mirror our own pain, our own issues, and we don't want to go there. The battle is always easier to fight when we can take the conflict outside of ourselves and turn it into a more tangible thing, be it an argument, a power struggle, or, on a more global scale, a war. In order not to allow the war to come too close to home — that is, too close to the real us, we create manifestations of the inner conflicts in our outer life in an attempt to keep the gun battle on the outside. None of us likes to fight the real battle — the battle which lies wholly within the confines of our individual beings. But ultimately, that's where the wars of the human race lie — deep within each one of us, deep within our many selves.

# Behind the Mask

In order to keep our own fears and anger from coming too close to our outer consciousness, we tend to stay safely protected behind various masks that we wear — masks of identity, occupation, protection, and lenses of perception. By staying safely protected behind these masks, we do not have to look at our own issues. By continuing to bounce around between those many inner selves, we protect ourselves from having to walk that initiation journey from the solar plexus to the heart. Most of us, at one time or another, have resisted taking that journey toward the unconditional self of the heart, because walking that road means a lot of work on our part, addressing our own "inner stuff." However, when we can realize that everyone feels that resistance, that everyone has pains and sorrows as well as joys and accomplishments, we can begin to take off the masks and begin to really touch, really experience our own deep feelings.

This process of taking off masks, of honoring the many selves within ourselves and others, is exactly what relationships are all about. Relationships offer us the opportunity to look within. Each person we encounter in our day offers us a glimpse into some aspect of ourselves. And each relationship that we pursue, whether it be business, friendship, family, or romantic, allows us to see our many selves and come to peace with their many aspects.

On the day that I was ordained as an Interfaith minister, Spirit spoke to me giving me these words which later that night became a song called "Behind the Mask."

*Into the stillness, Into the quiet,*
*Into the mystery Behind the mask;*

*Hoping and feeling, Knowing and wanting*
*To open a passage, One that will last;*
*Into the wonder, Into the magic,*
*Into the miracle Through the looking glass;*
*No more masquerading, No more pretending,*
*No more disguises, That's all I ask;*
*Silently passing, Piercing the veil,*
*Undressing hidden passions,*
*Motionless, Pale;*
*Aching and yearning, Touching and melting,*
*Breathlessly tender, Anguished desire;*
*Moment by moment, Hesitation falls away;*
*Frenzied dance commences, Ecstasy on fire;*
*Into the stillness, Into the quiet,*
*Into the mystery Behind the mask;*
*Hoping and feeling, Knowing and wanting*
*To open a passage, One that will last.*

"Hoping and feeling, knowing and wanting to open a passage, one that will last." That's what we're all yearning for. A passage to Love, a passage to acceptance, a passage to safety and security, a passage to that place where we feel at home and like we belong, a passage that never closes due to bad weather or construction. Deep down inside we all want to feel loved, safe, secure, embraced. Deep down inside, we yearn for reaching the point where we don't have to wear the mask anymore, where there are no more roles to play, where there is just simply Love flowing through us. That's what relationships are all about — learning who we are and honoring our own and others' journeys. Relationships are vehicles for Love.

# The Healing Balm of Love

This is the journey from the solar plexus to the heart. Relationships offer opportunities to work through our many selves to reach the unconditional love self of the heart. Only then we can meet one another face-to-face, heart-to-heart, soul-to-soul. These are the enlightened relationships that we can strive for in the 21st century. Making this journey to the heart is all about finding your way home — home to the essence of you, home to your heart. At home in your heart there is nothing to defend, there are no borders to protect, no wars to wage with others over freedom or its loss, no laws to break or uphold. There are no judgments of others or manipulation games to play, financial investments to protect or people or situations over which to exercise power and control. There is just pure Love.

There is an old spiritual that is very close to my heart that goes like this:

There is a balm in Gilead, to make the wounded whole;
There is a balm in Gilead, to heal the homesick soul.
Sometimes I feel discouraged and think my work's in vain;
But then the Holy Spirit revives my soul again;
There is a balm in Gilead, to make the wounded whole;
There is a balm in Gilead, to heal the homesick soul.

Where is Gilead? Deep in your heart. And what is the balm? Love. Relationships invite us on a journey deep into the heart where the mighty river of Love flows. As we have said, sometimes that river flows gently, and sometimes it comes as a torrential rapids. But however it flows, it brings its healing balm to the fears and pains of all those many selves. It gives us the strength and courage to take off our masks and live from our hearts.

In the next chapter we move on into the heart chakra. I encourage you to take your time with this relationship chapter before moving on. You may find that through this chapter you have spotted a few more dragons. If that is the case, take the time to go back to the previous chapter to work through those issues. There is no hurry in this journey. Give yourself the time you need to free yourself completely of the dragons. Allow yourself to be led through this initiation process that began in the solar plexus, continued through your work with the inner dragons and with relationships, and concludes in the heart chakra. This is a major turning point in the freedom journey. Give yourself the gift of honesty in recognizing where you are, and time for the process.

# 13

# Chakra Four: Love Enters In

The Heart Chakra
Color: green
Location: center of the chest

We begin our work in the heart chakra with an exercise for which you will need a partner. So call upon your adventurous friend once more if you are not in a group. You can also use a mirror to do the exercise alone if necessary.

## Exercise #25
## Soul Gazing

Sit facing your partner but not touching one another. If either of you are wearing eyeglasses and can still see without them, you may want to remove them. The exercise is simply to gaze into one another's eyes for a period of time — ten minutes or more — whatever seems right to the two of you. You are not to speak to one another, touch one another, or communicate in any other way. Just be with one another through your eyes. The object is not to see what you can learn about your partner, or even what you can learn about yourself. Just be with one another and take note of the feelings and emotions that arise within you. When you have finished the exercise, take a few moments to record your impressions in your journal before you talk together about the experience.

The first three chakras are related to physical reality and our relationship to our physical world. As we move into the heart chakra, we make the transition out of a purely physical consciousness into a consciousness that begins to integrate the physical and the spiritual. This chakra lifts us out of our purely physical, emotional, and intellectual planes of existence, and helps us begin to move beyond them to an understanding of a larger perspective, an understanding of our relationship to all of creation, from a spiritual point of view. For in the heart, we begin to become aware of relationships with all that is around us on much deeper levels. We begin to recognize that the feelings that we have for one another go beyond a purely physical or emotional response, toward a soul response. We begin to have an awareness that we are soul energies and that our souls reach out to connect with other souls as a part of their growth process.

## Expansion and Contraction

This is a chakra of expansion and contraction. Here we expand our awareness and energy to take in new experiences, and to explore new possibilities. Then we contract our energies, not to pull away from those experiences or create blocks, but rather to draw them back into our energy fields so that we can integrate them into our conscious awareness, into our lives. For instance, when you meet someone new, if the heart chakra is open you will extend your energy field to experience them and what this new relationship may have to offer you. Then you will draw that experience back into your body to see how it relates to the rest of your experiences. If the heart chakra is closed, on the other hand, you will probably be more hesitant to extend yourself, and not be very open to the other person. This is a higher development of the energies first experienced in the second chakra. There we first become aware of an "electricity" or "chemistry" between ourselves and others, and the possibility of establishing some kind of relationship with them. From that initial awareness, we move on to the solar plexus chakra, working out the issues of power, manipulation, co-dependence, and need. From the solar plexus, our awareness moves into the heart and a higher consciousness around relationships and their higher purposes. By developing the heart chakra, we reach deeper levels of comfort and security in opening ourselves to another.

# Capacity for Love

The heart chakra holds our capacity for love, both for a mate and for all of creation — our capacity for allowing ourselves to really experience love on all its many levels with another individual. Here we find our ability to give and receive love freely without expecting anything in return. When the heart chakra is closed, we will not be able to give love without the full expectation of it being a reciprocal arrangement.

Opening the heart chakra reminds us that we are a part of a larger whole. We get in touch with the soul essence here for the first time, and experience the longing of the soul to connect with other souls. Through the heart chakra we begin to understand the flow of both human love and universal or unconditional Love through our lives. And we begin to understand that our ultimate responsibility is simply to allow the Love to flow, not worrying about where it goes or how it comes back. When the heart chakra is open there is a constant circular flow of Love through you, out of you to the world, and from the world back into you.

# The Heart and the Immune System

The heart chakra is related to both the circulatory and respiratory systems, as well as the thymus gland. It effects how the blood moves through the body, bringing nutrients to every cell. It is also related to our breath. Without air, we cannot function as a human organism. Though we may be receiving a great deal of life-force energy through the root chakra, if the heart is closed, then we are still cutting ourselves off from essential life-giving energy. The thymus gland is strongly related to the immune system and the manufacture of T-cells. Many illnesses are caused or aggravated in part by a closed heart chakra, leading to a less active thymus gland, and a weaker immune system.

# The Melting Pot

You could think of the heart as a furnace or a melting pot, in a sense. We called the solar plexus chakra the "fire in the belly." It is the fire under the pot of the heart chakra. Whatever you put into this melting pot can be healed, transformed, transmuted to another form. The heart and solar plexus are the principal chakras of healing. Working together, they are capable of melting divisions, conflicts, and fears, opening to a flow of Love through our life situations. When we take the unresolved issues of our lives and put them into the heart's melting pot, we begin to see how to find peace, balance, resolution, and stability in our lives. We begin to gain clarity and understanding about the situation, and can open more easily to another's perspective. We begin to let down our defenses, and simply enter a place of Love where the issue can be resolved.

When you have done your work in the lower chakras, and the heart chakra is open, you are able to integrate yourself into your larger community and society as a whole without losing your sense of personal identity. You know who you are, and stand firm in your beliefs, while at the same time adapting to your surroundings. You are able to fit into many different scenarios and be comfortable. You can understand others' perspectives and be willing to accept another's point of view, even if it is different from your own. You feel no need to "defend" your point of view, because you are secure in yourself, safe in your heart home.

When this chakra is closed, on the other hand, you may distance yourself from others as soon as conflict or any difference of opinion arises. You are not able to discuss ideas and opinions freely and openly without feeling threatened. You may avoid conflict rather than facing it and the potential healing that lies within the situation. A closed heart chakra makes rationalizing your feelings and avoidance of issues easy. An open heart helps you face the conflict or difference with another and work with them to find a resolution.

# Attachment

Release of expectation and attachment to particular outcomes is an important part of heart chakra work. We begin to see how our ego expectations often create disappointment and pain. The more open the heart chakra, the more we are able to allow an experience to be whatever it is, opening our awareness to the lesson or the gift of the experience rather than becoming attached to a desired outcome. We are able to live our lives from a place of non-attachment, not becoming so caught up in the drama of all that is going on around us. There is a difference between non-attachment and detachment. When we detach ourselves from a situation, we have removed ourselves from it, not allowing the situation to touch or affect us emotionally. However, when we practice non-attachment, we can be fully in the experience, allowing our feelings and the situation to unfold without manipulation. Non-attachment allows us to respond to situations rather than react.

A perfect example of non-attachment is this story of Tony and Adria. They first met one another on the Internet, and began a "cyberspace" romance. Because they lived in distant cities, they had extensive telephone and electronic mail communications before they actually met personally. Tony and Adria are both deeply spiritually aware persons, and talked a great deal about opening to whatever gifts they were to receive from their meeting. They both pledged to themselves to not be attached to a particular outcome, and to allow the relationship to follow its own path. When they finally arranged to meet, they spent four days together. It was apparent fairly early on that this was not going to be a great romance, yet they found they had so much to talk about, to learn from each other, and to experience together. Had they been attached to a particular outcome, they probably would have come together, realized that their expectations were not going to be met, and parted company unhappily. As it was, they are once again in their separate cities, continuing their lives, and exploring all of the many gifts that their unfolding relationship continues to bring. Expectations can be very limiting. We focus our attention on one particular outcome, and when that exact outcome does not happen, we abandon the situation, calling it a failure. However, in the open heart chakra, we begin to learn to let go of our attachments, and let life lead us into often unexpected possibilities, many of which are much better than we could have possibly imagined.

# The Seat of the Soul

The heart chakra is the seat of the soul. It is where we come to know our divinity, our oneness with Spirit, with God, with the Universe. It is where we find our home. Through this oneness with the All, we begin to have a clearer understanding of eternity, even though we may not be able to verbalize that understanding. Here we have access to the Akashic Records, the records of all time. Akasha is a Sanskrit word referring to the fundamental life-giving substance of the universe. Theosophy defines it as an everlasting record of all that ever was, all that is, and all that ever will be. This is not to be confused with the memories that came to full consciousness through the root chakra. The root chakra accesses many personal memories of physical experiences from this lifetime and others. The Akashic Records hold all of the knowledge, information, and wisdom of the Universe, not just of our personal experience. Our access to the Akashic Records, even if usually on an unconscious level, allows us to see a larger perspective of our life circumstances than we are able to perceive with our outer senses.

# Dreams

An open heart chakra is often accompanied by a very active dream life. Dreams are a powerful healing tool of Spirit and of the unconscious mind. However, when the heart chakra is closed we may have little or no recall of dreams and the deep levels of the unconscious mind.

# The Balance of Love and Will

The front side of the heart chakra is the center through which we love. Here we find our sense of connection with all of creation. The more open this front side is, the greater our capacity to love in a constantly increasing circle of life. When it is open, you are able to see the whole person when you look at another, not just the aspect of themselves that they may be presenting at a particular time. You see the beautiful soul energy and inner beauty of the person.

The back side of this chakra controls your expression of outer will. Through this center you take charge of your life, going after what you want. It holds your fundamental beliefs about how the universe runs, how you can accomplish goals, and how other people support you or stand in your way for the accomplishment of those goals. When it is open, you will feel that your will and the divine will are working together, and that the universe supports you in your endeavors. However, when it is closed, you may feel that divine will is against you, and that others are purposely standing in your way to keep you from accomplishing what you desire. You may feel that you must "walk on" others in order to succeed in life, rather than seeing ways that you might work together with others to accomplish the same goals. You may attempt to make your world safe by controlling others.

The front and back sides of the heart chakra represent the essential balance in our lives of masculine and feminine, of the gentle embrace of Love, and the powerful Force of Love. Spirit speaks very clearly about this balance in a discussion about our essence and its relationship to Love.

*Essence. We would like to speak about essence. Essence of living. Essence of dying. Essence of creation. Essence of destruction. Essence. The essence of all is the same. It is Love. Love is the Force that moves through everything. Love manifests as matter as well as feeling, thoughts, ideas. When you can let Love flow freely in its purity, your feelings, thoughts, and ideas become of the highest vibration. However, when ego gets in the way and begins creating feelings, thoughts, or ideas, the Love is distorted or blocked. The same is true of matter. When the Love flows freely, the object of physical form vibrates on the highest frequencies, moving toward being pure Spirit in physical form. But when ego is the ruler of the physical form, then the Love-form becomes distorted, and the vibrational frequencies pulled to a lower level or rate. Here is the challenge that you have in physical form — letting the Love flow. Recognize that you are created of Love and let that creation blossom.*

*Too many of you stifle the Love flowering. There is very little you need to do to nurture the Love creation. It is more what you are not to do. The simplicity is this — just be aware that you are Love. Be aware in every cell of your being, honor it, and ask the Love what you need to do to allow it to flourish. The Love will tell you how you are blocking it or distorting its energies. Your only responsibility is to respond to the Love and remove the block. This is soul growth. This is essence. Pure essence. Getting to your truth, moving along on your journey. We ask you to enter more fully into this soul journey. Many of you have come a long way, but ego still enters in from time to time and distorts the Love. The soul simply wants to flower. The soul is Love. Love must be allowed to cascade through you in its own powerful force.*

*You tend to think of Love as this beautiful, gentle, embracing thing that is sweetness and light. Well, that is only*

208

*one part of the picture. Love is a full-spectrum Force. Force is the word you must come to grips with. Force much more fully describes what Love really is. If Love is the creator and the destroyer, the producer of both conflict and resolution, the initiator and the sustainer, then it cannot possibly be just a gentle, tender embrace. No, Love is a Force with which to be reckoned. It is the highest vibratory frequency in its purest form, and the strongest possible power. When distorted, it becomes great power used to the detriment or harm of others. When ego chooses to manipulate this energy for its own selfish desires or power needs, the Force can manifest in devastating ways. However, when the ego can be strong enough to surrender, allowing Love to flow unimpeded, it creates glorious kingdoms of existence. It is what you might call Heaven. Heaven can be wherever you are. It is not some special place high up in the skies. Your challenge is to let go of ego controls that manipulate or distort the Love power, and pull the vibrations down to the lower frequency, pulling you out of Heaven. This is the task of the human existence. This is the challenge that the ego presents. Without the ego, you cannot have physical form. However, in order to experience and find one's home in Heaven where you are, physical form must surrender to the potent Force that is Love.*

*Essence. The essence of your being is Love. It is your creator and your sustainer and it is you. Nothing can exist outside of Love. However, much can exist through distortion of Love. Allow the distortions to heal. Step out of the manipulation cycle and into surrender. Step into the flowing river of Love and float. Sometimes that river is a gently flowing stream, and other times it is a torrential rapids. Feel the Force of Love. Know it, and let it be your guiding Force. Let it create and destroy within your life. Let it show you how it is manifesting through you for your particular shape and form in this incarnation. The Force is overwhelming at times. The longer you have held Love at bay through your ego controls, the more powerful the back pressure of Love will be against the ego dam. When you open the floodgates, the Love will come pouring through. Prepare your mind for the powerful Force. Your heart is ready. Your heart is*

209

*waiting. Only the mind, an aspect of ego, may hold you in fear Sit in your heart, open the dam, and ride the powerful river of Love.*

Alan: Can you talk more about ego strength?

*Spirit: The ego must be developed and nurtured to be strong. This is not the popular opinion about ego these days. The ego gets a lot of bad press. But, when it is strong and secure it can surrender without fear of losing itself. Love is not out to destroy ego. Ego is essential, for it is the physical aspect of being. It, in fact, is created by Love. When ego is secure in knowing that Love is not trying to destroy it, but rather wants to work through it, using it, making it, in fact, stronger, then ego can surrender to the powerful river of Love. Nothing of ego's creation will be lost because of Love. Instead, everything of ego's creation will be transmuted and transformed to its highest form and realize its highest potential when ego allows the dam to open and the Love river to flow.*

In the solar plexus chakra we are able to get in touch with our knowledge. We can access great stores of information. In the heart, we begin to be able to transmute that knowledge into wisdom, taking all of that information and putting it into a more global perspective. We begin to move in the world in very different ways, being aware of Love as it flows through us to create in this physical world. In the heart, we begin to realize our oneness with all from a spiritual perspective. Therefore, we understand that improving our relationship with the self will improve our relationships with all. We understand that self-exploration and self-discovery are not selfish acts when undertaken through an open heart chakra, but rather help us further discover all of creation.

# Mercy, Grace, and Forgiveness

*Mercy is the Creator's greatest gift. For through mercy comes compassion, grace, understanding, non-judgment, acceptance. Through mercy you learn your own divinity. Here you are able to see the divinity in all and the oneness of all. For mercy is coming into acknowledgment of the One — the oneness of all of creation.*

*We have said many times that everything is energy. All energy comes from the same source, so when you move back through the chain of creation, you eventually come to only one source. You can call that source Love or the All or God — it doesn't matter. Move backwards on that chain of creation in every aspect of your life. You will see that ultimately every aspect of self, light and dark, comes from that same source. Therefore, when you can understand this oneness of self, you can have mercy with self. This is the first, most important, and most difficult task. When you can be merciful with yourself, then there will be no judgment or severity with others. Grace will be yours to have. Compassion will be your natural state. Understanding will become your primary vocation. Acceptance will be a way of life. Judgment will no longer be a part of your existence. When this point is reached, you will be free. You will have reached your destination on the freedom journey.*

*You may have noticed that we have never discussed forgiveness. Forgiveness is not a concept of the All. Forgiveness implies judgment. Forgiveness implies right and wrong. Your Western culture and religions have created the concepts of sin and forgiveness as a way of controlling people's minds. Judgment was created in this way. (You must understand judgment as being different from discernment. Discernment is an important skill to develop.) There is no place for judgment. The concepts of sin and forgiveness and redemption are not concepts borne out of Love. Love is within each one of you, bestowing mercy upon you in each moment of your existence.*

*You choose experiences and opportunities as a part of the learning process. You will find balance through those experiences*

211

over many lifetimes. This is the karmic law. Therefore, no judgment is necessary, in the larger scheme of the universe. What is necessary is for you to share mercy and grace and compassion with one another. Through mercy you can accept and love every soul for its inherent value — not for what your ego-personality-self and your society group mind tells you is the right or wrong action or behavior. Through every experience and action of every individual, learning occurs for many. Nothing effects only one. The ripple moves out from the center.

The great teacher, Jesus, taught mercy and compassion. He died because he dared to stand up and make a statement about the world that was far ahead of his time. He spoke the language of his people, and through that language, began to teach them of another way of thinking, doing, being. He opened another pathway for humankind's journey to the heart. The powers of the government at that time were very threatened by this man who had great charisma and spoke of freedom and non-judgment, and of a living, loving, creating God. He was put to death in order to stop his words, his teachings. He was put to death in order to bring the people back into the control of the government. But Jesus showed humankind that there is no death of the soul by walking the Earth again. Through this example of the master teacher Jesus, the people of the Earth were given the opportunity to see with their outer sight that there is no death. Life is eternal. One simply moves in and out of physical bodies.

Jesus taught mercy. The Western world has created a religion loosely based on the teachings of this great man. But Jesus did not teach concepts of sin and judgment. He did not teach control over people's minds and actions. He taught love and freedom and wisdom to make choices for one's own soul growth and liberation. Do not confuse this great master teacher Jesus and his God with the judging, restrictive, forgiving God of Western religion. There is nothing to forgive. God simply blesses, and helps to steer you on into the next experience from which you can learn. The creation came first. The creation continues now. Remember that destruction is a part of the creative process. Sometimes walls must be broken down so that bridges may be built.

212

*Mercy. Go deep inside to your own divinity, to your Love. Move toward your own perfection. See in your perfection that there is nothing to forgive. There is only "to learn from." Come to live in mercy, grace, and compassion, through your Love. And the blessed path of wholeness is yours.*

# Exercise #26
# The Heart Chakra

Allow yourself to move into a meditative state. Breathe deeply and let your body relax. Concentrate your breathing in the center of your chest and between your shoulderblades, the area of the heart chakra, with no pause between inhalation and exhalation in the breathing cycle. Visualize a beautiful green emerald light moving all through this region of the body. Feel the center of your chest and upper back become warm and relaxed as you continue breathing. Concentrate on your physical feelings in that area of the body. You may also experience emotional feelings. Just allow them to come to your awareness, without feeling that you must do anything about them. Allow the vibrations of the green color to move through you so that you may experience this color through all of your senses.

In order to heighten your experience, you may wish to tone on the vowel sound, "ay" (as in play), on the pitch F. Vocalize the vowel for as long as you wish, taking breaths whenever you need, and then continue. You will find that the sound vibration opens this chakra even more. The sound of your own voice is your most potent personal healing force.

. . .

In order to continue facilitating your process of self-discovery, as you continue to work with the color, your breath, and the heart chakra region, begin to move through the list of trigger words below. The words represent aspects both of an open and closed chakra. Some of the words will have no meaning to you at all, and some of them will spark strong, and perhaps even profound reactions. When you experience any reaction to a trigger word, allow yourself to remain there for a while and explore your feelings. Then, continue with the list when you are ready. As you explore this chakra, you may find other words that you wish to add to this list. Feel free to explore here in any way that you feel is right for you. Take as much time as you need.

| | | |
|---|---|---|
| love | universal love | green |
| heart | open | peace |
| joy | pain | God |
| eternity | soul | Spirit |
| knowledge of all times | partner | dreams |
| universe | center | blood |
| air | breath | balance |
| relationship | affinity | unity |
| hope | will | support |
| belief | faith | control |
| social awareness | sensitivity | diplomacy |
| children | parents | brothers/sisters |
| lovers | wholeness | expectation |
| healing | self-pity | compassion |

Take your time now as you continue to work in your meditation with whatever has come to your awareness. When you are ready, go to your journal to record any impressions, thoughts, or experiences that you had in this meditation.

# Unconditional Love

Unconditional Love is a term that is tossed about so easily in our talk of spirituality. But what does it really mean? Sometimes I think we stop our thoughts with the term itself and just assume that everyone knows what we are talking about, yet too often no one really has a definition. Not having a definition somehow makes the concept of practicing unconditional Love much easier — we aren't sure what it is, but we like the idea of thinking we are doing it. I asked Spirit to talk about this common term and bring it into perspective for me.

*Unconditional Love is simply non-judgment — acceptance of the soul essence of yourself and every other being exactly as they are. Unconditional Love does not mean romantic love, sexual love, familial love, friendship love, or any one of many other kinds of love that you speak of in your human state. You might call all of these other loves ego-loves. They are the ego's attempts at recreating the essence of what the soul is. Unconditional Love simply means allowing another soul essence to be as it is. There is no such thing as "conditional Love." That is a contradiction in terms. You may not like a behavior or action of yourself or another, but action and behavior are aspects of ego. When you sit in unconditional Love, you are sitting in soul. And the soul is a divine creation of God. When you add a "condition" of any kind, you have stepped out of unconditional Love and stepped into conditional ego-loves, or what you call co-dependence.*

*Ego-loves are activities. Through them you are given opportunities to learn. Unconditional Love, on the other hand, is a state of being. You come to know this state of being as a result of learning experienced through ego-loves. The more you open your awareness to see your experiences for what they really are, the more you are able to allow unconditional Love to flow more freely through your ego-loves. Each individual's lessons not only move that soul forward in its growth, but also move the entire civilization forward in its journey. You might consider all of the conditional ego-loves as stepping stones helping you to reach unconditional Love. Hopefully, through each experience in your many love lessons, you begin to see more clearly what is of consequence and what is not. You begin to understand your roles in the cosmos more clearly, and therefore begin to understand your lessons. You have a saying, "The whole is only as good as the sum of its parts." When all the parts are learning*

215

*their respective lessons, then the whole is developing, growing, transforming into higher and higher states. And you are all moving closer to unconditional Love.*

*The soul knows no expectations. The soul simply interacts with other souls — pure and simple. Through unconditional Love, you are able to experience yourselves and other beings as pure soul. When soul meets soul, you experience your own divinity. However, in your human state, you tend to relate to one another ego to ego. When you can relate soul to soul as a way of life, you can fully understand and recognize your own unconditional Love. Then no situation can make you uncomfortable or can take you from your own centering and balance, because you will be living in your point of stillness, a place of no ego expectations on yourself or others. In reaching unconditional Love, you are able to simply allow events and individuals to flow in and out of your life. It is from this place of unconditional Love that you find your home, that you know your peace.*

The following exercise is designed to help you experience your own unconditional Love. It is a long exercise, so give yourself plenty of time — at least 30 minutes — and see that you will not be disturbed. If you are not using the companion meditation tapes, I strongly urge you to first tape record the exercise in order to fully experience it.

# Exercise #27
# Touching the Soul —
# The Fire of Unconditional Love

Take deep and full breaths and allow yourself to settle into a deep state of consciousness. When you are ready, continue.

. . .

Balance comes from a place very deep within the self — the soul, your essence. Your soul is the light at the core of

216

your being. Go deeply within now and find this light at your center. Feel this light begin to glow. Let it shine brighter and brighter, and let the light guide you deeper and deeper into yourself. Continue allowing Love to flow through your soul — pure and unconditional Love. Move into a space where you know nothing but unconditional Love. All judgment of your body, of yourself, your behavior, your thoughts, your feelings, your emotions — all judgments now fall away. And there is only unconditional Love.

Let this light inside of you now become a flame. Allow the flame to begin burning off all the "conditions" — any way that you "conditionally" respond or feel or act. You must be in touch ONLY with your soul, with your essence, now. Let ego drop away. From your soul, you are able to respond to other beings and interact with them unconditionally. You are able to simply let the experience be whatever it is. Go to the center of yourself and let Love flow with no conditions. No strings attached. No expectations. Make no judgments. Recognize your divinity and let Love flow. All love begins with the flow of Love through self.

Breathe into the flame of your soul. As you continue to breathe, let your breath fan the fire, as it were, so that the fire of your soul, this fire of unconditional Love, grows. It expands to fill all of your being. This fire consumes your "conditions." It consumes judgment. It consumes fear. It consumes expectation. Let this fire grow up in you and transform you to overcome all conditions, so that all that is left within you is unconditional Love — unconditional Love for your self, for your body, for your entire being, with no judgment on any part of your existence. There is only unconditional Love. Through this Love comes understanding. Through this Love for self, you are able to experience unconditional Love with others. You are able to allow your self to be who you are, and every other being to be who they are. You may not choose to operate your life as another being operates his or her life. But you honor their soul, recognizing the difference between what is soul and what is ego, recognizing the difference between action and

217

soul essence, and give them space for their journey. The action and behavior is the expression of the lessons being learned at any given moment. And however their action and behavior affects you, that is your lesson. Through unconditional Love, you can learn the lesson with ease, because you are centered and balanced by sitting in the soul.

Take a few moments now. Allow yourself to breathe into the flame and fan it. Allow the flame to grow larger and larger — to consume you, transform you, and cleanse you, so that you become purified — purified in this flame of divinity — the flame of divinity that is you connected to the Divine Spirit. Let that flame overtake you, purify you, cleanse you. Allow yourself to feel whatever you feel with no judgments. Be consumed by the fire of unconditional Love. Take a few moments with this, and then, when you are ready, continue.

. . .

You may now be experiencing a new level of consciousness. As we continue, allow your mind to create a circumstance or an interaction with another person or group that would make you uncomfortable, that might threaten your inner peace and calm. Allow yourself for a moment to walk into that situation and see your "conditions." See your judgments or your fears or your anger — whatever your "conditions" are. And then, let the flame of the Divine Spirit, the fire of unconditional Love, rise up, and consume the "conditions." You are once again peaceful, centered, balanced. And you are once again unconditional Love. No conditions. No judgment. You can allow your essence simply "be" — to feel and experience pain, anger, love, or whatever, with acceptance, and allow these feelings to move through you and be cleansed by the flame of the Divine Spirit.

As you cleanse your soul and your body, you help all others in your presence cleanse themselves and find their center and balance. You help them find their own peace and calm, and ultimately, their own divinity.

Continue to feel this flame. Let it dance in your body. Let it dance out of your body and around the room. Let it be in touch with every other being that is in any way close to you — both the beings who are in physical bodies and those who are not. The flame of the Divine Spirit cleanses and purifies. It brings you to your center, to your soul, where you can feel peace and calm and balance — a peace and a calm and a balance that is unshakable, unflappable. Nothing can pull you away from this center. For you are unconditional Love.

You are coming to the core of your being. You are coming close to or even touching your essence. You are coming to know your own unconditional Love. And you are knowing your self, the true essence of your being. Through this knowledge of your soul, you are set free. You are reaching the destination of the freedom journey. You experience living in Heaven on Earth. Your entire existence becomes divine. Stay with this place. Stay with this essence of yourself. Stay with your soul, and stay with unconditional Love.

Take a few deep and healthy breaths, allowing your energy to begin shifting now as you feel this unconditional Love, this purity and divinity, integrating with every part of your life. Take deep and full breaths, breathing into every part of your body and soul and energy, allowing unconditional Love to integrate itself into every part of your being, every part of your life, every part of your existence. Unconditional Love. Peace. Centering. Balance. The heart is open — perhaps more open than you have ever felt it in your memory. And it feels safe and secure and full and joyous. Because now your heart only knows unconditional Love. And when any experience comes along that might bring you back to judgment, simply take it as an opportunity for you to fill your heart and soul and being with this fire of creation and purity and cleansing. And each time you do this, the energy of this fire will spill over out of you and embrace all those around you. It is through this process that we heal ourselves, and we begin to heal the planet. Let your life come from unconditional Love.

Sit for awhile now in your unconditional Love. Allow

yourself to be lost in it. And then, whenever you are ready, and please take as long as you wish, come back into this space. Allow yourself your own response. You may want to write, to take a walk, to reach out to touch someone who came to mind through this work — whatever feels right to you. Take your time and stay in your unconditional Love.

# 14

# From Belief to Faith

Once again we take a short break in the chakra journey to work with a transition. A part of the journey from the heart chakra to the throat chakra is one of moving from belief to faith. Working out the differences between these two concepts continues to be very important in my own journey. As I continue to gain clarity here, the process of the journey becomes simpler. A couple of years ago I had a combination of events in my life which helped to clarify these concepts even further.

Just returning from perhaps the most exhilarating rehearsal of my life, I received a telephone call from my father in which he told me that he would soon have cancer surgery. This was a total surprise to him and to me. I suddenly felt fear, anger, compassion, sadness, and had a multitude of questions about what this meant. Within a few minutes I went from joy and elation to fear and complete uncertainty. I was quickly getting lost in my projection of worst-case scenarios. After a little while, I finally stopped to say, wait a minute — what happened to those great beliefs you have, to that great faith in Spirit? There was my current inner struggle playing itself out in my outer life. My father was in a place of amazing clarity and strength. From his place of solid faith he had no doubt that everything would be fine. I, on the other hand, was not so clear.

The rehearsal was in the Cathedral Church of St. John the Divine in New York City. In a few days I would realize a dream of many years — to sing in that magnificent space. Dorothy Papadakos, the organist of the cathedral, and I were going to improvise the music for the procession of the New Seminary graduation ceremony. Singing in that space seemed to offer a confirmation of all that I believed about the basic concepts of working with Spirit. The energy of that holy place, the power and strength that poured through me from the massive organ sound, the Love that was driving up into my body and soul from the earth and beaming down into me from the heavens — it was a moment of total awareness of my full aliveness, knowing who I was, that my life was a miraculous gift, that I have a purpose in my life, and that Spirit is watching out and taking care of me. And then I came home to this news about my father, and visions of illness, cancer, fears, apprehension, and anxiety.

Ram Dass says that faith is what you find when all of your beliefs are shot to hell and you have nothing left.[1] I am understanding more and more that beliefs are there to be questioned. Beliefs are tools that help us make our way to faith. Faith is the bottom line. At various times in our lives we stand more or less in our faith. My pride wanted to believe that I was standing in my faith all of the time. But then my father called and the word cancer suddenly struck a little too close to home, and what happened to my faith? What happened to all of that Love that was surging through my body only hours before while singing in the Cathedral?

Everyone comes to faith by a different pathway. Part of the journey of the heart chakra is allowing everyone to have their own pathway, regardless of how different it may be from our own. The first step in this pathway, however, is giving ourselves the freedom to fully explore and question *our own* beliefs. Questioning and doubting beliefs can lead to very powerful experiences. Through the ensuing inner struggles for clarity and understanding, belief structures are more clearly defined.

Not all beliefs lead to faith. Sometimes we realize that some old belief structures are not ringing true for us anymore, and that they must die. This is the part of the belief to faith journey that happens in the throat chakra. These structures that need to die may have never truly been ours to begin with; we took them on from parents, schools, religious organizations, or society. As painful as it may be to allow a belief structure to die, to feel that for so long you have lived under the structure of some belief system that was not true to you, this is a tremendously liberating step forward. Through questioning, struggling, discarding, reshaping, and inner deaths, come the gifts of

222

clarity and knowledge of self, which can then begin to lead the seeker to faith.

The freedom journey is very much the journey from belief to faith. Freedom is knowing that no outer circumstance can touch the freedom of the soul. The soul knows nothing of beliefs, for they are of the intellect. Faith is in the domain of the soul. When I know the freedom of my soul, I am living my faith.

Some days, like the day when I sang in that rehearsal, I know I am really moving into the "faith" place. I am able to sit fully in my soul and follow my journey as it comes in each moment. And there are some days, like when receiving news of my father's impending surgery, that my belief becomes a "hoping for." Then I climb back into my meditation and keep wrestling with my doubts and fears, and begin working my way back to faith.

Beliefs are mental concepts. Faith is a body experience. I keep working with my beliefs, seeing which ones fall away, and which ones really settle in, so that I can come to live my faith. Spirit often says to me, *Honor your humanness, and allow yourself the journey from belief to faith. It is indeed a blessed journey. Many days you will* believe *that, and some days you will* know *it.*

# 15

# Chakra Five: Speaking Your Truth

### The Throat Chakra
### Color: light blue
### Location: the base of the neck

We begin our exploration of the throat chakra with a writing exercise for discovering your truth.

## Exercise #28
## Discovering Your Truth

Take a blank piece of paper and at the top write the word Truth.

Then on this paper write every word or phrase that comes into your mind from this word Truth. Just let yourself free associate, with no thought given to any word or phrase that comes to you. Write everything down that comes into your awareness as you think about Truth.

When you have completed making your list, turn to a clean sheet of paper and write in paragraph form anything that comes to you — anything at all. Once again, make no judgment over what it has to do with Truth, or whether or not it makes any sense to you. Just write.

When you are finished, read back over your list on the first page and your writings on the subsequent page or pages, and ponder what was written. You will probably find some significant food for thought on these pages. Regardless of the subject matter of your writing, look at it now from the perspective of Truth. What is it saying to you?

Having worked through the issues of the lower three chakras, passed through the initiation of the solar plexus into the heart chakra, and come to know a sense of unconditional love, we move on into the throat chakra. This is the first chakra in the spiritual realm, giving life-force energy to the upper chakras and the spiritual dimension in some ways like the root chakra feeds the entire system. This is because the throat is the chakra of speaking Truth. Here in this fifth chakra, we begin to speak and own in the world our personal Truth and sense of being. We begin to be willing to speak of our essence to others and to the world, and to know that this truth must be spoken in order to experience fully the grace and wonder of who we are.

In the solar plexus chakra we began to recognize our Truth, and to see how we might fit into a world of great diversity. In the heart chakra we explored unconditional love, and were able to find a place of peace in non-judgment of others' paths, knowing that each heart has its own story. And now, in the throat chakra, we step fully into who we are by learning to speak our Truth to the world. When we speak our Truth, we claim our power, because we are acting from our deepest and purest self.

# Assimilation and Reflection

The throat chakra is a chakra of assimilation and reflection. Here we are able to look down at all of the first five chakras and begin to understand all of our experiences within the context of our entire life. We are able to reflect on our path, and understand why certain things happened as they did. We are able to begin seeing the spiritual implications of our choices, decisions, experiences, and circumstances. Opening and clearing the throat chakra brings an integration of all aspects of our lives. Clearing and balancing the throat chakra helps to further clear and balance the lower four chakras as well. I call it the "adult" chakra, because here we finally are willing to live our Truth — to "walk the talk," to use a popular phrase. This is a major step in claiming who we are. Through opening and clearing the throat chakra, you no longer simply give lip service to an ideal or a belief — you live it.

# Taking Responsibility

The front side of the throat chakra is very much about taking responsibility for yourself and your personal needs. When this chakra is open, you accept every opportunity offered for learning, growth, and nourishment, because you recognize that it is your responsibility to do so. You cease blaming others for things that you lack in your life, and begin to take steps to create for yourself what you need and desire. However, when this front side is closed, you will tend to not take advantage of opportunities for learning and growth when they come along, often instead choosing an "easier" or "less effortful" path.

The back side of the throat chakra is related to your sense of self within your community and your work. It is usually open when you are successful and happy in your work. However, when this chakra is closed, you may tend to hold back giving your best. You may even be acutely aware that you are not giving your best, and become very defensive in trying to mask the fact that you are not doing the best you could. When the back side of this chakra is open, you are willing to take chances, to take risks for what you want in your life, not allowing yourself to become caught by ego traps. If the chakra is closed, you may experience tremendous anxiety over any action or decision that will include some risk, or does not have a sure guarantee for a positive outcome.

# Honor, Truth, and Prophecy

In an open and balanced throat chakra we express clearly and freely whatever we are feeling in any moment, spoken from a place of integrity and complete honor for self and for all others involved. We said in the solar plexus chakra that whatever you are feeling in any moment is your power and your strength, because it is your truth. Here in the throat chakra you step fully into that power and strength by expressing that feeling — by giving it a voice, not just to yourself, as you did in the solar plexus chakra, but now to those around you.

Ram Dass once described creativity as drawing truth into form. This is very much the realm of the throat chakra. We begin our creative process in the second chakra, the fundamental root of creativity. But in the throat, that creativity is given a voice. It is brought out into the world as an expression of your essence. The throat chakra is not only about verbal expression, it is expression of truth in all forms — action, thought, understanding.

The roles we choose to play in our lives, and the talents and gifts with which we are born, become fully developed through the opening and clearing of the throat chakra. This is obvious for those who choose a life as a singer or actor or public speaker. But the journey of the throat chakra is taken through any role that you choose to take on fully and honestly. That role becomes the vehicle for exploring your issues of self-expression. It does not matter what role you choose, or how long you play it, so long as you feel that through that role you can live in your truth. Earlier, in Part I of this book, we discussed gifts and talents and the language of Love. Through an open throat chakra, expressing the truth of an open heart that is fed by clear and balanced will and power, the language of Love is spoken.

The throat chakra is also the chakra of prophecy. Because of this, the gift of clairaudience, "clear hearing" or intuitive hearing, is associated with this chakra. The more we open to Spirit for guidance and direction, the more we can then begin to live that Love and truth of Spirit in our daily lives. Through the open throat chakra we begin to hear the guidance of Spirit and respond with choices and actions in our lives.

# Letting Go of the Past

Stepping fully into the path that we recognize as our truth means allowing who we thought we were in the past to fall away. There are many beliefs, concepts, and "rules for living" that we are taught by parents, teachers, religious training, and society, through our developmental years. (Incidentally, those developmental years are actually from birth until death!) We often take on the beliefs of others without giving them much thought. Our parents, teachers, and religious leaders are people we respect, and we accept their teachings because of who these role models are to us. However, as we move into the throat chakra, we begin to recognize clearly what is really our truth, and what is someone else's truth that we have taken on. We begin to say, "You know, this belief system just doesn't ring true for me. When I really sit in my heart with my feelings and my truth, I am hearing a different voice. I must now respond to that strong inner voice that is me." This is not to make a judgment on the belief systems of those whose guidance you received, but rather to take all of the information, sift through it, and recognize your truth in the middle of it all. The throat chakra offers the opportunity to look at everything you have learned so far in your life from a deep spiritual point of view, and then communicate your truths and revelations with the world.

Throughout our lives we tend to take on particular "roles" to play within our families and communities, and we put on what seems to be the appropriate costume to wear at the time. However, as we work through the throat chakra, we begin to see more clearly which roles are really true to our essence, and which roles we have taken on to please others or out of a lack of sense of self. The open and clear throat chakra gives us the courage and strength to begin taking off the costumes, to take off the "clothes" that we have worn for so many years, but now realize simply don't fit anymore. The throat chakra is death of the old so that the true can flourish. We must be willing to mourn and grieve those parts of us that we are letting go so that they can be fully cleared from our system. When we talked about energy patterns and habits, we discussed how our energy patterns form a matrix or weave a fabric that becomes an habitual thought process or

229

behavior. Here in the throat chakra is where we really do the unraveling process. We unravel the fabric and then begin to weave a new pattern that is true to who we really are. We come to the understanding that birth and death are really the same thing. As we let an old pattern die, a new sense of self is born. The old must fade away before the new can fully flourish. Through this process, we come to the ultimate realization that what *seems* new is not new at all. It is what has been there all along — the truth of who we are, our essence, finally coming to the full light of day.

Another important part of the throat chakra journey is healing traumas of the past. It is very easy to allow these traumas to become our excuses for non-action in the present. Difficult as those experiences may have been, they are the past, not the present. Continuing to dwell on those issues keeps us trapped in the past. In order to step fully into self-truth and self-expression of the throat chakra, we must be willing to finally let go of our remaining attachment to those past experiences. This process involves acknowledging those experiences, honoring ourselves for the pain and difficulties we have felt as a result of those experiences, and then finally moving on. As we said in the solar plexus chakra when dealing with pain and healing, the traumatic experience will be with you forever. It is a part of the fabric of your life. However, the whole bolt of cloth need not be ruined because of one tear. In the throat chakra we re-weave the fabric at the tear, and reclaim our true selves. Then we can focus on the whole bolt rather than just the tear, and take the next steps forward.

Spirit speaks so clearly and beautifully about these concepts of death, mourning, grieving, and living in truth.

> *Death is only a transition, a form of change. As you move through your journey, changes or deaths occur inside of you — death of the old so that the "true" can be brought forth. As you are born into physical life and move through infancy, childhood, and early adulthood, you put on more and more layers of "clothing." The fact that you are now consciously moving along your own spiritual journey means that you are now beginning to remove the "clothing" and come back to your truth, to the real self. This journey brings with it a lot of change, or at least what*

*appears to be change. But you see, the change that you are experiencing is actually a return to self, a return to the truth of soul.*

*As you begin to understand deaths within as simply a return to self and your wholeness, you can release your fears of death or change. You can approach your wholeness and truth in Love, and move in clarity and ease. As you move toward self and truth with no fear, you will realize that inner deaths have occurred without you even being aware of them. This is a true sign that you are on your way. For then you are just being, in whatever state that is, and simply allowing the "clothes" to fall away by themselves.*

*Mourning is a very important part of the change process, for in your mourning you find release. You all carry grief within you at times, but too often you try to speed up the grief process and its pain to create the illusion that all is well. But all is not well. The grief and pain become trapped inside.*

*Anything that has been part of your life for any length of time will take some time to leave, to die. You can't just expect to say it's gone and have it be so. It took time for that energy pattern to be woven, and it takes time now for it to unravel. A circumstance into which you enter with any kind of commitment, whether that be relationship or occupation, remains in your energy field for quite a long time. There are bands of energy that grow between you and the other persons or circumstances involved. As these bands of energy unravel, you often experience pain, because a connection is now being severed. Mourning is a part of the unraveling process.*

*You experience many inner deaths in your life. Your tendency, however, is to hold on to the old patterns, not acknowledging the deaths, and therefore not allowing yourself the mourning process. Or, you try to create the death of a situation by just "killing it off," fooling yourself into thinking that the death has now occurred, and that there is no mourning to be done because it was your own action that killed it. Unfortunately, it just doesn't work that way. The true death can only happen in its own time, as you allow yourself the unraveling process and experience the transition.*

231

*Energy patterns exist both in your thought process and within the physical body. While thought processes vibrate at very high frequency, the physical body vibrates at a much slower rate. Therefore, change within the physical body takes much longer than change in thought. Thoughts and attitudes about the situation may have changed, but the energy is still lodged in the body for quite some time afterwards. Mourning becomes the healing process.*

*Energy is Love. It cannot be destroyed; it can only be transformed. Everything and every being is, in its essence, Love. Therefore, nothing can be destroyed or lost. It can only be transformed. The transformation is a kind of death, in that the old form dies. The Love, however, continues in a new form. Energy patterns exist by habit. Your energy systems hold on to those habits. Letting go of habits is a death within, a shift in energy patterns. The soul is always shifting, changing, evolving. You must allow your ego to shift with the shifts in the soul. When your ego resists the energy shifts, you become stuck, and the resulting pain can be tremendous. This is because the soul keeps shifting and transforming, and the ego is trying to stand still. It is at this point that fear so easily steps in, because there is no motion. When Love is in motion, fear cannot enter. However, when Love is trapped in the body and not allowed to flow, fear can step in. Mourning and grieving are Love in motion — energy moving through the system and clearing it out — transformation of energy from one state to another.*

*Mourning and grieving are blessings, for through these experiences you open and grow, allowing Love to remain in its natural and healthy state, which is motion. Through this process, you end the separation of ego from soul, and of yourself from Spirit. When you experience loss of any kind and remain stuck in the loss, you are practicing separation — separation from the All, from God, from Self, from that which you feel you have lost. By mourning, you allow Love to flow, practicing union with the All, with God, with Self, with your feelings, and can therefore maintain your oneness with that which you thought you lost. Nothing or no one is ever lost to you. The forms simply change. When you allow your energy to move with the change, to fully*

232

*mourn and grieve the perceived loss, you can realize your union with the All, and you can finally understand that there can never be loss. There is only transformation.*

*Death of aspects of self are a part of the journey toward living your truth. As you come closer to living your truth, you are also beginning to live your greatness. For within your truth is your greatness. Within your truth is your power. As you move closer to your truth, it may feel like a flame within you — the eternal flame of your truth, of your soul. Let this flame of truth rise up within you and overtake you. It will purify and cleanse you. The energy will be overwhelmingly powerful and blissful and exciting, all at once. You will know that you have come home to your soul, to your essence, and that you stand embraced in God. Then you will know your own healing. There will be no more pain, because there will be no more resistance. You will know your own humanity and divinity and understand that they are the same. For to be human is to be divine. But first you must remove the layers of clothing of ego to get to the fundamental layer of human. The scriptures say that God created human in His and Her own image. That image is divine. That divinity is truth. That truth is Love. Go to the flame of Love and its power. Be in it and with it. Step into your own truth. Feel your greatness in your Love.*

*Wherever Love flows, there is truth. Everything else is busy-ness to keep you from truth — to keep ego happy in its separateness from soul. Let the busy-ness drop away. It impedes real growth. Real growth is simply truth blossoming further, Love flowing more freely. When you are constantly in truth, you are constantly in soul, and ego falls into its place as an aspect of soul.*

*Look at every aspect of your life, and every aspect of every aspect. What is the busy-ness and what is the truth? As you are ready, let the busy-ness die, and allow yourself the mourning and grieving process, as you move back to allowing Love to flow more freely. Come back to living only in your truth. Then every aspect of your life becomes an aspect of Love.*

233

# Sadness

There can be a lot of sadness associated with the throat chakra. It is often very hard to let go of the ways in which we've not been living our truth. Or, we experience great pain over the fact that we've not been in truth for so long. Spirit speaks of this with regard to sadness.

*You live in a culture that says you are supposed to be happy, a culture that does not support you in sadness or melancholy. But in sadness, you are simply entering into a deeper part of self. Ego says you must always be happy. But what is happiness, anyway? It is very hard to define what creates happiness, because what you think will make you happy changes constantly. You are not in a physical life to be happy or sad. You are just to be, and to know who you are, and to see where that takes you. You are to be honest — honest at the core of your being, true to yourself. Sadness teaches you about humility, grace, gentleness. Sadness often makes you very quiet, and in that quietness, you begin to hear the truth of your soul.*

*Wonderful gifts can come to you through sadness. Wonderful gifts come, in fact, through acknowledging anything that you feel. Whatever you feel in any moment is your fuel, your power. Don't run away from it. When you feel joy, step into it, live it. When you feel sadness, also step in, live your sadness. That's your power. That's your strength. Because that's your honesty. That's where you are right now. When ego surrenders to soul, there is a period of mourning. Ego, as an energy pattern, has many habits. When you let it surrender, at first your energy field doesn't know what to do. The aspects of ego are like pieces of clothing. They are the parts of who you are as a personality.*

*When ego surrenders, you have to learn new energy patterns, new vibrations. Every change you make in your life, every time you step from one place to another, every time Love manifests through you in a different way, then something has died at the same time. The energy has transformed into something else. It takes you time to make that adjustment. And that mourning often manifests as sadness. Let your sadness be your power, be your fuel. Don't be afraid of it. You don't have to wallow in it or get lost in it. You will find your soul in it. The sadness won't last for very long when you finally step in and really let it flower. Let your sadness bloom. Let it come all the way up and then transform to its higher form, which is peace.*

We find our truth in our greatest joys and in our greatest pain. If your essence was represented by a giant swimming pool, stepping into truth is like standing on the edge of the pool and being ready and willing to plunge in. In the throat chakra we are finally ready to take the risk and dive into the pool that is us — us and no other — pure, whole, divine essence.

# Emptiness is Wholeness

In one Spirit Circle, so many people came with questions about major life decisions. Spirit chose to speak about these questions in this way:

*By creating an emptiness within, you can begin to answer these questions for yourselves. The real issue has to do with the choices you make within your hearts. It has to do with creating a space — opening up and becoming empty — and being willing to step aside for some period of time to see what fills that space. It may be a person that steps into the space, a relationship, a job, getting fired from a job . . . In the empty space you can begin to receive your gifts, to receive your guidance. The important thing is to create the space. You are so conditioned in your society to stay busy — that if you aren't busy, there is something wrong with you. Sometimes you need to just sit. You have to create an empty space and then see what walks in. Nothing comes to you that you are not, at some level, ready to handle. Create an empty space on many levels of your life. You may need to create an empty day in your schedule, or an empty time period in each day, but also look to see where you need to create an empty space*

235

*within yourself. Then, see what walks in. See what your heart calls in to fill the space. What is your heart longing for?*

*Empty spaces need to be created in your energy systems in order to find your truth in the issues of your lives. And how do you do that? By cleaning out — by saying this and this and this I don't need anymore. This no longer serves me. This is no longer an appropriate part of my life. Let go of the things that no longer serve you. Let go of the old so that the true you can blossom. Not the new you — the you that you seek has always been there. It just got covered over by some extra clothing. What is it in your life that is no longer meaningful to you? That is where you begin to create emptiness.*

*You may need to start working in a very systematic way with this. One good way is through the phases of the moon. As you move from Full Moon to New Moon, what is called a waning moon, this is the time to let go of things in your life. Look at the moon every night, and, as you see it getting smaller and smaller, visualize the continued letting go. During the waning moon, clean out your closets, both in your house and in your inner self. That is the time to let go, shed the things no longer necessary, no longer important, no longer meaningful. Sometimes you will realize that something died a long time ago, but it keeps hanging around because you never buried it. Let go of the things that are no longer important. Create emptiness, and see what fills it. Then, when moving from New Moon to Full Moon, the waxing moon, allow new things into your life. See the new attitude or thing taking shape in your life as the moon gets larger and larger.*

*Sometimes what fills the empty space will create a major shift in your life. You may have invested a tremendous amount of energy in creating a particular aspect of your life, a particular role that you play such as profession or family position, only to see now that your heart is crying out for something else. There is no shame in changing your mind. Sometimes changing your mind is actually staying on the path, and letting the path lead you now to a different place. When your heart is full, when your mind is full, when your life is full and cluttered, you can't get any clear perspective on the next step. Take the time to create*

236

*emptiness, to clear away the clutter, to let go of the things that may have already died. Create emptiness and see where your heart leads you next.*

# Rites of Passage

Just as there is an initiation in moving from the solar plexus to the heart, there is also an initiation into deeper truth as we move from the heart to the throat. You might also think of these initiations as rites of passage. Rites of passage are transitions or changes in our lives, experiences that help us take another step toward our truths. We all experience these rites of passage, and we provide them for one another. For as any individual experiences a change or transition in life, they share that experience with family, friends, and loved ones.

In rites of passage, we experience the soul transforming, growing, shifting, continuing its journey. On the surface, we experience the event, such as mourning the loss of an individual or relationship, fear brought on by illness or tragedy, or perhaps the beginning of a new job or relationship. But what is really happening is the transition within — the death of an aspect of us that the event represents, and the beginning of a new page or chapter in our book of life. We help one another by sharing our events. In the larger picture, we are all one. We are all aspects of one another. Therefore, there is only *one* journey, which we all share. What happens to one happens to all, in one way or another. In some way, one's death is also another's death. One's pain is another's pain. One's joy is also another's joy. The rites of passage are simply opening us deeper into our hearts, allowing us to come closer and closer to our soul essence.

When we open our awareness to flow with these rites of passage, the transitions become much easier. We open to deeper levels of understanding with one another, and deeper levels of understanding with ourselves. In that moment, we come to a clearer understanding of our own grief or mourning process. We recognize that it may feel as though we are losing a part of ourselves, but actually we are just moving through another time of transition. When we recognize that we are all one, that everything is, at its fundamental level, Love, and that Love cannot be destroyed but can only be transmuted to another form, then we know that nothing can ever be lost to us.

Rites of passage are what we experience when we are able to clear away our emotions or reactions to circumstances in our lives, and sit fully in our souls, in our essence, in our truth. Then we can feel the inner shifts, and allow ourselves to step on up to the next rung on the ladder, rejoicing in the gifts that we are given, and in the gifts that we can give one another by living this journey together.

Opening your awareness, you can begin to see your personal relationship with all of the events of the world, and how they all effect you in some way. Some of these events create rites of passage for you. Take a few moments to reflect on the recent days of your life. What has happened in your life? How have particular events, circumstances, encounters affected you? Then consider events or things that happened around you, perhaps not involving you immediately, but still had some impact on your life. How were any of these situations rites of passage? How did they create a change in your life or a shift in your perception? Allow yourself to continue going deeper and deeper with each of these situations or encounters, and see what it has to teach you, how it might be guiding your life, if even in a very simple or subtle way. How might this be a rite of passage for you?

As you move on into the meditation for the throat chakra, stay aware of your rites of passage, and let your awareness open even further through the trigger words and working with color and sound.

# Exercise #29
# The Throat Chakra

Allow yourself to move into a meditative state. Breathe deeply and let your body relax. Concentrate your breathing in the base of the neck, with a pause after the inhalation, encouraging the energies to rise to this chakra. Visualize a beautiful light blue light moving all through this region of the body. Feel the base of your neck become warm and relaxed as you continue breathing. Concentrate on your physical feelings in that area of the body. You may also experience emotional feelings. Just allow them to come to your awareness, without feeling that you must do anything about them. Allow the vibrations of the blue color to move through you so that you may experience this color through all of your senses.

In order to heighten your experience, you may wish to tone on the vowel sound, "ih," on the pitch G. Vocalize the vowel for as long as you wish, taking breaths whenever you need, and then continue. You will find that the sound vibration opens this chakra even more. The sound of your own voice is your most potent personal healing force.

. . .

In order to continue facilitating your process of self-discovery, as you continue to work with the color, your breath, and the throat chakra region, begin to move through the list of trigger words below. The words represent aspects both of an open and closed chakra. Some of the words will have no meaning to you at all, and some of them will spark strong, and perhaps even profound reactions. When you experience any reaction to a trigger word, allow yourself to remain there for a while and explore your feelings. Then, continue with the list when you are ready. As you explore this chakra, you may find other words that you wish to add to this list. Feel free to explore here in any way that you feel is right for you. Take as much time as you need.

| | | |
|---|---|---|
| Truth | creation | expression |
| Self | death | hearing |
| receptive | love | original |
| being | warning | falseness |
| joy | ease | no blocks |
| honesty | frankness | faith |
| forgive | forget | me |
| speak | live | communicate |
| teach | guidance | receive |
| acknowledgment | God | human |
| responsibility for self | blame | self-esteem |
| giving your best | risk | reflection |

239

| assimilation | balance | trap |
| artistry | prophecy | claiming power |

Take your time now as you continue to work in your meditation with whatever has come to your awareness. When you are ready, go to your journal to record any impressions, thoughts, or experiences that you had in this meditation.

Before you continue on to the next chakra, you may want to go back to the beginning of this chapter and repeat Exercise #28. See what new insights you have into Truth after this journey through the throat chakra. This can be a very enlightening exercise to do periodically. It becomes a wonderful way of charting your own transformation.

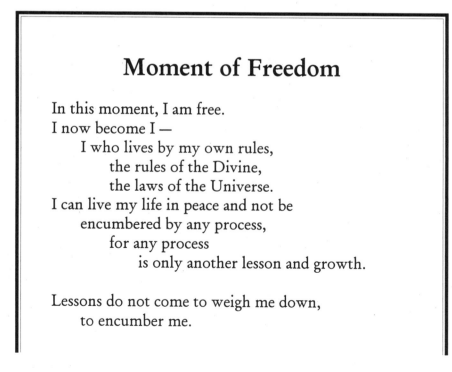

# Moment of Freedom

In this moment, I am free.
I now become I —
   I who lives by my own rules,
      the rules of the Divine,
      the laws of the Universe.
I can live my life in peace and not be
   encumbered by any process,
      for any process
         is only another lesson and growth.

Lessons do not come to weigh me down,
   to encumber me.

Lessons come as opportunities for growth,
    which means change,
        transformation,
            upward movement;
    not being pulled down into the lower vibrations
    of the lessons themselves.

Sitting in the lower vibrations of the lesson
    means being trapped.
Moving to the higher vibrations of the lesson,
    I learn to spread my wings
        and fly.

This is the real journey —
    to learn to always be able
        to spread my wings and fly,
    not being caught in any situation,
        circumstance,
            relationship,
                career step —
    any aspect of my life.
    And that includes my spirituality!
Instead, I must fly in relationship and
    career and
        spirituality.

The spirit of the Beloved lives within me.
I hear the trumpet call.
The shackles of conflict now lift away.
Together with the Beloved I create my life.
I spread my wings
    and fly in freedom
        through Love.

# 16

# Chakra Six: Clarity of Vision

The Brow Chakra
Color: indigo
Location: in the center of the head,
behind the eyes and between the ears

The upper two chakras, the brow and the crown, have much less impact on our daily lives than do the lower five chakras. As a civilization, we have not yet developed to a point where we are living our lives in these chakras, so to speak. For the most part, we live our daily lives working out the issues of the lower five chakras. You will see as we continue in these last two chakras, that there is much less to say about them, and probably less deep emotional work here for you to process.

## Light and Vision

As we enter the brow chakra, we enter the realm of light, vision, perception, inspiration, and imagination. This chakra holds our abilities to visualize, perceive, and project our images out into our world. The intuitive gift of clairvoyance is found here. When the

243

brow chakra, with its perceptual organ known as the "third eye," is open, we have the possibility of seeing beyond the realm of physical sight.

# Key to the Future

Because of its association with imagination and visualization, this chakra holds the key to accessing our future. When it is open, we are able to see many possibilities and options in our lives. We can make plans for our future based on our many ideas and possibilities. However, when this chakra is closed, imagination and visualization skills are greatly impaired. This can lead to great anxiety because we cannot see any other possibility than our present circumstance. We cannot see that there is a future, and feel hopelessly trapped in our current circumstances. Breathing into the brow chakra and chanting an "om" mantra can help open the chakra and relieve the anxiety.

# Transcending Linear Time

Both the brow and crown chakras are largely developed through meditation. Through this practice, we are able to move into a state of consciousness through which we can transcend time and space. In the brow chakra, we move beyond the linear time of our physical world to a limitless realm of no time. We will go into a much greater discussion of transcending linear time when we talk about working with Spirit in Chapter 19.

The chakras each have a very interesting relationship to time. In the root chakra, our awareness is focused on a very narrow span of the present moment. All we know is what we need and want right now for our survival and the satisfaction of our primal physical desires. As we move into the second chakra, we are still primarily focused in the present moment, but begin to have an awareness of the immediate past and immediate future. In the third chakra, we begin to focus on the future as we chart our course in the world beyond our immediate family. As we climb on up to the heart chakra in our development, we become aware of relationships between people, things, events, and circumstances. We become aware of cycles of time, and of the repetitive nature of seasons and events. We begin to associate events and feelings with particular times of the year. The throat chakra takes us back to the past to release those aspects of the past that no longer serve us, and then carries us into our future through our liberation into truth. In the brow chakra we enter a timeless dimension, much like the dream world, and finally in the crown chakra, we experience all time as simultaneous.[1]

# Visualization and Manifestation

The front side of the brow chakra holds our capacity to visualize and understand mental concepts. This includes our concept of reality. Here we project our perception of reality onto the world around us, and that is the world we create. If our concept of the world is that it is a difficult, challenging place that must be confronted at every turn, then that is the world we create for ourselves. If, however, we change our conceptualization of the world to be one of peace, support, love, and encouragement, then that is the world we begin to create. This may seem overly simplified, and to some degree, it is. However, think back in your life to how often what you expected in a situation is exactly what you got. If you expected to meet adversity, you got it, but if you projected a peaceful path, that is what you found. It is in the front side of the brow chakra that we work with these issues.

The back side of this chakra is related to the manifestation of the images created by the front side of the chakra. When the back side is open, you are able to follow through your ideas with appropriate action to bring them to manifestation. However, if it is closed, you will never seem to be able to bring any idea into reality.

The chakra system is a very powerful tool for manifestation. In Chapter Seven we spoke of the upward and downward flows of energy through the body (shakti and shiva). The manifestation process begins with the shiva (male force) energy entering through the crown chakra. The idea which you wish to manifest first appears in the

245

crown chakra. In the brow chakra you begin to visualize this idea in physical form or manifestation, and project that image out into your world. In the throat chakra you begin to give your idea a name and a voice, speaking it out into your world. The energy is now beginning to become more dense, and closer to a physical form rather than the very light energy of conceptual thought. In the heart chakra, you begin to see how this idea is going to help the world, and here make the necessary revisions to it so that it serves not only you, but those who follow you. (In the native American tradition, they speak of how any manifestation will affect seven generations to come. If it will not have a positive effect, then the idea should not come to fruition.) You begin to give it your love, and your passion intensifies. Bringing the idea down into the solar plexus chakra, you begin to look at the practical issues involved in making this idea a reality. In the second chakra, your passion becomes a drive for doing the work in the physical world, which carries the idea on into the root chakra where it can be grounded in physical reality and manifest.

# Exercise #30
# The Brow Chakra

Allow yourself to move into a meditative state. Breathe deeply and let your body relax. Concentrate your breathing in the center of your head behind your eyes, the area of the brow chakra, with a pause after the inhalation in the breathing cycle. Visualize a beautiful indigo light moving all through this region of the body. Feel the center of your head become warm and relaxed as you continue breathing. Concentrate on your physical feelings in that area of the body. You may also experience emotional feelings. Just allow them to come to your awareness, without feeling that you must do anything about them. Allow the vibrations of the indigo color to move through you so that you may experience this color through all of your senses.

In order to heighten your experience, you may wish to tone on an "ommmmm," with the emphasis on the "mmm," on the pitch A. Vocalize this sound for as long as you wish, taking breaths whenever you need, and then continue. You will find that the sound vibration opens this chakra even more. The sound of your own voice is your most potent personal healing force.

. . .

In order to continue facilitating your process of self-discovery, as you continue to work with the color, your breath, and the brow chakra region, begin to move through the list of trigger words below. The words represent aspects both of an open and closed chakra. Some of the words will have no meaning to you at all, and some of them will spark strong, and perhaps even profound reactions. When you experience any reaction to a trigger word, allow yourself to remain there for a while and explore your feelings. Then, continue with the list when you are ready. As you explore this chakra, you may find other words that you wish to add to this list. Feel free to explore here in any way that you feel is right for you. Take as much time as you need.

| | | |
|---|---|---|
| artistic | vision | clarity |
| divine love | balance | confusion |
| understanding | manifesting ideas | projection |
| anxiety | imagination | concentration |
| intuition | light | mystical |
| psychic | dreams | change |
| infinite | past | present |
| future | vastness | time |
| timeless | | |

Take your time now as you continue to work in your meditation with whatever has come to your awareness. When you are ready, go to your journal to record any impressions, thoughts, or experiences that you had in this meditation.

# Akashic Records

As we have said, through the brow chakra we transcend linear time, and move to a timeless dimension. The following exercise will take you on a journey into a timeless dimension. First we will travel into a dream-like time dimension, and then move on beyond that dimension to the Akashic Records, the mystical records of all time. You may be able to go all the way to this great source of wisdom and understanding in this first visit, and you may only be able to go part of the way. It doesn't matter. You will go as far as you are ready to go.

You will have an opportunity to ask questions once you have reached the Akashic Records. I only caution you to seriously consider the questions that you ask. Do not take this experience lightly, and do not ask to see or have information about anything that you really do not want to know. If at any time you become uncomfortable in this journey, simply open your eyes, which will immediately bring you back to your present moment in time and space. If you are not using the companion meditation tapes, I suggest you pre-record this meditation so that you can allow yourself to concentrate solely on your experience.

# Exercise #31
# Journey to the Akashic Records

Take your time to enter into a deep state of meditation.
. . .
See in your inner vision now a tunnel of light — a light of love and peace. The light may be of one color or many. It invites you to enter the tunnel. As you enter this tunnel, you begin to transcend time as you know it in your human existence. You move beyond all concepts of linear time, and enter a space where everything simply is — where there is no such thing as past or future. Linear time does not exist here.

As you move deeper and deeper into the tunnel, you may notice that the colors in the light are changing. They may become more cosmic in nature, and you may see and experience colors that you have never encountered before in your earth life. Let yourself experience these colors in every possible way. Some of them will speak to you very strongly, and you will recognize them as your own cosmic colors — colors with which you feel deeply connected in ways you never imagined before. Feel their energy, and let your energy become one with theirs. Ride on these cosmic color energies, these beams of color light, and allow them to take you deeper into the tunnel towards the Land of No-Time.

. . .

As you begin to reach the Land of No-Time, you may be aware that you have come to a very new place. You may see familiar faces, places, events, occurrences, or you may see completely new people, circumstances, happenings. There is no past or future here. You have now reached the area of No-Time Land where you come in your dreams. Move on into this area and explore. Allow yourself to experience whatever there is for you to learn at this point in the Dream area of No-Time Land. Take as long as you need here, and then continue on with this exercise.

. . .

Remain on your color beams of light now, and begin to go deeper through the tunnel. As you continue in your journey, you may begin to experience visions for which you have no known connection, at least as far as you are aware. You may begin to see into the Universal Library, the Akashic Records. Allow yourself to look around here, knowing that in this place you have access to all the knowledge and wisdom that there is — all of the information that exists in the universe and of all time. Take as long as you wish to become comfortable here, learn how this great library of wisdom and knowledge works, and then explore. You might want to ask a particular question or questions while you are here in the Universal Library. I only suggest that you seriously consider the questions you ask, so that you only ask questions for which you truly want an answer. If you ask, but do not receive an answer to your question, consider the question once again to know whether or not it is appropriate for you to have this information at this stage of your journey. Again, take as long as you wish here, and then continue with the exercise.

. . .

When you feel that your work is complete for now, get back on your color beam of light, and begin to move back through the tunnel of light, back toward this present time and space of your life. Come back slowly through the tunnel, bringing your awareness of your cosmic colors with you, as well as complete memory of what you experienced in the Universal Library of the Akashic Records, and in the Dream area. Ride your cosmic beam of light back into this physical reality once again, and open your eyes. Before you become too grounded in this physical world, take time to write in your journal about this experience. Afterwards, take a few minutes to move around, perhaps jump up and down or do some physical exercise for a couple of moments to insure that you are fully present once again in this physical reality. You have traveled far. Be sure you are completely back now before going on about your daily life.

# 17

# Chakra Seven: Opening to Spirit

The Crown Chakra
Color: violet
Location: the crown of the head

In the brow chakra, we moved beyond linear time. Now as we enter the crown chakra, we move beyond physical space. The crown chakra takes us into the spiritual realm and into the integration of the whole being: physical, mental, emotional, spiritual. Through the crown chakra we come to know our oneness with our ancestors, with the past and future, with angels and spirits, and with all other dimensions of time and space. In the brow chakra, we took a journey to the Akashic Records where we could access all of these other dimensions. In the crown chakra, however, there is no longer any need to take a journey to that place — you are there already, at the same time that you are here.

## Action and Understanding Are One

In the crown chakra, action and understanding become one. This is the highest level of human development. Living in the crown chakra means living the Love language with no thought given to doing so. It simply is who you are in every moment of your existence. Living in the crown chakra also means being fully aware and present in all of the other chakras at the same time, perfectly balanced in your relationship to heaven and earth.

Spirit speaks of this level of understanding:

> *When you finally reach the stage of development where you can live in the crown chakra, you realize that becoming one with Spirit does not mean walking side-by-side, hand-in-hand with Spirit. It means being fully within Spirit and Spirit fully within you. You reach a point where you realize that you are in God and God is in you, and this is not an ego-trip. This is realizing the oneness of all — the humbling, profound, quiet, still oneness — a silent ecstasy of the soul experiencing its full oneness once again with the divine, no longer pulled away by ego's ministrations, desires, or demands. The realization of oneness is simply everything. Ego and soul and all their components are in perfect balance and communion with one another.*

# The Other Side of Passion

When our consciousness is centered in the crown chakra, we enter into a profound state of peacefulness about our lives. This peace or bliss seems to be void of passions for or attachments to ideas, activities, or aspects of our lives. This was very confusing to me when I first began to experience this absence of passion. I thought there was something wrong with me because I no longer felt driven to accomplish an ego-created goal, or to defend a particular belief system. But once again, Spirit spoke to help me understand what was happening.

> *Being passionate about your feelings or your beliefs is an essential step toward non-attachment, toward the "other side" of passion. You could not possibly understand the concept of non-*

*attached living in its essence if you did not know from experience the passions of attachment to particular aspects of living, the driving forces of desire and yearning to be all that you can be, to have all that you can have, to win others over to your way of thinking, in whatever arenas. It is through the journey of your passions that you come to the other side — that you finally are able to let go of the passions or the attachments, and that they let go of you! This is the full journey of the chakras. For in the crown chakra is the ultimate letting go — your arrival in the unadorned essence of the heart. You have not lost your passions. Quite the contrary — the essence of your being is more alive now than ever. And this new level of aliveness will create more wondrous living than your ego's passions could ever imagine.*

# Higher Consciousness

In the crown chakra, we reach our highest consciousness. Here we come to the full understanding that consciousness is pure order and organization — the design, the pattern, the intelligence in all. It is not something that we create or develop; it has created us. We are created of consciousness and surrounded in it. What we think of as developing consciousness is actually a matter of discerning that force, and then developing our awareness of it, so that we can work with higher and higher levels of that consciousness. This brings us full circle back to our initial discussions of Spirit at the beginning of this book. For consciousness could also be called Spirit, God, Love, The Great Mystery. We come to know our oneness with this most powerful force of all of creation through the crown chakra.

When the crown chakra is closed, there is no experiential connection to spirituality. You may experience depression, alienation, confusion, apathy, or an inability to learn and comprehend. However, when it is open, your awareness goes way beyond the physical world and creates within you a sense of wholeness, peace, and faith, and a sense of purpose in your life.

# Exercise #32
# The Crown Chakra

Allow yourself to move into a meditative state. Breathe deeply and let your body relax. Concentrate your breathing in the crown of your head, the area of the crown chakra, breathing evenly with no pause between inhalation and exhalation. Visualize a beautiful violet light pouring down through the top of your head. Feel the crown of your head become warm and relaxed as you continue breathing. Concentrate on your physical feelings in that area of the body. You may also experience emotional feelings. Just allow them to come to your awareness, without feeling that you must do anything about them. Allow the vibrations of the violet color to move through you so that you may experience this color through all of your senses.

The sound of the crown chakra is silence. Before moving on to the trigger words below, take time to sit in the silence of the crown chakra. Allow the divine energy of the universe to come pouring into all of your being through the crown chakra.

. . .

In order to continue facilitating your process of self-discovery, as you continue to work with the color, your breath, and the crown chakra region, begin to move through the list of trigger words below. The words represent aspects both of an open and closed chakra. Some of the words will have no meaning to you at all, and some of them will spark strong, and perhaps even profound reactions. When you experience any reaction to a trigger word, allow yourself to remain there for a while and explore your feelings. Then, continue with the list when you are ready. As you explore this chakra, you may find other words that you wish to add to this list. Feel free to explore here in any way that you feel is right for you. Take as much time as you need.

| | | |
|---|---|---|
| spirituality | integration | wholeness |
| peace | faith | infinity |
| transcendence | sense of purpose | bliss |
| depression | confusion | apathy |
| comprehension | beliefs | Spirit |
| consciousness | Universal Force | silence |
| meditation | enlightenment | |

Take your time now as you continue to work in your meditation with whatever has come to your awareness. When you are ready, go to your journal to record any impressions, thoughts, or experiences that you had in this meditation.

# The Winds of Time

The winds of time
shatter all thoughts in the night;
and the days of yore
come back to haunt you;
or was it the longings for more?

You are not lost to time —
time flies past you as you stand your ground,
ever moving,
ever straining,
against the wings of the dove.
You must travel inward
to the heart of love.
You must journey onward
to where others dare not to tread
for their hearts are not so empty
as yours.
Their hearts are full
of their fears and their dreads,
their lies and their hopes
that seem to be so easily dashed.
You, dear one,
now come with an empty heart;
a heart that can be filled
with the Spirit's love;
a heart that can be filled
with the earth-bound song
of the falling leaves,
the falling snow and rain,
the crackling fire,
the driving wind,

*as well as the celestial song*
*of angels all around.*

*You are now traveling*
*on the winds of time.*
*These winds blow irrespective*
*of others' directions —*
*no attention given*
*to the ways of the world.*

*You are the light.*
*You are the dark.*
*You are the infinite void of all creation.*
*And there you remain,*
*peering into the time-full world,*
*and wondering how it all*
*could possibly make sense.*
*You stand still in these winds of time,*
*for you are all time.*
*You are all space*
*and all of infinity.*

*Stand still in the winds of time.*
*Know your love.*
*Know your self.*
*Now you must come to truly see*
*where you stand —*
*to know your place in the universe.*
*You will see that your place*
*is not in this physical world*
*where your body resides.*
*Your place*
*is standing in your empty heart*
*receiving God.*

# Part III

# Working with Spirit — Embracing Intuitive Living

The essence of God lives in me.
The essence of God lives in all.

O Great Spirit,
prepare me and move through me
as I serve you among your people.
Bless me and strengthen me
for the journey ahead.
Give me sustenance —
all that I need.
And give me time —
time to sit and be and listen
so that You might create in this world
through me.

# 18

# Awakening the Inner Senses

The more we become self-aware and are able to open to Spirit for guidance and direction, the more the details of our lives seem to fall into place. Our personal responsibility in this process is first to remove any obstacles that might keep us from hearing and seeing clearly what is being given to us, and then to listen and receive guidance, and respond in the appropriate way and time. Spirit uses our brains, our minds, and our feelings and emotions to communicate with us. When working with Spirit and the intuitive mind, thoughts, images, and sounds often come very quickly. One of my teachers described Spirit communication as "being on the phone long distance with someone who is talking very fast and will not slow down." When we stop to analyze the flow of information, more often than not we lose the "connection," and the flow of images stops. The goal is to reach a point of having a constant stream of images through our conscious awareness so that we can receive the guidance and proceed accordingly. It is very much like watching a movie. The movie doesn't stop for you to analyze or think about what is happening. It just keeps going. When you go home from the movie you can begin to think about it or analyze it. So it is with the intuitive mind and with Spirit. The information comes pouring through you, sometimes at lightning speed. In that moment, you must just take in the information and then process it later.

The following exercise is designed to help you learn to allow thoughts, images, and sounds to flow through your awareness without holding on to any of them. The idea is to never allow yourself to focus on or stay with any particular thought, image, or sound, but rather to let them pass continually, as if in a movie. No image should be held still for your observation or analysis. This may be difficult or challenging at first, because you will find yourself wanting to "think" about what you are experiencing. The object here is not to think at all, but rather just to observe, letting the information pass by.

# Exercise #33
# The Movie of the Mind

Lie comfortably on the bed with a pillow beneath your head. Close your eyes and allow your breathing to fall into its own natural and steady rhythm.

. . .

Lift your head up off the pillow, and then let it drop heavily, sinking deeply into the pillow. Now lift your right arm and let it fall as dead weight on the bed beside you. Do the same with your left arm. Now your right leg — lift it up above the bed and let it fall heavily as if it were a dead weight. Do the same with your left leg. Then, lie still, and for the next 10 minutes, simply allow thoughts, feelings, images, and sounds to flow, not holding on to any of them, and not making any judgment on what they should or should not be. Just be aware of the constant flow.[1]

Do this exercise once a day for a couple of weeks until you have mastered an easy and uninterrupted flow of events. If there is a particular image that keeps coming up for you, Spirit may be showing you something with which you need to do some work. Spend time with this issue in your meditation, but not in this exercise.

Another important skill to develop as you open the intuitive mind is sensory awareness. This means being aware, with all of your five inner and outer senses, of your experience and of all that is around you. The more your sensory awareness is developed, the more you are able to sense the energy in a place, feel someone else's energy (what might be called empathy), and be aware of the presence of Spirit around you. The next two exercises are designed to help you step into your imagination to heighten your senses.

# Exercise #34
# Sensory Awareness I

In the midst of the sirens, the traffic noise, the boom boxes and the shouts and screams, we can come to find our silence and our peace. And even in the midst of all of this turmoil, this constant energy that never stops, we can come to Mother Earth for her teaching, her guidance, her love, her nurturing, her blessing.

Close your eyes and, as you breathe and move into a meditative state, focus your awareness on Mother Earth. Feel her power and strength, as well as her gentle and loving embrace. Take a few moments to let yourself settle deep into the arms of Mother Earth.

. . .

Open your awareness to the ocean. Within your meditation, step into the waves of the ocean as they come upon the shore. Feel the rhythm of the waves, the rhythm of the ocean. Feel how the rhythm of the Earth flows through the ocean.

. . .

Now step into a rushing river and let yourself flow with its rhythm. Become that energy. Know the rhythm of the Earth through the river.

. . .

Step into the wind and become the wind, feeling the rhythm of the Earth in the wind.

. . .

Listen to a bird sing. Step into the bird and become the

263

bird singing. Know the bird's rhythm and the way the bird knows the Earth's rhythm.

. . .

Step into a volcano that is just ready to erupt, and feel that power. Know the Earth's energy as it is about to give birth, to stretch, to open.

. . .

Step into the crevice that becomes the center of the earthquake. Feel that energy. Become one with the rhythms of the Earth.

. . .

Feel your own body rhythms. How do they dance with the Earth rhythms? Do these rhythms complement one another, or clash with one another? Is the dance an easy one or a difficult one?

. . .

Mother Earth can help show us the way through our journeys. When she experiences changes, we often refer to those changes as "natural disasters" or "catastrophes." But if we can look from a much larger perspective, we begin to see how these disasters are opportunities for understanding. Our Earth is shifting, stretching, opening her joints, growing. Just as your body changes throughout your lifetime, so does our Earth's body change throughout her lifetime of millions and millions of years. It is part of a natural process. The changes are only "disasters" in our perceptions. We get caught up in the resulting unexpected life changes, and are not able to flow with Mother Earth's rhythms. However, when our lives are changed so unexpectedly by these "disasters," our hearts are opened. Sometimes a powerful jolt is needed to open our hearts. The "disasters" are simply yet another way that Mother Earth guides us and encourages us in our journeys.

Allow yourself to step into the energy of Mother Earth, into the flow of her rhythms, and then to understand how your individual rhythms interact with her rhythms. When all of humankind can allow their energies to align with Mother Earth's energies and the energies of the Universe, there may not need to be any more "natural disasters," because we will all be flowing together in our grace-ful, open-hearted dance.

We are not here to control the Earth. We are here to learn from her. She will continue changing, because she is a living, breathing, evolving being. As we align our energies with her, we are able to understand those changes, and learn to flow with them rather than fight against them. Mother Earth's soul must be honored. She is here to teach us, to guide us, to nurture us, and move us on as she herself moves on.

# Exercise #35
# Sensory Awareness II

Make yourself comfortable and allow your breath to carry you into a deep state of consciousness.

As you settle deeper and deeper, allow your heart to open. Your heart brings together the life-force of the Earth with the universal connection of the heavens. Feel your heart and the light inside of you. Allow the Light of the Universe to come in, touch your soul, and be reflected out again. Take several deep and full breaths, realizing that with each inhalation, you are bringing in the energy and Light of the Universe. And your exhalation carries that Light on through you and out to the world.

As you work with breathing this energy into your body, begin to feel a wonderful, warm, emerald green light all around you. Let that light come into your body and weave through it like ribbons dancing all around you and playing through your body. Feel the green color.

. . .

Imagine a pathway now through a lush green forest and beautiful meadows. Experience the green of the trees and the grass. Feel your heart opening more and more as you walk this path, allowing the green energy to move through you.

265

Breathe it in, so that with each inhalation, the energy of the Universe comes to you through this green healing light.

. . .

Now look down to the ground, and see the reddish-brown, reddish-orange colors in the earth. As you are walking down this pathway in your imagination, reach down and pick up a handful of the earth. Feel it run through your fingers. Look at the many colors that are there in the earth. Feel the textures. Feel the power in the earth, in the soil, and how this earth and soil gives birth, gives new life, gives energy to living and growing things. Feel that energy, and feel the colors of red and orange coming through this soil, this earth that is running through your fingers. Dip both hands into the earth. Feel the life. Bring it to your nose and smell it. Allow this red and orange earth energy to move through all of your senses, hearing through your inner ear what the earth has to say to you, smelling it, imagining its sweet taste — the sweet taste of life and of birth.

. . .

As you continue down the pathway, it opens into a meadow, and you feel the sun streaming down on you. Feel its bright yellow and white light. Feel this light move through your body. Smell its freshness. Feel its warmth on your skin. Let it touch you and move all through you. Feel your safety and security as you stand basking in the warmth and glow of the sunlight.

. . .

The pathway takes you back into the forest now, where you are once again enveloped in green. While you are walking in the green, you realize that the green is brought to life through the red and orange of the earth, and through the bright yellow of the sunshine. You realize that without those elements the green could not come to be.

. . .

As you go on down the pathway you come to another clearing where all you see is bright, blue, clear sky — the most brilliant and clear sky you have ever seen. It goes on forever. Feel that blue, and realize that the heavens and its boundlessness, are all things to strive for, to reach out for, and bring into your life. As you breathe the blue color into your life, let yourself feel a new freedom to express who you are. Feel your own personal universe expand as far as the sky goes. There are no limits. Your being can open to embrace the entire universe. Let yourself fly through the sky, and know that your energy is boundless, that your soul knows no limits, no boundaries, no cage. Know that the physical body in which you live is only a house where the soul comes to live. But the soul must still be free to fly.

. . .

As you come back to the earth and continue on your pathway, you are once again in the woods. Soon you come upon an enormous bed of violets — deep blue, indigo, and purple violets. You have never seen such an expanse of violets. It is as if there is a carpet of indigo and violet. Lie down in this sea of color. As you lie down, so many pictures come into your mind. Allow yourself to see your own life very clearly — where you have been and where you are going. Feel the indigo color wash through your body, opening the area in your forehead between your eyes to a tremendous flow of energy. The purple, violet, deep blue, and indigo colors wash through your brow. Feel a new energy surge through you as your vision expands. This can become your way of seeing the world. This can become your way of opening to poetry, to music, to art, to relationships, to career, to life — seeing and understanding at deeper and deeper levels with greatly heightened awareness.

. . .

Arise from the bed of violets, carrying this purple and indigo energy with you. Become aware that in the violet is also the green, and how the green moves through the violet. For each of those violets grows on a green stem, and they have green leaves to take in the nourishment of the yellow sunlight.

. . .

Move back into the sunlight, and as you feel the sunlight pour over you, allow it to take on a golden-white color that pours into your body through the crown of your head. Let it move down through your entire body, taking in the indigo color and the bright blue, and then move out through the green of your heart. At the same time, feel the red, orange, and yellow energies of the Earth moving up through the soles of your feet, pouring up into your heart and out. Open to receive the fullness of heaven and earth. Feel these energies pour through your body, coursing through your veins. Let every cell of your body be energized, enlivened, and invigorated. Experience new birth from the earth and the heavens. Your heart brings these energies together and gives them full expression. Through your heart you can live and sing, dance and play, cry and mourn, and love.

As you continue through each day, remember this walk through the woods. Remember the soil running through your fingers, that wonderful earth energy, and the power that you felt in your hands and surging through your body. Feel the sunlight, the yellow warmth of safety and security. Feel the expanse of the sky and know that you can fly forever — that your soul has no bounds in its understanding and in its expression. Through the indigo color in the bed of violets, you are able to see this great expanse. You are able to see clearly the totality of life, and understand more clearly your place in this life. You can feel the golden-white light of the sun pouring down through the top of your head, and all of these energies meeting at your heart. Every day you can carry this wonderful light and love through your heart. Let your heart sing! Let your heart cry! Let your heart laugh and weep for joy! Let your heart experience its pain. Let all of the feelings that come through your heart be real. Let them have their full expression, for this is living. This is opening to fullness as a divine being. And when you open in this way, you help others touch their own heart centers.

Take your time to rest in this wonderful feeling. Let these vibrant colors be an active part of your life. And when you are ready, go to your journal to record your experiences.

# 19

# Working with Spirit

We have spoken a great deal about working with Spirit. Having explored many other aspects of the 21st-century mystic's journey, and worked through emotional blocks through the chakras, it is now time to step more fully into what working with Spirit really means. We begin by looking at the concepts of time and space, which become vastly different when entering the Spirit realm.

## Linear Time vs. Simultaneous Time

Here on planet Earth, we live within a framework of linear time — past, present, and future. There is another dimension of time, however, that goes backward and forward at the same time — one that encompasses past, present, and future simultaneously. We call this simultaneous time, the time of the Spirit realm and of the akasha. In simultaneous time, everything occurs at once. There is, in fact, no sense of past and future — everything is now. All experiences are happening at the same time.

Our framework of linear time, on the other hand, with past and future clearly mapped out on a time line, allows us to learn from our past and make plans for our future. This is very important for our learning and growth process. If every experience of our lives was happening at the same time, we would be completely overwhelmed, and never accomplish or learn anything. However, by remaining fixed in the linear time frame, we do not have the ability to see the "bigger picture" of our situation. We have memory of the past, but can not literally re-experience it. We know our present circumstances, and can perhaps predict the events of the immediate future, but we are not able to go there and see it or experience it. We are also in a realm of physical space, only able to experience our present physical environment. By merging our energies with Spirit and moving into the realm of simultaneous time, we are able to see the "bigger picture," to gain a greater perspective on our lives and our situations. We are able to move into a state of awareness where all time and space becomes one.

The Spirit realm can be thought of as a single universal point which contains all of creation — all of what we know as past, present, and future. You might think of it as a hologram. Between this point and our physical realm, you could imagine a giant magical lens or mirror, which not only reflects that point, but also protracts it into a line creating the principle of linear time. Time is then "spread out" across the linear time line, so that there is a past, present, and future, relative to any particular point along that linear time line. When we become one with the universal consciousness, we are, in effect, starting from our particular point on the linear time line and jumping through the magical lens into a realm where all time and space become one. From here we are able to get a much larger perspective on our spot on the linear time line and our current situation or circumstance.

# Three Levels of Development

Generally speaking, our energy systems vibrate at very low frequencies as compared to the high frequency vibrations of Spirit. At this much slower frequency vibration, most people can only stand on one point on the linear time line at any one moment. Therefore, most people can only *experience* one thing at a time. In order to move beyond that single point, we must raise our vibratory frequency to a higher level. The higher our vibrational frequency, the more we are able to become one with Spirit, which determines how much of the "bigger picture" we are able to see and experience.

In simple terms, there are three levels of development in learning to raise frequency vibration to become one with Spirit. At the first level, the individual is able to function only on one particular point of their linear time line at any given moment. Generally speaking, individuals at this level are aware of their present circumstance or situation, but do not reflect on the past for recall of past lessons learned, or make clear plans toward the future. They tend to be easily caught up in fears related to past experiences or the unknown, or in anxieties concerning their future.

At the second or intermediate level, individuals are able to function both on the earth-plane linear time line *and* have access to a broader vision of past and future within their individual time line. Here they have opened their awareness to possibilities of a broader world and have a greater perspective on their experiences and circumstances. As individuals reach more advanced states of this level, they may be able to see far beyond their individual time line into past history and far into the future.

The highest level of development is the ability to see the entire Earth-plane linear time line and into the universal point or the Spirit realm. Through this universal point, the individual at this level of development is able to see, know, and understand all.

The fact that you have chosen to read this book shows an awareness within you that places you at least within the intermediate level. Through disciplined work and commitment, all of us have the potential of reaching the third level.

# Orientations of Perception

Working with Spirit on any of these levels of development involves our senses of perception. There are three principal orientations of perception: visual, aural, and kinesthetic. Those individuals whose primary perceptual orientation is visual will learn the fastest or grasp concepts more quickly when they can see the information presented in a visual form, whether that be through a picture, a written description, or a demonstration. For instance, a visual person may have difficulty comprehending verbal directions about how to get to a particular destination, but if he is shown a map, everything is clear. For a person with an aural perceptual orientation, the information is grasped through verbal explanation. They will understand the directions to their destination very clearly when someone describes the necessary turns, while a map might really confuse them. Finally, individuals with a kinesthetic perceptual orientation will learn the fastest through actually experiencing the concept. They might have difficulty with a map or hearing directions, but if they can drive the car there once with someone navigating the trip, they will then be able to go there by themselves.

You probably already know which of these categories best describes your primary learning orientation. At times, more than one perceptual orientation and process may emerge. If you are not aware of your primary perceptual orientation, just pay attention for a few days to the ways that you take in information. Under what circumstances does information come easily to you, as opposed to other circumstances where you remain very confused, and just can't seem to "get it." Notice the words you use in conversation. Does "We'll *see*," come up, or "I can't *imagine* that," or "I don't know how I *feel* about that." This will give you some indication of your primary learning orientation.

# Clairvoyance, Clairaudience, Clairsentience

Intuitive gifts also fall into three categories which correspond to those of perceptual orientation. Clairvoyance, or intuitive sight or vision, corresponds to a visual orientation. In simple form, it involves perceiving images through your inner vision. In its more developed form, the clairvoyant is able to see spirit beings, non-physical energies, and auras.

Clairaudience, intuitive hearing, corresponds to an aural orientation. The clairaudient perceives messages either as an inner sound or an outer voice. The Bible tells of many such clairaudient experiences, as God spoke to prophets.

Finally, clairsentience, intuitive feeling, corresponds to a kinesthetic orientation. Clairsentience may include perceiving fragrances or odors, tastes, emotional feelings, or tactile sensations.

Our perceptual orientations give us strong indications as to which of these gifts might be the strongest for us as we begin to open our awareness. As we continue developing our gifts, all three orientations begin to open more and more, but, at first most people receive information in one way more than the others. We all have these abilities if we are willing to discipline ourselves to refine our skills.

# To Each His Own

It is very important to note that everyone has their own way of perceiving, of processing, and of working with information. It never fails in classes that someone is able to "see" intuitively, and everyone else immediately wants to be able to "see," while not noticing that they are receiving such beautiful and clear information through their hearing or feeling. Please do not compare yourself and your intuitive gifts with someone else's. One person may see clearly but not be able to hear a thing, while another hears whole symphonies played by the angelic realms. Just go with your strengths, and let all three areas of awareness and perception open for you in their own time.

# Grounding

One of the primary rules in working with Spirit and the intuitive realm is to stay grounded in a strong sense of physical and material reality while opening awareness to the intuitive world. This means maintaining a strong sense of personal identity and of what is real and tangible in the physical and rational-thought world. Being grounded means not letting yourself be swept away by the fascination of spiritual or psychic phenomena, but rather learning from it and applying what we learn to our physical life experiences. One of my teachers used giraffes to illustrate the perfect balance between the rational and intuitive realms — their feet are firmly planted on the ground while their heads are in the clouds! We live in a physical dimension. We must never forget that. One of our primary spiritual

273

lessons as human beings is to learn to bring heaven to earth — to be able to live in physical form with a clear understanding, knowledge, and communication with the heavenly realms. When we can keep this clear balance in our lives, we can understand the different levels of spiritual energy, and develop our intuitive gifts to their greatest potential.

# Three Levels of Spiritual Energy

There are three primary levels of spiritual energy: the physical level, the mental level, and the spiritual level. The physical level is the realm of the physical body and ego, and includes all those currently in a physical existence as well as those recently crossed over into the spirit realm. The mental level is the realm of the soul, and includes spirit guides and teachers. The highest level, the spiritual level, includes guardian angels and angels. Pythagoras spoke of these levels as the Inferior World, the Superior World, and the Supreme World. In his system, the Inferior World was the home of the mortal gods, demons, humans, animals, and all physical matter. The Superior World was the home of the immortals, while the Supreme World was the true plane of God.[1]

While we are obviously at the physical level, our ultimate goal in this work is to be able to become one with the spiritual level — to move through the magical lens to the other side where we can see, hear, and feel all of the knowledge and wisdom that there is in the universe. However, this demands tremendous strength on our part to raise our vibrations to such a high level that we can meet with this angelic energy. Therefore, many people work with spirit guides and teachers from the mental level. Later in this chapter we will discuss the angelic realms in more detail.

# Three Levels of Spiritual Energy

| | | |
|---|---|---|
| Spiritual Level | Spirit | guardian angels and angels |
| Mental Level | soul | spirit guides and teachers |
| Physical Level | body/ego | physical beings, and those recently crossed over |

Pythagoras referred to this trinity as:

| | |
|---|---|
| the Supreme World | true plane of God |
| the Superior World | home of the immortals |
| the Inferior World | home of the mortal gods, demons, humans, animals, and all physical matter.[1] |

# Spirit Guides and Teachers

A spirit guide or teacher is a nonphysical entity that makes itself known to you in some way through your intuitive mind. The guide's purpose is to help and protect you, and to assist in your spiritual development and understanding of daily life. We all have guides and teachers around us who are with us from birth. We may or may not be aware of the presence of spirit guides, but they are there. Children often have imaginary playmates, which can be a sign of their awareness of their guides. Individuals who are aware that physical death is approaching often speak of perceiving guides from the other side who appear to assist them in making their transition back to the spirit realm. In the great deal of research done in recent years with those who have had near-death experiences, most people report being met by spirit entities or relatives or friends who have crossed over. All of these occurrences tell us something more tangible about the

275

existence of spirit beings.

Spirit guides have described themselves to me as being like training wheels. Their purpose is to help us communicate with the spiritual level by being the "middle man," the translator of energy essence between spiritual and physical levels, until we are able to raise our vibrations high enough to make a direct connection. When we are able to communicate directly with the highest realm of Spirit, the spirit guides will step out of the way. Remember that we described soul also as the aspect of our being that is connected to the spiritual realm. This is why being in touch with soul, the essence of ourselves, is so important in opening to communication and guidance from Spirit. Sitting in soul greatly facilitates opening to Spirit.

# Belief in Spirit Guides and Teachers Through History

Our Western awareness of spirit guides comes from the ancient Greeks. They believed that there were spirits who served as intermediaries between man and the gods. They believed that these spirits could be either good or bad, and therefore could be either a protector or lead you astray. It was considered very good luck to have a good spirit guide, because the guide would give you good advice and ideas. Both Socrates and his student, Plato, in fact, claimed to be guided throughout their lives by guardian spirits in whom they put their supreme trust.

With the exception of the concept of the guardian angel, the Christian church considered all spirit guides to be evil, and condemned all spirit communication. This led to great persecution of many people throughout history for their practice of "witchcraft." However, there are many accounts of great Christian mystics, such as Hildegard von Bingen, Thomas Aquinas, Teilhard de Chardin, Meister Eckhart, St. Teresa of Avila, and Joan of Arc, to name only a few, whose work was inspired by their direct communication with Spirit, and their mystical experiences.

# The Band of Seven

In the old-time Spiritualist tradition, everyone was considered to have a band of seven spirit guides. The first is the Gatekeeper, who is responsible for protecting you in the spirit realm, making sure that nothing can come to you that could harm you. The Gatekeeper decides who from the spirit realm may communicate with you. It may also seek out a particular spirit guide who can be of help to you. The Gatekeeper is sometimes a child guide, and is known in some circles as the Joy Guide.

The Philosopher, sometimes called the Doctor, serves as your daily philosophical guide and teacher in the spirit realm. Opening to its wisdom will give you guidance in the practical aspects of daily living. The Ethnic Guide brings understanding of Earth and Sky, and of cultures beyond your own understanding and experience. It is called the Ethnic Guide because it will rarely be of your own ethnic origin. The Chemist gives guidance about your physical health and well-being. The Teacher brings wisdom and understanding of a higher philosophical nature. The Guardian Angel usually remains very far away from you because the angelic realm is such a high vibration, but communicates with you through one of the other guides.

According to the Spiritualist tradition, these first six spirit guides remain with you for your entire life. However, the seventh guide, the Master Teacher, will change as you evolve in your understanding. As you are ready to receive higher and higher levels of teaching, you will receive a new Master Teacher to take you on to the next level.

Various cultures have their own understandings of spirit guides and teachers, each having their own task. If you come from a Catholic background, you may feel the presence of saints around you. If you come from a Native American spirit tradition, or from a Yoruba (African) or South American tradition, or from a Hindu or Sufi tradition, you may wish to work within that orientation. What is important in working with spirit guides and teachers is the realization that they are here to help us experience our mystical selves, and know our oneness with the divine.

# Are They Real?

In the course of your meditation, you may meet your spirit guides, and they may appear in some of the roles discussed above. But a spirit guide may also appear to you in the form of an animal, a color, a sound, or a feeling. One of your first questions may be, "Are these spirit guides real entities from the spirit realm, or are they aspects of my personality manifesting as guides and teachers assisting in the learning process?" From my perspective, it is not so important to determine the "reality" of spirit guides. What is important is to access the information that is available when energy is focused on communication with Spirit and spirit guides. I have had very powerful and transformative experiences with spirit guides and Master Teachers. If a spirit guide becomes a tool that works for you, then use it. Spirit comes to work with us in many ways. Our responsibility is to use the tools that Spirit gives us in the best way we are able. Accept the lessons as they come. Embrace them and take them into your life. Getting caught in the web of questioning the reality of spirit guides can cause you to miss the lesson or the wisdom they are trying to share.

# Spirit Helpers

It is very common for someone to speak of feeling the strong presence of a loved one, such as a parent or grandparent, who has crossed over to spirit. Many people speak of being visited by these spirits, of seeing them or hearing their voice as clearly as if they were standing beside them. This brings us to a discussion of spirit helpers as opposed to spirit guides, two distinctly different categories of beings. Spirit helpers are loved ones or friends who have passed over into the realm of spirit, but whose presence you continue to feel very strongly. They are still at the physical level of the spiritual world. They have lifted out of physical bodies, but remain very close to the earth plane vibration. They often serve as intermediaries between us and spirit guides and teachers when we are not yet able to access the higher vibrations of the mental and spiritual levels. Their perspective and understanding of earth-plane existence may or may not be higher than ours, but usually they have not yet lifted far enough above the earth-plane vibration to have the perspective of those spirit guides and teachers in the mental level.

The true teacher guides always come from a higher level of vibration than ours, usually from the mental level. They appear as conscious beings who may or may not have ever had a physical incarnation in the earth plane, or who may have had their physical-plane experiences in other galaxies of the universe. These entities become our chief spirit teachers and Master Teachers. However, once again, please do not get caught up in trying to analyze who a spirit guide or teacher is, or where they come from, or whether they are an aspect of your personality or separate entities. If a guide makes itself known to you, and you are comfortable with its presence and wish to work with it, dive into the work. Everything you need to know about the guide will be revealed in time.

# Angels

We have said that most guides and teachers come from the Mental level of the spiritual world. You may be wondering why they don't come from the highest level, the Spiritual level. The energy in the Spiritual level is called the Devic essence, or what we call angels. Angels are such a high level of energy that they are electrical structures only, while we in the physical form are atomic structures. We are made up of molecules, cells, and atoms. We have an atomic form of bonding that holds our physical bodies together. Angels, however, have no bodies. They usually appear to us as mists. They have the ability to take their electrical charge and form shapes for us to see them, but there is no atomic structure. Although spirit guides and teachers are no longer in atomic structure form, they are very familiar with that vibratory rate, having been in that form in some physical dimension. Therefore, they have a much clearer understanding of how to communicate with those of us in physical form. This does not mean that angels are not very present in our lives.

279

They are all around us, and as your intuitive senses open, you will become even more aware of their presence. However, communication with them will usually happen through one of your other spirit guides.

## Learning to Work Together

Spirit guides and teachers must learn to work with our energies just as we must learn to work with theirs. As we raise our energy vibrations to try to match theirs, they lower their vibration somewhat to meet us. The more we can expand our energies, the higher the teacher is going to be. Eventually, we learn to expand so far that the spirit guides step out of the way so that we may become one with the universal energy. This is the goal. It may happen for you in the next few days or weeks, or it may take years. Joey Crinita tells of sitting in a development class for seven years before anything happened for him at all! Please try not to be in a hurry. Just work with the tools and guides that Spirit brings to you. Be patient and, once again, allow yourself to move at your own pace.

## Talking with a Spirit Guide

When you become aware of a spirit guide or teacher around you, always ask how it wishes to be known by you so that you may get to know its energies and can help facilitate the communication. Ask what it wishes to be called, and how you will know that it is with you. Ask what its purpose is in your life, and what guidance it has to share with you. I refer to the guides in a non-gender form, because often they do not really have gender. Please let go of any preconceptions of how spirit guides should appear or name themselves. Let them show you the way that you will recognize them. It may be by their name or title, by a sound, a color, a vision, or a feeling. Again, Spirit is giving you a tool with which to work. Use it.

# Invoking the Highest Realms of Spirit

Finally, in working with spirit beings, whether they be helpers, guides or teachers, remember that you are always in charge of the situation. Never let a spirit "take over," so that you feel you have lost physical control of the situation. If you ever feel uncomfortable with a spirit entity, demand that it leave. Invoke the Christ consciousness, the Light and Love of the Universe, as your protector by reciting a prayer that is sacred to you in your particular tradition. Common protective prayers in western traditions are The Lord's Prayer, the 23rd Psalm, or the Kabbalistic Prayer, which I use to begin each meditation session, channeling session, or work with a client:

Holy art Thou, Lord of the Universe;
Holy art Thou whom nature hath not formed;
Holy art Thou, the vast and the mighty one;
Lord of the Light and of the Darkness,
Amen.

The following meditation is to help you become aware of the presence of a spirit guide. You will also have an opportunity to begin working with this guide, asking its role in your life, and how it wishes to help you. You may wish to use this meditation several times to meet each of the above-mentioned spirit guides, one at a time. Each time you use it, enter into the meditation with an open mind and heart, and allow the experience to unfold. Again, remember that Spirit is giving you a tool for higher understanding. Try not to get caught up in the "reality" of what is happening, and just go with your experience.

# Exercise #36
# Meeting a Spirit Guide

Allow yourself to move into a deep meditative state.
. . .

In your imagination now, see yourself in a very beautiful place. It may be a room of a house, the seashore, on a mountaintop, or in a meadow — just let your imagination create a spot that feels right for you.

. . .

Take a little time now to experience all of the details of this spot. See the colors and shapes — every detail of the things that are in this place. Hear the sounds. Notice the smells. Feel the textures of the various things that are here. And even taste this place in your imagination. Take time to feel at home here, and then find the spot that you wish to stand or sit or lie down — a spot that you feel is your special place to do your inner work.

. . .

After becoming comfortable in your special spot, ask of the universe if there is a guide or teacher from the realm of spirit who would like to work with you. Is there a spirit guide who is waiting to make itself known? (If you are using this meditation to meet a specific guide, such as the philosopher or gatekeeper, ask specifically for that guide to make itself known to you.) Ask the guide to appear to you, and take note of how this being enters your space. Let go of any preconceived notion of how the guide should appear. Allow it to appear in any form — as a color, a sound, an animal, or a human form. Thank your guide for coming to you and for being with you.

. . .

When the guide has appeared, ask how it wishes to be known to you. It may give you a name, or it may simply call itself "The Guide." Or, it may make itself known only as a feeling of a presence, a color, or a sound. It doesn't matter — just accept whatever way the guide wants to be known to you at this time.

. . .

Ask your guide if there is something that it would like to tell you now. Again, allow this information to come as words, as a picture, or as a feeling or impression. In whatever way the guide is communicating with you at this point, accept the communication and work with it.

. . .

Ask your guide what its general purpose or agenda is in your life.

. . .

One of the first and easiest ways to work with a spirit guide is by finding answers to "yes or no" questions. Ask your guide to show you a physical or energetic feeling in your body that means "yes." . . . Then ask your guide to show you a sign that means "no."

. . .

Your spirit guide has now given you a clear tool to use in every day of your life. When you need some advice in making a decision, turn the decision into a series of "yes or no" questions, and let your guide help you make the decision through your body signals. Try this out now by asking a simple question about which you would like some guidance. Let your guide and your body show you the yes or no answer.

For the next several days, you may want to continue asking your guide or Spirit to show you "yes" and "no" so that you get a strong confirmation of this physical sign. You will then more easily trust the signals.

. . .

Now ask your spirit guide to take its place in your energy field. Where does your spirit guide live around you? You may feel it behind you, over your head, or over a particular part of your body. Ask your guide to show you its place so that you always know where to find it.

. . .

It is very important when working with spirit guides to thank them for their help. Thank your guide now once again for being with you and for the guidance you received during this meditation session. Know that you can call upon this spirit guide at any time for advice, guidance, and understanding. You do not need to come back to this place to find your guide, for now you know exactly where it lives in your energy field. However, you may choose to come back to this very beautiful place at any time to work with Spirit, or to meet other spirit guides.

Once again, thank Spirit and your guide for being with you. And slowly open your eyes, coming back into your own space now. Go to your journal and record your experiences and what you learned from your guide.

# 20

# On Your Way to Intuitive Living

This chapter is devoted to three exercises whose aim is to further stimulate your intuitive process. The first two exercises focus on developing concentration. Highly developed concentration is necessary in learning to raise your energy vibration and become one with Spirit. This is because when you begin Spirit communication, you must remain intensely focused in order to keep attuning your vibration to the high frequency of Spirit. This first exercise will help you build your concentration, as well as stimulate the third eye, the psychic organ of perception, essential for the development of clairvoyance. You may feel like you are physically exercising a muscle here, and will probably feel a tremendous pressure in the area between your eyes. Therefore, you are only to do this exercise for a few minutes at a time. As you continue working with it, you will find that you can work with the exercise for longer and longer periods of time.

## Exercise #37
## Opening the Third Eye

Sit comfortably in a chair and focus your gaze on the tip of your nose. Your eyes will cross and you will feel a tremendous amount of pressure at the third eye (located just above and between your eyes in your forehead). Keep your gaze focused on the tip of your nose for 30-60 seconds at first. Then release your eyes and rest briefly. Repeat the process several times.

. . .

Repeat the exercise, but this time focus your gaze on the bridge of your nose, the spot directly between your eyes.

. . .

Do this exercise several times daily, but never for more than a few minutes at a time. As a variation to the exercise, you can close your eyes, while still focusing your gaze on the tip and then the bridge of your nose.

The following exercise will help you learn to block out all extraneous thoughts so that you can more easily concentrate on the task at hand.

# Exercise #38
# Concentration

On a sheet of 8 1/2" x 11" white paper, draw a circle in the center about the size of a nickel and color it in with black ink. Place the paper on a stand or tape it to the wall approximately 8-10 feet in front of your meditation spot.

Stare at the dot from this distance of 8-10 feet, and focus your gaze and concentration totally on the dot and nothing else. Silently, begin counting slowly from 1 to 100 (approximately 1 count every 2 seconds). Your entire attention must be focused on the dot and on your count. If any other thought comes into your awareness, you must stop and begin counting again at 1. Continue this exercise for 10 minutes, and then stop until the next day. Do not concern yourself with how far you get with the numbers. The important thing is the exercise itself, not whether or not you get to 100. The first few days you may never get past 10 or 15 because your concentration continues to be interrupted by other thoughts. It doesn't matter. Just stay with the exercise for 10 minutes, and then leave it. If by chance you do get to 100, then count backwards from 100 back to 1.

Do this exercise daily for at least a couple of weeks until you are easily able to maintain your concentration and count to 100 and back. Then, from time to time, return to this exercise to brush up your skills. If, after a couple of weeks, you feel you are getting nowhere in your concentration development, put the exercise aside for a week and then come back to it.[1]

The last of these three exercises will help you begin to work with Spirit guidance for clearer understanding of situations in your life now or of different aspects of yourself. It may also give you glimpses into other lifetimes. Just allow yourself to be guided by Spirit, and see where you are led. At the end of the exercise, record your impressions in your journal.

# Exercise #39
# Exploring Different Aspects of Self

Make yourself comfortable and allow your breath to carry you into a deep state of consciousness.

. . .

Imagine yourself alone now in a very beautiful and peaceful space. This space can be anywhere and anything that you wish — outside or inside, large or small — whatever comes to your inner senses. Take a moment to let the entire space come into your awareness.

. . .

You are here alone, physically, but you begin to feel that you are being welcomed here by a host of spirit friends and helpers, guides and teachers. One by one these spirit friends and helpers begin to materialize so that you see them appear before you. Do not be limited by your preconceived ideas of how they should appear, for a guide may come to you as an animal or as a sound or as a color or as an energy form, as well as in human form. One by one, the guides greet you and give you some brief word about who they are to you and how they will help you. Take a moment to allow these spirit guides to come to you.

. . .

Now that you have met some of these guides, you will see that one of them is coming to you with an outstretched hand and inviting you to join it on a journey. Your guide now leads you into a great, long, bright hallway. Along this hallway you see hundreds of doorways. Each one is different. Some are large, some small, some ornate, some simple, some painted, some natural wood, some very antique, some very modern or even futuristic. As you walk down this hallway, along with your guide, choose a doorway that piques your curiosity — a doorway that you would like to open to see what is inside. Ask your guide to please wait for you in the hallway, and slowly open this doorway and step through it. Notice your surroundings, which may be anywhere, anything, any time. Take it all in. Move around and look at the people or things there. Now look at yourself — what are you wearing? Who are you? How do you fit into this picture? What does your face look like? Explore this place, and this new physical identity. Know that you are perfectly safe here, for at any time you can go back to the doorway, out into the hallway to your spirit guide, and close the doorway. Take a few moments here for your exploration.

. . .

Now begin to wind up your investigation of this place and time and find your way back to the hallway, closing the door behind you. Greet and thank your spirit guide. Notice that you once again look like yourself as you know yourself.

Continue on down the hallway until you and your guide find another doorway that you wish to open. Ask the guide to wait for you, and slowly open the door and step inside. Notice once again your surroundings and your own identity. Spend a few moments exploring this place and who you are. Know that you are perfectly safe and that at any time you can come back to the hallway and your spirit guide.

. . .

Now begin to wind up your investigation of this place and time and find your way back to the hallway, closing the door behind you. Greet and thank your spirit guide. Notice that you once again look like yourself as you know yourself.

Repeat this process for one or two more doorways. Take time to explore there and then come back to your spirit guide.

. . .

Along with your spirit guide, make your way back down the hallway to the beautiful and peaceful space where you began. Thank your spirit guide for accompanying you on this journey. While still here in the presence of these many guides, ask them anything you wish about where you have just been.

. . .

Know that what is behind all of these hundreds of doorways are parts of you in one form or another. And all of the people that you found yourself as are aspects of you. You can call upon these aspects of yourself at any time to glean information, to help you develop a skill, to help you relate to a particular person, or to help you understand a particular circumstance or a facet of your life.

Thank these spirit guides for appearing to you and helping you. They now begin to disappear so that once again you only feel their presence. Know that they are with you at all times. Any time that you wish to speak face-to-face with them or to visit the Hallway of Doors again, you have only to return to this space and ask them to join you.

# 21

# Gaining Confidence Through Giving Intuitive Readings

The exercises in this chapter focus on giving intuitive "readings" or "messages" to others. Some of you will be very interested in these exercises because you want to develop your abilities as intuitive readers. Others of you may have no interest in giving readings at all. However, doing readings as a part of your intuitive development process is very important. By giving a reading to someone else and receiving feedback from them about your message, you learn how your own intuitive process works. You learn to know the difference within yourself between "making the information up" and "receiving" the information intuitively from Spirit. Through this experience, you gain confidence and trust in your own intuitive process, and have more faith and trust in receiving guidance for yourself. So, whatever your interest in using your intuitive gifts in your life, let yourself enter fully into these exercises for your personal learning and growth.

## Am I making this up?

As you begin to give messages or readings, it will often feel like you are making the information up. In Chapter 6 we talked about moving into altered states of consciousness, a place where you are able to access many levels of awareness at once. When you move out of rational thought and into intuitive mind, you are in that altered state. Your rational thought mind cannot function there. As long as you keep talking and stay with the flow of information, you help yourself stay in the intuitive mind. However, when you stop to "think" about what you are saying, you have just left the intuitive mind and its many levels of awareness, and stepped back into the rational mind which can only function on one level of awareness at once.

When you step into the intuitive mind, you are stepping into a realm of which you have no conscious knowledge. That's what imagination is — a realm where you can function on many levels of awareness at once, where there are no boundaries or restrictions. So you see, in a way you are making it up, because the intuitive mind and the imagination are very much the same thing. However, you will be amazed at how often the person who receives your intuitive message will respond by saying that they understood exactly what you were talking about, and that the reading made perfect sense to them. I encourage you to take the first thought or impression that comes to you as you begin, and go with it. Start talking and do not stop. As long as you keep talking without judging or editing, you keep the energy connection with Spirit intact. When you stop talking or "think" too much, however, you break the energy contact, and the message process is much more difficult. (This is why the Movie of the Mind exercise in Chapter 18 is so important.) This all may sound overwhelming at first, but it gets very easy if you will just let yourself have fun and go with your impressions.

# The "Double Check"

It seems to be our human nature to look for guarantees. While there are no written warranties or guarantees when working with Spirit, there is what Joey Crinita calls the "double check." A double check is simply a message that keeps coming to you in different ways. Let's say you are considering a move to Colorado to start a new career in holistic healing. At first you have a quiet inner voice saying that Colorado is the place for you. Then for some "coincidental" reason, several people mention to you their love of Colorado and how much they want to live there. You happen to turn on the television one evening and find a travel documentary about the Colorado Rockies. Then your favorite magazine just happens to run a story about the growing holistic health care industry in Colorado. Finally, a friend you haven't seen for a long time calls to say they've been thinking about taking a vacation to Colorado and wonders if you might like to come along. Are you getting the picture? These are all double checks. When Spirit has an important message for us, it will keep coming in many ways. This is Spirit's way of giving you confirmation.

# Symbols and Metaphor

Spirit speaks often in symbols and metaphor, so this may further confuse the readings that you give or receive at first. Even if a reading makes no sense to you, open to its possibilities and allow yourself to sit with it for a few days. In time the truth in the message may be revealed.

# Intuitive Readings vs. Giving Advice

When giving intuitive readings, do your best to be sure that the message is coming from Spirit. Especially when you know your partner well, it is very easy to get caught up in giving advice based on what you know about the situation or the person. Do your best to stay away from giving advice and only report the impressions you are receiving. When you feel that you are having difficulty remaining objective, do not hesitate to suggest to your partner that they should seek out someone else for a reading on that particular subject.

# How much should I say?

You may also receive information that you are not sure is appropriate to share. When in doubt, first ask yourself if this information will be helpful to the person who will receive the message. Your role as a reader is to help bring clarity and understanding, not stir up fears or anxieties. Any time that you have any doubt about whether or not to pass on information in a reading, honor that doubt and keep the information to yourself. If it is important that the information be given, it will come out in some other way and you will know that sharing it is appropriate.

Enough talking about it — it is time to dive in and begin. So here we go with our first intuitive reading exercises. Several of these exercises will require a group setting, so if you are not in a group, gather a few more adventurous friends and have fun.

Giving intuitive readings in a group setting is often very intimidating at first. This first exercise is a great way to break the ice, and let everyone begin to feel comfortable with letting Spirit speak to them in whatever form they may receive information.

# Exercise #40
# Introduction to Intuitive Readings

Begin by having your group sit in a circle. In turn, each person goes around the circle giving a one-word only message to each person in the circle. They should say the first thing that comes into their mind as they look at each person. Do not think about what to say — in fact, try to get "thinking" out of the picture completely. Just allow your intuitive self to be open and say the first word that comes to you. It will almost feel like free association.

After doing several rounds of one-word readings, move on to several rounds of one-sentence readings. Again, follow the same format, and simply say whatever comes into your mind. Do not concern yourself with whether or not the message makes any sense at all. You will be surprised how often it will make perfect sense, or at least relate in some way to the person receiving the message, even though it means nothing to you.

The above exercise is a great way to "warm up" your group each time you gather to give readings. Once everyone is getting comfortable with the process, you can skip this exercise and go directly to the following more advanced methods.

# Psychometry

Psychometry is a method of psychic reading by which you hold an object and speak the impressions you receive from that object. We will use a slight variation of this principle here, moving it into a more spiritual realm. You will not be so much tapping into the energy of the object itself, but rather using the object to connect you to the soul energy of the individual to whom it belongs.

# Exercise #41
# Psychometry Readings

As your group gathers, place a basket by the door and ask each person to anonymously place a personal object in the basket as they come in. It can be a watch, a piece of jewelry, a crystal — anything that has been in their possession for at least several months and is close to them. (I discourage the use of wedding rings because from a distance they can all look alike. You will understand why this is important in a moment.)

When you are ready to start the readings, sit in a circle. You might like to begin with a brief meditation, inviting the highest realms of Spirit to be in your midst, and asking for guidance and wisdom as you begin your work. If individuals in the group are working with spirit guides, they will want to invite those specific guides and teachers to be with them as they give their readings. Then choose one person to begin the readings.

The first reader takes an object out of the basket and holds it up for the group to see. No one should acknowledge that the object is theirs, but the owner will recognize that this reading is for them. The reader is using the object simply to connect to the owner's energy, and then speak their impressions. When the reader is finished, they continue to hold on to the object, and the next person in the circle takes an object from the basket, holds it up for all to see, and begins their reading. Continue in this manner around the circle until everyone has given a reading and the basket is empty. After all of the readings are completed, the first reader asks for the owner of their object. The owner can then respond to the reading and give feedback about what made sense from the reading and what did not. Continue moving one at a time around the circle again so that everyone gets feedback on their reading, and all objects are returned to their owners.

When your turn comes to give a reading, hold the object in your hand, and begin speaking about your first impressions. For most people, the hardest thing to do is to begin speaking. You may feel that you have nothing to say, or be afraid to keep talking because you have no idea what you are going to say next. But the important thing is to just start talking and let Spirit or your guide do the work for you. Your only responsibility is to receive the information. You are not even responsible for interpreting the information, for the message may make no sense whatsoever to you, but may make perfect sense to the person receiving the message. Never assume anything. Just go with your first impressions and keep talking until you know that the message is over.

Each time you meet as a group to do this exercise, you could do several rounds of readings, using different objects each time. In my classes, the students know that if there are baskets on the table when they come in for class, they automatically put an object in each basket and then we are ready for as many rounds as we have time. By the time we have done several sessions of giving readings, most people look forward to this part of the class, because it is a wonderful feeling to invite the energy of Spirit to move through you and to work with your intuitive mind.

# Tarot Cards as an Intuitive Tool

Tarot cards are a wonderful tool for intuitive development because of the magical illustrations on the cards. Pay a visit to your local spiritual or metaphysical bookstore or any other bookstore that has a large selection of tarot decks and spend some time looking at the many decks available, choosing a deck whose pictures "talk" to you. When you get home and open your deck for the first time, you will find that it includes a booklet giving you brief interpretations of each of the cards. Put that booklet away for now and do not refer to it as you are getting to know your deck. We want to use the cards as a tool for accessing your intuitive wisdom, not an exercise in remembering what the cards are supposed to mean.

Spend your first few days with the tarot cards just looking at them one by one, and letting images and symbols jump out at you. Become aware of the use of color, of archetypal symbols, of anything in the illustrations that speaks to you. Let go of any preconceived notions about what an individual card is supposed to mean, and just let yourself develop your own interpretation of each card as you look at it. Keep in mind that each time you look at that card, it may mean something completely different to you, because you will be coming to the card as a different person than you were yesterday, with different thoughts, concerns, feelings.

After spending a few days getting to know your cards, spend the next few days drawing a card from the deck each day and letting that card give you a message for that day. It may give you insight on how to handle a situation you will encounter, help you solve a problem, help you understand a feeling you have been having, or suggest a theme or point of focus for your day. Just allow the card to speak to you.

After you have spent a couple of weeks with your cards and you are getting comfortable with them, invite a willing and interested friend to sit with you so that you may give a reading from your tarot cards. Explain that you are just beginning to explore this avenue of intuitive development, and you would like their help. You will be surprised how many friends jump at this chance!

# Exercise #42
# Intuitive Reading with Tarot Cards

Sit opposite your friend and shuffle the cards by mixing them, not by a traditional card shuffling style. (This breaks the energy in the cards.) Ask your friend to cut the cards, spread them out between you, and choose three cards. Put the rest of the cards aside. Turn the three cards face-up between you. Do not worry if the cards are upside down or right side up. You are just going to work with images on the cards, and the messages that you receive through them. As in the previous intuitive exercises, take your first impressions. Let the cards "talk" to you, and, as you receive impressions, share them with your friend.

If you are in a group for this exercise, divide up into partners. After each set of partners has read for each other, trade partners and read again.

If you already have knowledge of the tarot deck and the traditional meanings of the cards, let your knowledge mingle with your intuitive impressions as you give the messages, so that you are not giving a "textbook reading." You may also want to choose a deck that you are not familiar with for awhile in order to get the full benefit of this intuitive development exercise.

When you feel very comfortable with three-card

readings, expand to five cards and let Spirit guide you as to how you wish to proceed. Should the five cards be laid out in a certain pattern? Should the position of the cards mean something? Again, let yourself be guided as you explore this tool for intuitive development. You may also want to allow your partner to ask you a question or suggest a situation about which they would like insight, letting that question guide the reading.

When you have become comfortable with this level of readings, invite your partner to ask a question or suggest a situation to work with, and then seek Spirit's advice for how many cards should be drawn and what the layout pattern should be. By now you are really flying with the cards, and enjoying an ongoing dialogue with the cards as you work with them.

# Direct Readings — The Ultimate Practice

Finally we come to the most challenging, yet most practical form of giving readings. I call them direct readings, because you simply ask Spirit to speak to you, show you pictures, or give you feelings — to somehow impress upon you the information you are to share with the person you seek to help. When you have developed your skills to this point, you will really know the tremendous benefits of all of the work you have done. Psychometry and the tarot are important tools for helping you develop your abilities, but now we take the tools away. After all, when you are in a meeting being offered a contract, you can't ask the other party if you can hold their ring first in order to decide whether or not you want to do business with them! When you are suddenly confronted with a friend in crisis and must help them sort out their situation, you don't have time to run home and get your tarot cards. In the real world, there are no tools — there is just you and your ability to see, hear, and know. The more you use your intuitive skills, the more you will begin to trust them.

If you pay attention, you will see that every day presents countless ways in which to practice. The more you do, you will find that you are integrating your intuitive process into your everyday living, and that you are living on many levels of awareness at once. This is our goal — to be aware of any situation from many perspectives, and then be able to proceed calmly and assuredly with the appropriate words or actions.

These last two exercises will help you practice doing direct readings. They are both group exercises. The first is to be done in the dark, or with as little light in the room as possible. Although this might make you uncomfortable at first, I find that most groups really come to love doing readings in the dark. First, they become much less subconscious because no one can see anyone else. Secondly, they begin to have impressions, and see and hear intuitively in a different way. The darkness heightens the senses in new ways.

# Exercise #43
# Direct Readings I

Gather your group in a circle. Assign one person to be the light keeper. They should be seated beside the lamp or light switch so that they can safely find the switch to turn the light back on at the end of the exercise.

When everyone is in place, turn off the light. Begin your session with a prayer, such as the Kabbalistic Prayer or another powerful prayer of protection. Then allow time for everyone to become acclimated to the darkness. When someone has a message or reading for anyone else in the circle or for the group as a whole, they should speak freely, sharing their message. Everyone should be encouraged to share any intuitive impressions that they have. The session should last 15 minutes to an hour, depending on the level of your group, and the comfort of the group with the process. When you have completed your work for the session, thank Spirit for being with you, and once again say your prayer. At this point the light keeper turns the light back on. (Be sure to warn the group to close their eyes before the light comes back so that their eyes can adjust to the light.)

For this last intuitive exercise, your group will gather in a well-lit room. The process is very much the same as for the previous exercise, except that now the lights are on.

# Exercise #44
# Direct Readings II

Gather your group to sit in a circle. Begin your session with a prayer, such as the Kabbalistic Prayer or another powerful prayer of protection. Then, when someone has a message or reading for anyone else in the circle or for the group as a whole, they should speak freely, sharing their message. Participants may find it easier at first to receive messages with their eyes closed. However, the ultimate goal is to do the entire exercise with eyes open. Everyone should be encouraged to share any intuitive impressions that they have. The session should last 15 minutes to an hour, depending on the level of your group, and the comfort of the group with the process. When you have completed your work for the session, thank Spirit for being with you, and once again say your prayer.

## Variations on a Theme

After several sessions of doing these last two exercises, I encourage you to continue working in your group, creating variations on the direct readings. You might take turns, with each person giving a message to each member of the circle. This is what is known in the Spiritualist tradition as "platform work," and what I do in the Spirit Circle. One person stands in front of the entire group and gives messages to individuals in the circle.

You might also choose a particular topic on which to focus for a particular session, such as "creative and professional life," or "emotional life and relationships." Everyone in the circle then focuses on receiving guidance from Spirit for the others in the circle on that particular topic. When I do private clairvoyant readings, I work in this way. I begin the reading by looking at the underlying spiritual essence or lesson that is moving through the client's life at this time. Then we move on to the categories of physical energy and health, creative and professional life, emotional life and relationships, and finances. The reading concludes with any questions the client may have.

As your development circle continues to work together, you might also invite the members to ask for guidance on particular issues in their lives. In this format, the entire circle focuses on giving messages to one person at a time. That person asks the group and Spirit for guidance on a particular issue, and then the members of the circle report their impressions. Here again, it is important that this not become an advice session. Be clear about what is coming from Spirit and what is your opinion.

The possibilities are endless. Be creative about the many ways you can use your intuitive gifts to enrich your life. The rewards are truly magnificent.

# 22

# Being Present with Spirit

In the meditation of the Spirit Circle in New York City on May 19, 1995, Spirit spoke these words:

*It's a holy place. This place that you gather, it's a holy place. What does that mean — it's a holy place? It's a place of wholeness. It's a place of peace. It's a place of quiet, and it's a place of divinity. It's a place where we from the Spirit realm can move in and out of your lives easily, freely, and you can move in and out of our vibrations. It's a holy place, this place that you gather.*

*And where is it that you gather? My dear ones, you gather in your hearts. It seems that you have come into this room to have this communion with one another and with Spirit. But in order to truly commune, you enter your heart. And it is when you sit in your heart that you truly meet one another, for you meet one another heart to heart, soul to soul, essence to essence, truth to truth. So, welcome to this holy place. Welcome to your heart. And let your breath keep carrying you, and allowing you to settle into a deeper and deeper place in your heart, sinking deeper into that comfortable chair in your heart, where you know your truth.*

*Tonight we would like to talk about enlightened being. What does it mean to be enlightened? It's very simple, you know. To be enlightened only means that you are open to the flow of Love through your being in every moment. Pure and simple. An enlightened vocation is one that allows the flow of Love in every moment. And an enlightened relationship is one that allows the flow of Love in every moment. And an enlightened existence for each of you, personally, means allowing Love to flow through your existence in every moment. Such a simple and basic concept, and so hard to live in your world.*

*But what we really want to get to tonight is the concept of enlightened being and awareness, because awareness is the key to your enlightenment — awareness of your circumstances, of the energy around you, and the energy within you, and how those two energies are interacting. Open your consciousness to be aware of when you are open to that Love flow and when you close yourself off. The greater definition of Spirit is simply that Spirit is "the all of the everything that is." It is the essence. And Spirit is made of Love. And the Love is always flowing. However, it's your choice as to whether or not you let that Love flow through you. Now everyone in this room knows this as a very simple and basic concept, and everyone in this room would like to think of themselves as moving toward some state of enlightenment — of Love flow. But the practical matter is that, in your world, stress and conflict and all of those things that you deal with on a daily basis very easily close you down, and you forget to be open to the Love flow. That's the important message tonight. Opening your awareness helps you know when you are open to the Love flow, when you are open to Spirit, and when you are closed. As you move through every moment of your day and night, it is important to become aware of the times when you shut down, when you close off to allowing the flow of Love. When you close down, your enlightenment can only be a mental concept, not an experiential truth. Because experiencing enlightenment means the Love is flowing through every cell, every atom, every molecule of your being, and every bit of your energy field, however far that happens to extend from your physical body.*

*As you sit right now in this holy place where we are all meeting in your heart, just take a moment to look back over your life today. Was your energy system open in such a way to allow Love to flow, or did you get caught up in your ego agendas of the day and shut off the Love flow, just to accomplish whatever it was that your ego thought you needed to accomplish? How did your energy feel within your physical body? Was it calm and peaceful and flowing and fluid and gentle, or was it jerky or a little bit too-fast paced? Was the sound of your body revved up to a too-high pitch? All these are signals to help you know when you have shut off to the Love flow. When you feel your life flowing and gentle and smooth, you know the Love is flowing. When you find that you can handle any situation that comes to you, ANY situation, then you know that the Love is flowing.*

*An enlightened being is not necessarily one whose life is free of conflict. An enlightened being is one who can let the Love flow through the conflict, experiencing the lesson and the growth and the healing that comes from that conflict. If you get stuck in the conflict, there's not very much Love flowing. Please don't make any judgments about where you've been today, or any day, or for your life. Just open your awareness a little further. Just say maybe I'm starting to understand something a little differently now, and I can make a change from here out.*

*Take a moment, and, as you reflect upon your day, allow your energy system to soften and open to the Love flow. Allow this moment in your life to be enlightened — in Light — in the Light of Love — in the Light of the Spirit — in the Light of the Beloved — in the Light of the Divine — enlightened. Let your armoring and your walls and your difficulties and your resistances fall away for a moment, and experience enlightenment. Experience a full flow of Love through your entire being. It's a wondrous healing. It's a wondrous gift.*

*Just as you receive the gift of Love, it's important that you give your gift back to Love. And your gift back to Love is simply to be open to receive it. As you receive the gift, you are giving back. That is the only necessary response. Open your awareness to the flow of Love through your being. And experience your enlightened self.*

*Blessings upon you, children of the Light! Blessings upon you!*

And so we come full circle. We began this journey together talking about enlightenment and the language of Love. Spirit is always present with us. Love is always present with us. Our task is to *be present with Spirit and Love.* We end this leg of the journey in simplicity, with an exercise and a benediction from Spirit. But the key words here are "this leg of the journey." For now, you may want to take some time off from the rigors of your work, and then, after a little rest, start at the beginning of the book again. I can promise you that each time you return to this book you will find a new leg of the journey. I say that out of my own experience. I've been living with this material and these concepts for many years, yet every time I return to these fundamental principles, I go deeper, fly higher, and my life gets simpler and clearer. I see the same thing with students in classes. In the last several years, many students have returned to take the same classes again, and their experiences are very different each time.

So I offer you my best wishes and send you off into this last exercise and Spirit's Benediction and Blessing.

This is an exercise/meditation to be done with a partner. Sit facing one another, but not touching. You will begin this exercise in your own space, and then, at a later point, you will take your partner's hands for a few moments. Then you will come back to your own space.

# Exercise #45
# Being in the Moment

Take time to settle into a deep state of consciousness. Go to your own special place of peace and calm within.

When you have reached a very deep state of consciousness, a place where you can freely speak with Spirit, ask Spirit to show you what you need to release in order to let go of the past. What person, concept, thing, or belief of the past must you now let go of? Take whatever comes and visualize or feel it in front of you. Let it be. Have a conversation with it. Make peace with it.

. . .

When you have made your peace, say to this image in strength and confidence, "We are healed in one another. We have only pure and unconditional love for one another." Use both affirmations or just one, whatever feels right for you. Or, if you prefer, make up your own affirmation that feels right. "We are healed in one another. We have only pure and unconditional love for one another." Remember that any belief, situation, concept, thing, or person is simply an energy pattern. You and this image are now healing your energies together. Continue saying and affirming these statements to your image for a few moments. Feel yourself becoming more and more liberated from this image.

. . .

When you have completed this work, release the image, knowing that it is gone, and that you are no longer locked in the past by what this image represented.

Ask Spirit now to show you what you need to release in order to let go of the future; what person, concept, thing, belief that represents the future to you? Take whatever comes and visualize or feel it in front of you. Accept it. Let it be. Have a conversation with it. Make peace with it.

. . .

Say to this image in strength and confidence, "We are healed in one another. We have only pure and unconditional love for one another." Say your affirmation over and over again. Feel yourself becoming more and more liberated from this person, concept, thing, or belief.

. . .

Release this image when you are ready, knowing that it is gone, that you are no longer locked in the vicious circle created by what this image represents, by anticipating the future.

While remaining in this very deep state of consciousness, take the hands of your partner, perhaps move a little closer together, open your eyes, and just "be" with your partner for a few moments. Simply look into one another's eyes. Do not try to see anything. Do not look for any images. Just be. Allow yourself to be lost in one another for a few moments. Then, when you are ready, continue with this exercise.

. . .

In "being" with one another, you are experiencing the Now. You are so wrapped up in one another that you have forgotten the past or the future. This is the Now.

. . .

Close your eyes, release your hands, and come back into your own space. Continue aligning your body, mind, and emotions with the Universe, with Spirit. Bring yourself into quietness and calmness and a feeling of rest and repose. Be firm, quiet, still, tranquil. Feel a peacefulness, a stillness, a nowness in yourself. Open your mind — have a look inside. Does your mind tell you that you have to do something or that you have to become something? Does your mind say that sometime in the future you will get around to being happy or to being spiritual or to becoming your best person or to being healed? The great teachers of all times have all said that there is no place to go, nothing to become, nothing to do. They all taught that you must only look into yourself and see your truth. In each moment, keep aligning yourself with your truth, no matter what the circumstance. As you hear your mind speak, keep bringing yourself back to peacefulness and calmness and tranquillity. Keep bringing yourself back to the Now. Throughout the day, test yourself — see if you are relaxed and just being in the moment. If not, tell yourself mentally to let go. Relaxation lets the energies flow through all of your body, all of your cells, out through your aura. This can be done no matter where you are or what you are doing — walking down the street, riding on the train, sitting at a desk, cooking, sitting in a class, cleaning, meditating, or waiting tables. The more you become aware, the more you will realize when you and your body become tense, and the more you will realize the times when you are living in the past or the future, not in the Now. Awareness is the first step toward reclaiming all of you for you. It is the first step for reclaiming the Now and living in it.

Become aware of your breathing. Watch it going in and out. Exhale all that is past and inhale into this moment. Consciously follow your breath, letting each exhalation free you and each inhalation bring you to the moment of the present. That is all there is. Take a few moments now to practice this.

As you can come to be in each moment, you can be one with Spirit, one with self, one with God. You can touch the divine place in your being where you are meant to live. Carry this with you into each moment, releasing each past moment, and have a wonderful dance with this new rhythm of your life.

As you are ready, prepare to open your eyes and step back into your physical reality, fully present in this moment in time.

# Benediction and Blessing

*Go forth in peace in the name of Love. You will know when the time of initiation has come, and you will know that you must make that journey alone. You will find that some souls will remain with you throughout the journey, and others will drop away. Your relationships with those who remain with you will transcend to a higher level. You will move to a new level of understanding and love and cooperation and support with one another.*

*As the initiation begins, you will feel the purification fires raging within. What you experience in the beginning may be only little flickers compared to the raging flames that will come. When the raging flames come up they will consume parts of you in a very short time. You will experience periods where large parts of your ego will quickly be consumed by fire and you will feel that you have nothing left. Yet your guides and teachers in Spirit will be with you to help you see that you have everything. After the fire, once the smoke clears away and your mourning and tears clear away, you will see your everything. You will see the real essence of Self. You will find your new set of tools waiting to be used to create the wondrous gifts that are waiting to be created by you for the world. This is the journey. This is the initiation. Many will be the trials. But if you remain clear in your understanding of the process, you will see that, although the fire rages on, you, your soul essence, can never be consumed.*

*Go forth in peace in the name of Love. Let us go a little further with the three parts of this benediction.*

*"Go forth" — This means picking yourself up and moving on from where you are now. This is not a change in location, necessarily, but rather a change in your being. You begin taking firm steps, strong and large steps, forward into the unknown. Those in Spirit who are guiding you know it as the known. Have faith and trust, and walk knowing that as the flames consume aspects of ego, the new tools for the work will be uncovered.*

*"in peace" — Yes, go in peace, not confusion or turmoil or torture. Move in peace within yourself. Remain calm and allow yourself to feel and experience, and the feelings and experiences to move through you, be consumed by the purification fire, and be cleared away.*

*"in the name of Love." — You are blessed by Love and your guides and teachers in Spirit. Know that your journey is blessed, and that you are protected, and walk on, calmly and confidently.*

*You are a divine essence. All beings are, but few recognize their divinity at this time. Move in the journey to burn off all that separates you from your divinity. Until now you have perhaps only been able to see your divinity from afar. You have had to look through a great fog to see it. Through the journey, you burn off the fog and all of the barriers you have created over many eons of time, so that you are no longer separated from your divinity. Through the journey you will come to live in your divinity. This is your initiation. This is your beginning. Your early "deaths" will show you courage and faith. And your soul will be made stronger by these experiences. In the purification fires, only the clothing, the outer structures, aspects of ego will burn. The soul essence will take on a new flame of Divine Light and live in its purity until the great Homecoming once again.*

*Go forth in peace in the name of Love.*

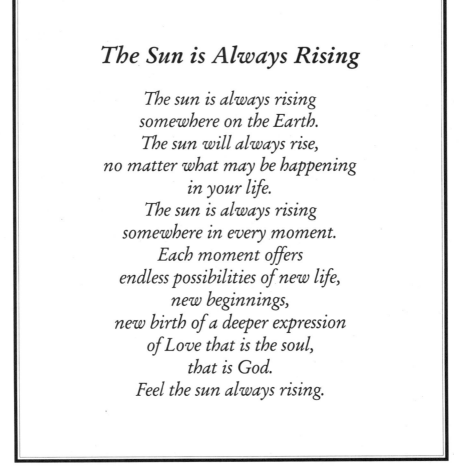

## *The Sun is Always Rising*

*The sun is always rising
somewhere on the Earth.
The sun will always rise,
no matter what may be happening
in your life.
The sun is always rising
somewhere in every moment.
Each moment offers
endless possibilities of new life,
new beginnings,
new birth of a deeper expression
of Love that is the soul,
that is God.
Feel the sun always rising.*

# Epilogue

# The Quiet Place

It's very still here.
There is a peace and silence that is deafening.
It is a place where nothing seems to be able to touch me.
It is a place where I can stand and
　　watch the whole world spinning by,
　　　　whirling in its array of activities
　　　　　　and struggles
　　　　　　　　and conflicts
　　　　　　　　　　and joys
　　　　　　　　　　　　and anguish;
　　yet I remain still, untouched.
It's neither a warm or a cold place.
It's neither an easy or a difficult place.
It's neither a sad or happy place.
It just is.
There is no activity here.
There is no hurry to get to the next appointment
　　or finish the next project or to . . .
　　　　　　there is just IS.
There is a certain detachment that allows observance here.
There is no judgment,
　　but rather a tremendous and profound permission granted
　　　　from some unknown source
　　　　　　to simply be and accept.

313

Others could confuse this place with depression,
    for in this place there is such an absence of emotion.
But when you settle into this place,
        you realize that there is profound peace.
            This is not depression.
            This is oneness.
            Feelings run deep here,
                yet merge into the oneness of being.
                    Pain and joy are one.
                    Sadness and elation are one.
                    Ecstasy is the constant state — yes, bliss.
            Yet this is not how I would describe those terms
                in my human ego's perceptions.
        Ecstasy and bliss are states of being,
            not states of doing.
        And the ego knows nothing of being.
        The ego only knows doing.

How does one get to this place?
Everyone is on their way to here in their own time.
Every experience is preparation.
Every moment is a step closer,
    even when you feel like you are running the other way.
It's all part of the journey to the quiet.
It's a place where everything is reduced
    to its simplest form and meaning.
It's a place where the criteria for choices becomes
    whatever allows you to continue being;
        not getting caught up in doing.
Many struggles may lead you to this quiet place.
Yet when you arrive,
    suddenly there is peace.
Everything else has simply fallen away.

How did I get here?
Carrying wood.
While carrying and stacking firewood to provide heat for the winter,
    I suddenly arrived here.

Carrying wood made sense to me.
Carrying wood helped me get to "being" instead of "doing."
How long can I stay here?
Each time I arrive here I am able to stay longer,
    but then my ego pulls me back into "doing."
Yet each time I come back here,
    I get into deeper chambers of this quiet place,
    and I get more comfortable with "being" and not "doing."


It's very still here.
This place is where God lives within me.
This place is my soul.
This place is my oneness with every creature
    and with every point in time.
This place is my truth, my essence.
This place is sacred and to be honored above all else.
This place is Love.

# Glossary

**akasha** — Sanskrit term borrowed by Madame Helen Blavatsky to represent universal life force.

**Akashic Records** — mystical records in the spiritual dimension of all that has ever been and will ever be.

**aura** — electromagnetic field of energy surrounding all matter.

**chakra** — Sanskrit term meaning "wheel of light;" refers to energy centers in the body through which we exchange information and energy with our environment and the universe.

**clairaudience** — intuitive hearing; perceiving messages or information either as an inner sound or an outer voice.

**clairsentience** — intuitive feeling or knowing; may include perceiving fragrances or odors, tastes, emotional feelings, or tactile sensations.

**clairvoyance** — intuitive sight or vision. In simple forms, it involves perceiving images through inner vision. In its more developed forms, the clairvoyant is able to see spirit beings, non-physical energies, and auras.

**co-creation** — a process of creating your life in full partnership with Spirit.

**consciousness** — the underlying framework of all; the pure order, organization, design, pattern, intelligence, in all that exists. We are created of consciousness and enveloped in it.

**ego** — the vehicle for the soul's journey in the physical dimension; the physical body and personality; the mind and analytical thought process.

**intuition** — a process of tapping into one's deep sense of inner wisdom, the place inside of you where you know your oneness with All. At its highest level, the intuitive voice is the part of you that is one with the Great Mystery, that is Love, that is the voice of God within.

**intuitive living** — living moment-to-moment in an awareness of Spirit and the intuitive mind as a fully integrated aspect of your total being.

**kundalini** — the life-force energy that is released from the root chakra and travels up the spine, awakening all the other chakras.

**mystic** — one who seeks to have a constant awareness of Spirit throughout every moment of daily life.

**21st-century mystic** — one who comes to know and experience oneness with God through:
1) spiritual awakening — an opening in conscious awareness to the existence of a universal force that is the creator and sustainer of All.
2) self-exploration — embarking upon a journey to uncover and know the divine essence of being.
3) removing blocks — recognizing, acknowledging, and working through emotional blocks and inner resistance or fears that hinder a full awareness of your own divinity, and the constant flow of Love through you.
4) intuitive development — developing the intuitive mind as an aspect of Spirit, of Love, of God, of the Great Mystery.
5) surrender — complete surrender to the guidance of Spirit.

**mystical experience** — that which is very real to the experiencer, but cannot be explained by the rational mind.

**mysticism** — an acute awareness of Spirit, its influence on and movement through daily life.

**point of stillness** — that quiet and still place deep inside where you can simply "be," accepting and embracing your feelings and circumstances. From this point you are able to hear Spirit and know the wisdom of your heart.

**soul** — the aspect of you that is timeless, that is one with Spirit, and that is Love; your divinity.

**Spirit** — the all of the everything that is. It may also be called God, Source, Love, the Universal Creative Force, the Great Mystery, Universal Wisdom, or Higher Power.

**spirit guide or teacher** — a nonphysical entity that makes itself known to you in some way through the intuitive mind. The guide's purpose is to help and protect you, and to assist in your spiritual development and understanding of daily life.

**spirituality** — a sense of one's personal relationship with the divine, with God, with Spirit, or the ultimate Creative Force of the Universe.

**talent** — any way that one allows Love to flow through them into action.

# Chapter Notes

## Chapter 4

1) Sule Greg Wilson, *The Drummer's Path – Moving the Spirit with Ritual and Traditional Drumming* (Rochester: Destiny Books), p. xv.
2) Agnes de Mille, *Martha: The Life and Work of Martha Graham* (New York: Random House, 1956), p. 264.

## Chapter 6

1) Sources: Barbara Brennan, *Hands of Light: A Guide to Healing Through the Human Energy Field* (New York: Bantam Books, 1988); Rosalyn Bruyere, *Wheels of Light: Chakras, Auras, and the Healing Energy of the Body* (New York: Simon and Schuster, 1989); Rosemary Ellen Guiley, *Harper's Encyclopedia of Mystical and Paranormal Experience* (San Francisco: Harper San Francisco, 1991).
2) *Holy Bible*, John 14:12.
3) Sources: Brennan, Bruyere, Guiley
4) Sources: Brennan, Bruyere, Guiley
5) Sources: Brennan, Bruyere, Guiley
6) Rosalyn Bruyere uses these terms of direct and alternating current to explain raising energy in her book *Wheels of Light*, p. 95.
7-10) These exercises were inspired by similar exercises in Barbara Brennan's *Hands of Light*, p. 41-42.
11) L. W. de Laurence, *The Master Key* (Chicago: The de Laurence Company, 1941), p. 81-82.

## Chapter 7

Sources: Ted Andrews, *Sacred Sounds: Transformation through Music & Word* (St. Paul: Llewellyn Publications, 1992); Brennan; Bruyere; Anodea Judith, *Wheels of Life — A User's Guide to the Chakra System* (St. Paul: Llewellyn Publications, 1990); Klausbernd Vollmar, *Journey Through the Chakras* (Bath: Gateway Books, 1987).

1) Judith, p. 3.
2) Anodea Judith describes the chakras and their relationship to the elements throughout her book, *Wheels of Life.*
3) Judith, p. 68.

## Chapter 8
Sources: Andrews, Brennan, Bruyere, Judith, Vollmar.

1) from a lecture by Matthew Fox at the Omega Institute Conference in New York City, spring 1995.
2) from a lecture by Deepak Chopra at the Omega Institute Conference in New York City, spring 1995.
3) Bruyere, p. 164-165.
4) Ibid., p. 159-160

## Chapter 9
Sources: Andrews, Brennan, Bruyere, Judith, Vollmar.

1) from a lecture given by John Nelson on human sexuality and spirituality at Chautauqua Institution, Chautauqua, NY, summer 1995.

## Chapter 10
1) from a lecture by Stephen Levine at the Omega Institute Conference in NYC, spring 1994.
2) Rick Jarow, *Creating the Work You Love* (Rochester: Destiny Books, 1995), pp. 45-46.

## Chapter 13
Sources: Andrews, Brennan, Bruyere, Judith, Vollmar.

## Chapter 14
1) from a lecture at the Omega Institute Conference in New York City, spring 1994.

## Chapter 15
Sources:  Andrews, Brennan, Bruyere, Judith, Vollmar.

## Chapter 16
Sources:  Andrews, Brennan, Bruyere, Judith, Vollmar.

1) Judith, p. 348-349

## Chapter 17
Sources:  Andrews, Brennan, Bruyere, Judith, Vollmar.

## Chapter 18
1) de Laurence, p. 79-80.

## Chapter 19
1) Guiley, p. 494

## Chapter 20
1) de Laurence, p. 80-81.

# Bibliography

Allen, James. *As a Man Thinketh*. Marina del Rey: DeVorss & Company.

Andrews, Ted. *Sacred Sounds: Transformation through Music & Word*. St. Paul: Llewellyn Publications, 1992.

Bartholomew. *From the Heart of a Gentle Brother*. Taos: High Mesa Press, 1987.

———. *I Come as a Brother*. Taos: High Mesa Press, 1986.

———. *Planetary Brother*. Taos: High Mesa Press, 1991.

Brennan, Barbara Ann. *Hands of Light: A Guide to Healing Through the Human Energy Field*. New York: Bantam Books, 1988.

Bruyere, Rosalyn. *Wheels of Light: Chakras, Auras, and the Healing Energy of the Body*. New York: Simon & Schuster, 1989.

Campbell, Don G. *The Roar of Silence*. Wheaton: The Theosophical Publishing House, 1989.

Capacchione, Lucia. *The Power of Your Other Hand: A course in channeling the inner wisdom of the right brain*. North Hollywood: Newcastle Publishing Co., Inc., 1988.

Crinita, Joey. *The Medium Touch*. Norfolk: The Donning Company/ Publishers, 1982.

*Emmanuel's Book: A Manual for Living Comfortably in the Cosmos*. Compiled by Pat Rodegast and Judith Stanton. New York: Bantam Books, 1987.

*Emmanuel's Book II: The Choice for Love*. Compiled by Pat Rodegast and Judith Stanton. New York: Bantam Books, 1989.

*Emmanuel's Book III: What is an Angel Doing Here?* Compiled by Pat Rodegast and Judith Stanton. New York: Bantam Books, 1994.

Fields, Rick, Peggy Taylor, Rex Weyler, and Rick Ingrasci. *Chop Wood Carry Water: A Guide to Finding Spiritual Fulfillment in Everyday Life*. Los Angeles: Jeremy P. Tarcher, Inc., 1984.

Fisichella, Anthony J. *Metaphysics: The Science of Life*. St. Paul: Llewellyn Publications, 1988.

Guiley, Rosemary Ellen. *Harper's Encyclopedia of Mystical and Paranormal Experience*. San Francisco: Harper San Francisco, 1991.

Hendricks, Gay and Kathlyn Hendricks. *Centering and the Art of Intimacy*. New York: Prentice Hall Press, 1985.

Jarow, Rick. *Creating the Work You Love*. Rochester: Destiny Books, 1995.

Judith, Anodea. *Wheels of Life – A User's Guide to the Chakra System*. St. Paul: Llewellyn Publications, 1990.

Lansdowne, Zachary F. *The Chakras and Esoteric Healing*. York Beach: Samuel Weiser, Inc., 1986.

de Laurence, L. W. *The Master Key*. Chicago: The de Laurence Company, 1941.

LeShan, Lawrence. *How to Meditate*. Toronto: Bantam Books, 1974.

Kabat-Zinn, Jon. *Wherever You Go, There You Are*. New York: Hyperion, 1994.

Karpinski, Gloria D. *Where Two Worlds Touch: Spiritual Rites of Passage*. New York: Ballantine Books, 1990.

Kornfield, Jack. *A Path with Heart: A Guide Through the Perils and Promises of Spiritual Life*. New York: Bantam Books, 1993.

Levine, Stephen. *A Gradual Awakening*. New York: Anchor Books, 1979.

———. *Who Dies? An Investigation of Conscious Living and Conscious Dying*. New York: Anchor Books, 1982.

Martin, Joel and Patricia Romanowski. *We Don't Die — George Anderson's Conversations with the Other Side*. New York: Berkley Books, 1989.

de Mille, Agnes. *Martha: The Life and Work of Martha Graham*. New York: Random House, 1956.

Moore, Thomas. *Care of the Soul: A Guide for Cultivating Depth and Sacredness in Everyday Life*. New York: HarperCollinsPublishers, 1992.

*The Perennial Dictionary of World Religions*. Edited by Keith Crim. San Francisco: Harper & Row, Publishers, 1989.

Ram Dass. *Be Here Now*. San Cristobal: Lama Foundation, 1971.

———. *The Only Dance There Is*. Garden City: Anchor Books, 1974.

Ram Dass with Stephen Levine. *Grist for the Mill*. Berkeley: Celestial Arts, 1987.

Ram Dass and Paul Gorman. *How Can I Help? Stories and Reflections on Service*. New York: Alfred A. Knopf, 1990.

Redfield, James. *The Celestine Prophecy: An Adventure*. New York: Warner Books, 1993.

Shannon, William O. *Silence on Fire: The Prayer of Awareness*. New York: Crossroad Publishing Company, 1995.

Sinetar, Marsha. *Ordinary People as Monks and Mystics: Lifestyles for Self-discovery*. New York: Paulist Press, 1986.

Three Initiates. *The Kybalion: A Study of the Hermetic Philosophy of Ancient Egypt and Greece*. Chicago: The Yogi Publication Society, 1912.

Thunder, Mary Elizabeth. *Thunder's Grace: Walking the Road of Visions with My Lakota Grandmother*. Barrytown: Station Hill Press, 1995.

Underhill, Evelyn. *Mysticism: A study in the nature and development of Man's spiritual consciousness*. New York: New American Library, 1974.

Vollmar, Klausbernd. *Journey Through the Chakras*. Bath: Gateway Books, 1987.

Walsch, Neale Donald. *Conversations with God: An Uncommon Dialogue — Book I*. New York: G. P. Putnam's Sons, 1996.

White Eagle. *The Gentle Brother*. New Lands: The White Eagle Publishing Trust, 1968.

———. *Jesus Teacher and Healer*. New Lands: The White Eagle Publishing Trust, 1985.

———. *Spiritual Unfoldment 1*. New Lands: The White Eagle Publishing Trust, 1961.

———. *The Still Voice*. New Lands: The White Eagle Publishing Trust, 1981.

———. *The Way of the Sun: White Eagle's teaching for the festivals of the year*. New Lands: The White Eagle Publishing Trust, 1982.

Williamson, Marianne. *A Return to Love*. New York: HarperCollins Publishers, 1992.

Wilson, Sule Greg. *The Drummer's Path: Moving the Spirit with Ritual and Traditional Drumming*. Rochester: Destiny Books, 1992.

# Index of Teachings from Spirit

# Index of Exercises

# General Index

# About the Author

Alan Seale is an ordained Interfaith Minister of Spiritual Counseling, Peace Elder, and a spiritual/clairvoyant counselor, as well as a professional singer and voice teacher in New York City. He has led workshops and classes in spiritual and intuitive living throughout the United States since 1988.

In 1990, Alan developed the concept of Creative Energy Dynamics, a method of working with performing artists to help them be clearer channels of their own higher creative energy. After teaching this method to many performers in New York City, he developed a teacher training program in Creative Energy Dynamics in 1994, to help other teachers in the arts develop their clairvoyant skills and intuitive awareness in order that they might incorporate Creative Energy Dynamics in their work.

As a singer, Alan has appeared as soloist with the New York Philharmonic, the New York City Opera National Company, the Spoleto Festival (Italy and USA), the Baltimore Chamber Orchestra, and in solo recital throughout the United States and Europe. He has also appeared in cabaret as a singer/songwriter in New York City and throughout the country. His first solo CD recording, *Child of the Moon*, was released by I Virtuosi Records in 1996. His voice students have appeared in leading roles in most of the major opera houses of the world, including New York's Metropolitan Opera, Seattle Opera, the Salzburg Festival, Vienna State Opera, and Paris Opera, as well as on Broadway, and in many regional musical theaters throughout the country.

Alan is available as a guest speaker, for workshops, Spirit Circles, concerts, or private consultations. He may be contacted through Skytop Publishing, P. O. Box 134, Cathedral Station, New York, NY 10025, (212) 932-0858.

For additional copies of
*On Becoming a 21st-Century Mystic,*
or for the companion meditation tapes,
please contact:

Skytop Publishing
P. O. Box 134
Cathedral Station
New York, NY  10025
(212) 932-0858

Quantity discounts are available on bulk purchases
of this book for study groups, educational
purposes, or fundraising. Special books or book
excerpts can also be created to fit specific needs.
For information, please contact Skytop Publishing.

Alan Seale is also available for speaking
engagements, workshops, Spirit Circles, concerts,
or private consultations. Please contact him
through Skytop Publishing.